Our readers write:

Awesome! Polancy strips away many ster ~~meaningful information and specific assist~~ *~~without~~ destroying the romance and opportunity that still is Hawai`i. The book is a must for visitors and kama`aina alike.*

If you are thinking of moving to Hawai`i do it with your eyes open! Read this honest and informative book.

Highly recommended for large public libraries.

This book is the model for what hopefully would be a book for every place...a tutorial for what anyone should think about before moving anywhere.

After 25 years on the mainland, I moved back home to rejuvenate my soul with Aloha Spirit. **So You Want to Live in Hawai`i** *peels away romantic blinders and enables a more realistic view of* **kama`aina** *life.*

I have always felt a deep down desire to move and try life in these very special islands. This book has the answers to just about everything I really need to know.

More readers' comments on the Internet:

The most even-handed review of Hawai`i...

Of all the books on moving to Hawai`i that I have read, this one gives the best discussion of reasons not to move to Hawai`i...

The book is the most true portrayal of Hawai`i I've ever read...

I think this book's secret interest is to dissuade any more people from moving...

If you've ever wanted to move to Hawai`i, this is THE book to read...

Thoroughness of information, excellent organization, balanced viewpoint and... honesty!

So You Want to
Live in Hawai`i

The Guide to Settling and Succeeding in the Islands

by Toni Polancy

Barefoot Publishing, Inc.: *Practical Books About Paradise*
Kihei, Hawai`i

Disclaimer

This book is designed to provide suggestions and resources regarding the decision to move to and live in Hawai`i. It is sold with the understanding that the publisher and author are not engaged in rendering legal or professional advice or services. This book should be used only as a general guide. In no way is it to be regarded as the ultimate source of information regarding your move to the islands or your success there. You are urged to read all available material before making such decisions. Every effort has been made to assure this information is accurate and timely, however there may be mistakes both in typography and in content. Facts and figures may have changed, and probably will have changed, from the time of writing and time of purchasing and reading this book. Figures quoted are used only as examples of prices and amounts and neither the author, the publisher nor the sources of such information should be held responsible for changes. The author and Barefoot Publishing, Inc. shall have neither liability nor responsibility to any person or entity with respect to loss or damage caused or alleged to be caused, directly or indirectly, by the information in this book.

So You Want to Live in Hawai`i
The Guide to Settling and Succeeding in the Islands

First edition, November 1998
Revised edition, May 2005
Some statistics updated late 2007
Revised, 2010

Library of Congress Catalog Card Number: 98-073548

Printed in China
10 9 8 7 6 5 4

Polancy, Antoinette
So You Want to Live in Hawai`i: The Guide to Settling and Succeeding in the Islands
Includes index

ISBN 0-9666253-6-6

Maps ©2005 by Bob Franklin

G Brad Lewis

Matthew Thayer

Photos by

G. Brad Lewis

and

Matthew Thayer

Additional photos by

Steve Brinkman

Steve Strand

Bob Fijal

Matthew Thayer

G. Brad Lewis

This book is dedicated
to my mother,
Josephine Jaskiewicz Falk,
made strong by life

Table of Contents

Introduction

A fax full of questions arrives one afternoon in my office. It is from a Texas woman. Her questions are simple; the answers are not.

If my family decided to move to one of the Hawaiian Islands, what can we expect to find there besides the ocean, beach, tropical vegetation and the lovely resort areas?

Aside from the breathtaking beauty, the romance of paradise...

Can you give any information for family living?

Beyond the beachfront estates and the golf villas...

Are there any hospitals or medical centers?

Are there any schools?

Are there any churches for Sunday services?

What conveniences are available for shopping for daily needs?

Thank you for your information!

Sincerely, Sandra

Aloha, Sandra,
Yes. All of the six habitable islands offer all of the amenities and necessities you mention. But you have asked the wrong questions; living here is not that simple.
What will your life in Hawai`i, paradise, really be like?
Most likely, buried deep in your subconscious is a special image of the islands that we all share. You live in a solitary shack on a secluded beach. Wearing a sarong, you step out and sniff the flower-scented air. You pluck a banana from a bunch hanging conveniently near the door, gather a coconut off the ground, and stretch out on the sand to enjoy dinner. The setting sun tinges ocean waves with gold while, in the distance, Elvis Presley sings "Blue Hawai`i."

Our visions of Paradise are similar because neither you nor I created them. Hollywood and our school books did.

This is reality: bananas are picked green; if they are allowed to ripen on the stock, hundreds of ants invade them. Palms need trimming; their fronds can weigh as much as 30 pounds, and a falling frond or coconut could give you a concussion. Elvis Presley is dead — although if he ever does come back it's a wise bet he'll visit Hawai`i.

Day-to-day, real life here is probably very different from life as you live it now; it is certainly different from a vacation at a posh resort, and it is a far cry from the picture painted by movies. This book is about living here as a longtime resident, as *kama`aina*. It is about real life in Hawai`i, about surviving and succeeding in this incredibly beautiful paradise.

In a kind of giant swap-meet of lives, thousands of people move to Hawai`i each year, and thousands leave. Some stay only a few weeks or a few months before packing up knapsacks, cardboard boxes, or *Louis Vuitton* luggage and traveling back to where they came from.

"So many people move here and then go back. After a while, you find yourself being a little careful," says one longtime Hawai`i resident. "You don't make close friends as fast with newcomers. You kind of wait a year or two to see if they will stay."

"Hawai`i is beautiful, but it is not for everyone," declares a prominent Realtor. "Sometimes I spend the first half hour with a client helping them decide if they belong here at all."

Much has been written in recent years about Hawai`i's struggling economy, about its high prices. Still, 1,285,500 people do live here, most of us happily and many of us successfully. For optimistic newcomers eager to work and daring *malihini* willing to take a chance, Hawai`i offers opportunities for success beyond what you can imagine.

Will you "make it" in Hawai`i? If you decide to join the more than 40,000 people who move here each year, will you be among the many who leave? Or those who stay? Can you find satisfying work? Will your children, if you have them, be content? Do you have the flexibility and perseverance to succeed here? This book should help you answer those important questions.

Four little words

Come to Hawai`i and you will learn some new words. Hawaiian words, like *malihini* (mal-a-HEE-nee), *kama`aina* (ka-ma-EYE-na) and *haole* (HOW-lee) are spoken nowhere else in the world. Familiar words, like "local" take on new meaning. You will begin using these words yourself, in everyday conversation, barely thinking. You will forget that these words, uttered a certain way, with a curl of the lips, with a soft smirk, become tiny daggers of discrimination.

Kama`aina* is a positive term. It literally translates as "land child" and, according to Hawaiian dictionary, means "Native born, host... acquainted, familiar." *Kama`aina refers to someone who has lived on the islands for a long time and is *akamai* (smart) about life here. *Kama`aina*, like most Hawaiian words, also carries more subtle meanings: acceptance and belonging in the islands.

Malihini, usually a neutral term, means newcomer. "They are *malihini*," simply states a fact.

The other two words, "local" and *haole*, are used often in everyday conversation. "Local" indicates a person who was born and raised on these islands. "Local" usually refers to anyone except Caucasians, and sometimes connotes a darker-skinned person of any race. "Local" can also be derisive: "A truck full of locals sped by."

Haole once meant foreigner; today it means a white person. Like "local", *haole* can be derisive. A *haole* may say about himself: "No thanks! This *haole* doesn't like fish!" But a local hollering at a light-skinned tourist "Go home, *haole*!" is hostile.

We use the words *kama`aina*, *malihini*, "local" and *haole* often in this book because they are specific. Here, they are meant in their most positive connotations.

The islands are its people:
here's what we say about us

"For me, moving to Hawai`i was a matter of surrendering to forces. It's spiritual. It was a leap of faith."
— businessman, Maui

"I worked many years for the success I've had. I pushed my children to get a lot of education, to be somebody and have good jobs. And then I retired and I moved here. And I say, what's that all about? All that Mainland bullshit about getting ahead in life?"
- retiree, O`ahu

"There's more intellectual freedom here, more openness and acceptance of ideas. In my hometown, I was a crazy guy with wild ideas. Here, everyone has hopes and dreams and schemes and it's okay. We're allowed to dream here. If we fail that's okay too. But we can dream."
— entrepreneur, Kaua`i

"You're at a restaurant and you look up and the guy waiting tables by night is your attorney by day."
— realtor, Kaua`i

"The culture, the traditions are very different here. It's America, but it's not the Mainland. You need to know that."
— social worker, Oahu

"Plastic people don't make it here. Fake nails, fake tits don't make it here."
— architect, Big Island

"If you are a man in your 20s or 30s there's a pecking order here and you should know it."
- violin maker, Maui

ka poʻe

the people

At the Hawaiʻi Tomorrow Conference
in Honolulu, hundreds of citizens of
various races and ages explored ideas
on improving life in the islands.
(Photo courtesy of Deborah Booker, *The Honolulu Advertiser*)

"I came for the

scenery and weather;

I stay for the

beautiful people"

– writer, Maui

We enjoy, and survive, a variety of lifestyles

Toni Polancy

A multi-million-dollar mansion on Kahala Avenue, O`ahu, left. A homeless man scavenges in a middle-class O`ahu neighborhood, below.

Matthew Thayer

Real lives in Paradise

It is 5:30 p.m., a Monday in December. Tourists and *kama`aina* gather on beaches as the setting sun slashes the sky with bronze and vermilion and spills gold across the ocean. The sound of conch shells echoes across the islands, signaling the end of day.

- On the island of Kaua`i, Bob Jasper comes home from work, flips on the television in his living room to catch the national news, and without looking at the screen, heads out to the lanai of his house along the Wailua River and breathes deeply, relaxing. As the heat of the day recedes, animals venture out of their hiding places on Mount Wai`ale`ale and drift to the river to drink. Tonight, as a television newscaster tallies the toll in Iraq, Bob counts two wild boars, a horse and a family of five ducks.

'The islands take care of their own. You'll either make it here or you won't, and it has more to do with what kind of person you are than how much money you have."

Daryl Davis, professional bellhop

- In her tiny apartment at an O`ahu complex, Erica Maluski, 24, dons running shorts and a T-shirt, skips expertly down the few steps from her apartment, and jogs through the parking lot. For Erica, sunset is the most beautiful time of day, and it is also the most lonely. The six-hour time difference means it is too late to call friends and relatives back in New York. She speeds up a little and waves to a neighbor pushing a stroller.

- At the Kamakou Preserve atop a mountain on the rural island of Moloka`i, Scott Hemenway, 31, high school teacher and volunteer guide, leads a group of Japanese tourists and walks just a little faster to finish the hike before dark.

- At Renaissance Wailea Beach Resort on Maui, Daryl Davis helps a honeymooning German couple into their rental car, stacks the luggage into the trunk and repeats directions to the airport. As the car pulls away the reflection of the setting sun reminds him that his shift is over. Daryl glances at his watch; he'll have time to stop at the Kihei Canoe Club on his way home, to help to clean the beach and grounds.

- On the Big Island's rural Hamakaua Coast, Susan Friend returns from a grocery trip to Costco, 50 miles away. As she lugs supplies from the car, she admonishes Jack, 3, and Lucky, 2, to behave, to stop throwing grapes at the peacocks. She glances at the sun and hopes her husband Tim will be home before it sets.

Life here goes on much the same as it does anywhere. Learning, working, playing, celebrating, surviving. But here, it is eternal summer. Breathtakingly beautiful. And very expensive.

"We are so busy trying to survive financially," says one ten-year resident, "that it doesn't matter that we live in Hawai`i. We are in our own little houses, our own little cubicles, working, working. Then a visitor comes from the mainland and we look up and say, 'Oh that's right! We live in paradise. Let's go enjoy it.'"

We work long hours, yes, but despite the rush of everyday life, despite the stress of making ends meet, the beauty of this land influences our lives in many ways. We work at resorts or on tour boats, sell art or activities, clean condos or paint pictures, sit at computers creating vacation brochures — all because Hawai`i's natural beauty lures tourists and provides about 40 percent of us with our livelihood.

We live on six small islands thousands of miles from the nearest continent, and no matter how busy we are, most of us acknowledge the ocean that surrounds us. Several times a day we feel compelled to check its condition, simply because it is an ever-present part of our lives.

Each morning most of us awaken to the scent of plumeria or pikake, to the cries of exotic birds, or, occasionally, as the islands grow and develop, to the smell of car exhausts. We end each day watching sunsets or at least noting the sun's glow tingeing our computer screens or glinting off the chrome on the cars in the office parking lot.

Newcomers may spend their first year here drunk on an overload of beauty. Flowers, fragrances, rainbows. Double rainbows. Triple rainbows. "Moonbows" — ghostly brushes of color against a dark sky.

- A 34-year-old computer specialist quit consulting positions that paid six-digits, left his mom and dad and siblings back in New York City, and moved to the Hawaiian Islands where he expects to start his own business.

Four more little words

Many visitors and newcomers to the islands simply assume that everyone who lives in Hawai`i is a Hawaiian. However, as newcomers quickly learn, when someone from Hawai`i says "Hawaiian," they tend to mean an indigenous Hawaiian, one who was born here.

To clarify, they will often say "I mean native Hawaiian." But even the term "native Hawaiian" is confusing, at least when it comes to how the state and federal governments define things. In at least one federal law, the Hawaiian Homes Commission Act of 1920, Native Hawaiians (note the °capital N) are defined as those having 50 percent or more Hawaiian blood. Many state laws, however, refer to native (small n) Hawaiians, which means anyone with indigenous Hawaiian blood.

To get around all of these definitions, some Hawaiians refer to themselves only as *kanaka maoli*, which translates as real, true or original (*maoli*) man or person (*kanaka*). At the same time, those of us non-*kanaka maoli* who call Hawai`i home are left with the similarly awkward term "Hawai`i resident" instead of simply "Hawaiian."

(Contributed by Jonathan Scheuer, an editor of this book.)

"I tell friends back there: You will work until you are 60 or 65 and then retire so you can spend five or six years doing what I am doing now, living in warmth and sunshine. Paradise. Even if I can only enjoy this on weekends," he says.

• Two sisters have lived on Maui for several years. One is a graphic artist, the other a high school teacher and, like many longtime residents, neither has had an easy time making ends meet. They occasionally lie on a beach near Maui's main airport, watching planes soar into the sky. "We look up," says one sister, "and raise our arms up high and laugh, 'Ha-ha, ha-ha... we live here! We don't *have* to go home! We *are* home!'"

The best things about Hawai`i — warmth and beauty — are free, delivered democratically to bank presidents and condo cleaners alike. Beyond that, the day-to-day structure of your life will depend here, as it does everywhere, on your circumstances and your priorities: How much do you *want?* How much do you *need?*

Being rich and/or famous in paradise

Both newcomers and *kama`aina* express a common fear: that Hawai`i is becoming a land of the poor and the very rich, those who serve and those who are served. Our nation's ever-widening income gap has long worried mainland sociologists too, but the division between haves and have-nots is more visible where sleek limousines with darkened windows glide past battered Hawai`i cruisers, where homeless people spread towels on beaches in front of million-dollar homes.

There is so much wealth here.

- A South African family, worried about violence in their hometown, buys mom a practical birthday present: a million dollar home and luxury car so she can move to safer Hawai`i.

- A young Maui woman lives on a luxury estate, free. "I house-sit for a gentleman," she says. "He comes from Japan just two or three times a year for a couple of weeks, but he likes to entertain and everything has to be just right. All I have to do is make sure everybody does his job: the pool man, the gardener, the cleaning lady."

All of the islands have posh neighborhoods where seclusion, a back-yard beach or an ocean view are status symbols. On O`ahu, cruise Kahala Avenue, Pacific Heights or Portlock; on Kaua`i, `Anini and Po`ipu beaches; on the Big Island, Waimea, Kohala and Keauhou Estates; on Maui, Makena, Wailea or Kapalua. Ornate gates shield entrances to modern marble and stucco palaces.

Our transplanted rich include successful writers, entertainers, sports figures, and entrepreneurs. Usually, the famous are allowed their privacy. Residents barely react when they encounter Jim Nabors walking his dog on a Diamond Head road; Kris Kristofferson jogging a Hana roadway; Willie Nelson at a favorite Pa`ia restaurant; Michael Jordan standing tall in line at Longs Drugs; Alice Cooper or Arnold Schwartzenegger enjoying a family dinner at a Wailea restaurant. Also among Hawai`i's privileged are "trust babies" — heirs and heiresses whose biggest worry is whether the trust check is deposited to their bank accounts on time.

Being poor in paradise

A family — mom, dad, two teenagers — helps prepare dinner at a Hawai`i homeless shelter and tells this story: They sold their Iowa home and moved to the islands several months ago. Dad, a highly qualified handyman, was sure he could easily find work here. He did, and life was beautiful, until he was installing a window and severely cut the ligaments in his arm. The family has no health insurance; dad cannot work for several months; the funds they brought dwindled and the bills mounted, landing the family at the shelter. Still radiating the awed glow of island newcomers, the family is overwhelmed, mom says, by Hawai`i's kindness and generosity.

Many *malihini* (newcomers), like this family, have no health insurance or job benefits when they first arrive and are just a bit of bad luck away from poverty. Fortunately, gentle Hawai`i is probably one of the best places in the nation to be broke. There is no residency requirement or waiting period to qualify for state aid. And a family of four can collect tax-free income, including cash grants, housing, food stamps and medical benefits, to a total of $15,482 a year in 2005.

Should you come to the islands expecting to live on the public dole? Absolutely not. Consider that living here can cost as much as 40 percent more than in some states, and $15,000 barely covers a year's rent for most homes.

About half of all shelter residents are families and about 8,000 families at any one time seek permanent public housing. They will wait two to seven years, according to an aide at the state's public housing/rent subsidy office. The office passes out 30 to 50 applications a day for subsidized housing.

The rest of us

And what about the rest of us, that 70 or so percent who comprise the middle class and working class, we who foot the bill for government and life in general? Most likely, when you first move here you will live in an apartment. If you are single, you might consider sharing expenses with a roommate. If you are a couple, probably both you and your mate will work. These days, if you have a skill and experience and are flexible in the job you take, you should find little difficulty finding work. In Honolulu, you may be able to wait to purchase a car, since bus service is efficient. In rural O`ahu and on the neighbor islands, you will need a car as soon as you arrive. These everyday aspects of life are discussed in other chapters of this book.

The real question is, what will your life be like once you have settled in? Once the thrill of life in this new, incredibly beautiful place, has worn off? *Will* it wear off?

You may work longer or harder than you do now, or you may be forced to work in a position other than that for which you are trained; but if you do survive paradise — and remember why you came: to enjoy it — your life here may be simpler and more easy-going. Your co-worker is apt to tell you he cannot come to work tomorrow because the surf is up. He loves to surf. He lives in Hawai`i to surf, not work. He hopes you understand.

That's nice. Relaxing. Pleasant. If there's just you to worry about. But if you have children to raise… well, you'll have to decide whether Hawai`i will supply you with the means you need to support them. Some of us grow wealthy here beyond our wildest dreams; some of us can hardly make ends meet. That's probably also true where you live now.

Your priorities change

Maybe it's the warm soothing weather. Maybe it's the serene atmosphere. Maybe it's the gentle spirit of the people here. But after you've lived on the islands awhile, your priorities change. The sprawling house with koa floors is nice, but the trade winds blow in dust that coats those floors. The long white Cadillac has a lot of surface to polish, metal to rust in the ocean air. Mahogany antiques can be invaded by termites. Silver tarnishes in the humidity. And all those material possessions are not what you came to the islands for, anyway. What you are coming for is there, right outside your window, whether that window is in a condo, a tract home or a marble mansion. Sunshine. Fresh air. An ocean to swim in. A beach on which to jog.

The economy

It's not easy to live an easy life here. The old pineapple and sugar industries that supplied the bulk of jobs and money for so long are phasing out, moving to parts of the world where labor is less costly. Ideally, tourism is supposed to pick up the slack, but competition for the world's visitors is tough. And relying on tourism for our income puts us at the mercy of events around the world. In 1991, the Gulf War and economic

Some good advice for *malihini*

- **Slow down, speak softly, relax.** The islands are changing in many ways, but among long-time residents some customs remain and one of them is "talking story," an old term for relaxing and chatting about nothing in particular. Long sessions of "talk story" are apt to precede business deals, especially on the neighbor islands, and newcomers who want to fit in should respect that tradition.

- **Don't try to speak pidgin**, the *patois* of the islands. "Newcomers don't know how to speak pidgin and it is almost insulting when they try," says a local man. "It sounds as though you are speaking down to us."

- **Avoid honking your car horn.** Nothing is absolute, but for the most part, people here are courteous and patient when they drive. It is considered very rude to honk your car horn.

- **Smile. Make eye contact.** It is the custom in most parts of the islands to make eye contact and smile at people you pass on a street, on the beach or in a mall. That's friendly, part of the *aloha* spirit, but it's also smart. A frown can be mistaken for "stink eye," an antagonistic or challenging expression.

- **Come with a plan.** Then have a backup plan. Try, but don't count on finding the job of your dreams. Have a second plan, one that you'll settle for. Then work hard to make the first plan succeed.

- **Don't talk stink.** Say something negative about a neighbor or co-worker and you are apt to be met with silence or a stare. As a rule, we avoid bad *mana*, spreading negative thoughts and words.

PEOPLE

troubles in Asia and the U.S. set off a drop in tourism and the real estate market from which it has taken Hawai`i several years to recover.

A popular saying here is that the islands are about five years behind the mainland economically. At this writing, Hawai`i, as much of the rest of the nation, is suffering economically. Jobs can be hard to find.

Meanwhile, each island competes for visitors and looks for other ways to bolster its economy, to keep the good times rolling. High-tech development, movie-making and exotic produce and coffee production are the enterprises most often mentioned. (See the Working chapter of this book.)

Unwritten rules

More than 200 people were interviewed for this book, and many of them voiced the same concern: that giving back to the community is especially important here. Newcomers on these small, isolated islands, we must be each other's caretakers, each other's `ohana, or family. To succeed here, to be considered `ohana, you must contribute in some way to the overall welfare of island residents, or to the preservation of the islands, whether by performing a song, cleaning a roadway, serving on a town development committee, or dishing out food at a homeless shelter.

Many people here are also spiritual; they feel drawn to the ocean and mountains, which exert a mystical pull. And there is an almost religious fervor here, as though nature is a being in its own right. *Kama`aina* tend to speak of God and the Hawaiian goddess Pele in the same sentence, giving due respect to each.

Mable Haas, wife of a retired veterinarian, had lived on Kaua`i for 40 years and raised four sons there. Sipping coffee at a Kapa`a music store one rainy Sunday morning, I told her my story — that I gave up a good, steady, dependable job, came to Hawai`i to start a business and made little money for the first two years; how scared I sometimes was. She gazed over the rim of her steamy cup, a gentle smile on her creased face.

"But after you were here awhile," she murmured, "you realized that you were accepted, that you'd be taken care of."

"The islands take care of their own," said another longtime resident. "You'll either make it here or you won't, and it has more to do with who you are — what kind of person you are — than how much money you have."

"Hawai`i is selective," says another *kama`aina*, echoing an often-heard refrain. "Hawai`i will either accept you into her arms... or she will spit you out and throw you away, send you back to the real world."

Another person said this, and it's true: "If you are happy and successful there, where you are now, you'll be happy and successful here."

And still another wise person added: "You have a history, in your life, of either making good decisions or poor decisions. Moving here isn't going to change that."

You are still *you*, good or bad, wise or wanton.

Most Common Surnames on
Birth and Death Certificates

| Rank | Birth certificates | | Death certificates | |
:---:	Surname	Births	Surname	Deaths
1	Lee	77	Lee	67
2	Smith	66	Wong	50
3	Williams	55	Ching	37
4	Johnson	49	Kim	37
4	Nguyen	49	Nakamura	37
6	Wong	46	Higa	32
7	Jones	45	Young	32
8	Brown	44	Chun	29
9	Silva	43	Tanaka	29
10	Ramos	41	Smith	28

Source: Hawaii State Department of Health, Office of Health Status Monitoring, records.
The State of Hawai`i Data Book 2008 http://www.hawaii.gov/dbedt/info/economic/databook/db2008/

Smith, Brown, Johnson, Anderson. Birth Certificates illustrate a growing Caucasian influence.

Prejudice and aloha

The fact that prejudice exists in Hawai`i comes as a surprise to many newcomers. Tourist brochures never mention it, nor do Chamber of Commerce or visitor bureau materials. Guidebooks offer only a half-hearted warning suggesting visitors stay off some beaches at night.

Yet :

- A middle-aged woman, visiting the southern tip of the Big Island, a traditionally local area, hears a hiss behind her as she enters a food market. When she turns around, a young local couple behind her snarls, "Go home, *haole*."

- A young homosexual man tells of threats and beatings on Maui.

- A 44-year-old Pennsylvania attorney, tall and blond and very *haole*, visits the islands annually. At least once every year someone yells *"Haole!"* or "Go home, *haole*!"

- At a beachfront wedding celebration, a group of local bodyboarders advances threateningly toward the Caucasian bride and groom, murmuring *"Haoles*, go home." When the groom's local friends show up, the hecklers apologize. The groom, who has lived here for several years, warns, "If you are in your 20s or 30s, there's a pecking order here and you should know it."

- An elderly woman wants to live on the Windward side of O`ahu, but concerned friends warn her that the area is "too local" for her to live there alone. One day she talks story with a young local couple, sitting on a park bench in Ha`aula, and tells them of her desire to live in the area. She asks their opinion. Would she be safe? The local man thinks a minute and then responds, "Yes. You old woman. You be okay. Young *haole* man, not so good. Trouble."

- A Big Island family with a twenty-year history on the islands leaves after the father is involved in an altercation at a sovereignty protest. It is one of several reasons the family left, but the mother warns, "The sovereignty issue is heating up and it added to our decision."

Hawai`i's 1,295,000-plus people are an eclectic mix. Recruited as labor in the sugar and pineapple plantations, a potpourri of races came from around the world: Chinese, Filipino, Japanese, Portuguese, Russian, Norwegian and others. Plantation owners encouraged ethnic groups to live apart, each in its own company-owned "camp," small neighborhoods isolated deep in the tall cane fields. Labor unions, voted in during the 1940s, advocated brotherhood, the bringing together of races, and camp families began to mingle more.

Today, everyone in Hawai`i is a minority. Asians make up the largest single group and about 37 percent of the residents are *hapa* or mixed race, but neither constitutes a majority.

Today, as the islands grow more crowded, few residents ask who belongs in Hawai`i and who does not, but the topic — accompanied by a shrug of the shoulders, a shake of the head — surfaces occasionally. Does a person whose ancestors sailed here in a *wa`a* (canoe) hundreds of years ago have more claim than one whose grandfather shipped over as a plantation worker several decades ago? Does either have more claim than someone newly arrived on a jet plane?

Several of the people interviewed for this book echoed this statement: "This is America, but it is not the United States. You have to respect that." What they mean is that living in Hawai`i is living with people of many cultures, all of which must be acknowledged.

"Here, you are no longer American, top dog," commented another person. "Here, you are one of at least thirty cultures that make up the islands, and many of those cultures have prior and more valid claims to power then we do."

"It's misleading," says a transplanted New Englander. "We use American currency and have American laws; English is the primary language. But other than that, you are living in a foreign country."

An unlikely U.S.

Hawai`i will never be the United States as mainlanders know it, with one primary culture that dictates beliefs and customs. The European and Asian immigrants who came to mainland America in the late 1890s and early 1900s aspired to become part of the American culture, to meld into it. Today, the nation's newest immigrants — Mexicans, Cubans, Koreans and Eastern Europeans — have that same goal.

But in Hawai`i, perhaps because of our geographic isolation, ethnic groups struggle to retain heritage, cling to and promote old customs.

Ethnic Stock

Ethnic stock	State total	City and County of Honolulu	Hawai`i County	Kaua`i County	Maui County
All groups	1,257,607	880,308	172,004	62,669	142,626
Unmixed (except Hawaiian)	699,622	493,181	88,041	33,796	84,604
Caucasian	256,381	138,078	54,860	16,707	46,736
Black	7,380	6,842	195	144	199
Japanese	220,201	179,755	20,273	7,258	12,915
Chinese	47,767	44,706	1,688	405	968
Filipino	148,773	106,394	10,455	9,156	22,768
Korean	8,001	6,989	547	66	399
Samoan/ Tongan	11,118	10,415	24	61	619
Mixed (except Hawaiian)	252,147	185,796	31,991	11,674	22,685
Hawaiian/ part Hawaiian	305,838	201,331	51,971	17,198	35,337

Source: Hawai`i State Department of Health, Office of Health Status Monitoring, special tabulation from the Hawai`i Health Survey.

The State of Hawai`i Data Book 2008 http://www.hawaii.gov/dbedt/info/economic/databook/db2008/

Steve Brinkman

Descendants of Ali`i (chiefs) and leaders of high-ranking families gather in an `awa ceremony. People who have lived in a town or area for a long time are welcomed into the community as official members with this ritual.

They have no desire to be "Americanized"; instead they see the islands as a place where various cultures can flourish, not diminish. Hawai`i businesses boast of the state as being "like a giant cultural stew." In truth, it is more of a traditional Hawaiian plate lunch, each food item sitting separately on the same plate, yet contributing to the overall meal.

The disdain some locals have for Caucasians has roots in recent history. During the 1800s and early 1900s, most of the powerful plantation bosses were Caucasian. These days, displays of prejudice against Caucasians or Japanese are apt to be spurred by the huge influx of both ethnic groups during the past 30 years, buying up property and driving up land prices, claiming higher-paying jobs and, in some cases, desecrating the land.

Resentment against Asian residents is apt to be tinged with respect, and perhaps, envy. Their grandparents were imported to work on the plantations, but today's Hawaiian Asians are often highly educated and prosperous. For many years after World War II, Asians dominated business and politics.

> "Given the uniqueness of Hawai`i, where nobody's a minority because everyone is, it's very difficult to tell whether someone was targeted because of their ethnicity...

In *Honolulu* magazine (July, 1995), the Rev. Al Miles, an African-American, argues there is relatively little racial bigotry here compared to the mainland. He says Caucasians feel prejudice because they are so accustomed to special treatment by virtue of being white. Nevertheless, some sociologists predict ill-will and ethnic unrest will escalate as the islands become more crowded. And in the second volume of *The Price of Paradise*, Franklin Ode, director of Ethnic Studies at the University of Hawai`i, and Susan Yim, a freelance journalist, conclude, "The truth of the matter is that ethnic tension in Hawai`i is growing and a tradition of tolerance tends to mask this."

Ethnic crimes: It's not that 'anyone's naive'

Hawai`i's diversity leads to thousands of cases involving minority victims, but there are few examples of a victim being singled out specifically for their ethnicity, culture, sexual orientation or other differences, officials say.

A hate crimes unit, mandated by the federal government, was set up in Hawai`i in 2001, but very few crimes are reported or judged to be hate crimes.

"Given the uniqueness of Hawai`i, where nobody's a minority because everyone is, it's very difficult to tell whether someone was targeted because of their ethnicity or they became a victim for some other reason," Paul Perrone, chief of research for the state attorney general, said in a *Honolulu Advertiser* article.

"There's the ongoing problem of locals and military mixing it up in bars, but attacks against the Asian community or other communities are rare," said Honolulu police Capt. Doug Miller in the same article.

"It's not that nobody cares about these crimes, or that anyone's naîve enough to believe it doesn't happen here," Miller said.

Most incidents — threats, name-calling, "stink eye" — fall short of being crimes under existing statutes and so go unreported.

African-Americans: segregation 'prevalent'

African-Americans are a true minority on the islands, just over two percent of the population. And, in a state so proud of its ethnic mix, this race suffers the most from prejudice.

"Hawai`i can be brutally racist in its treatment of this particular minority," Franklin Ode, director of Ethnic Studies at the University of Hawai`i, and Susan Yim, a freelance journalist, comment in *The Price of Paradise.* A longtime Hawai`i schoolteacher concurs.

"There is much discrimination against blacks and you see it particularly in the schools," says the Caucasian middle school instructor. "Here, African-Americans are called *popolo*, which is very derogatory. It's ironic. We have so many dark-skinned people, but somehow if they find out there is just a little bit black, there is this extreme prejudice."

Gilbert Githere, an award-winning Kenyan filmmaker who lived on O`ahu for several years, says smiles and aloha are an easy way out, a method of covering racial prejudice.

"Segregation, although not part of the law, although not admitted, is prevalent in Hawai`i. Segregation means 'cutting away from livelihood.' Prejudice becomes economics," Githere says. "They [other races] are polite, but they are waiting for you to go away. They make it very difficult for you to stay. [They say] 'Why are you giving this man a job? Why is he living in Hawai`i?'"

'Basically gay friendly'

Hawai`i is very gay friendly, says David Morehouse, director of the gay and lesbian community center on O`ahu. "Well, *basically* gay-friendly," Morehouse corrects himself. "Hawai`i does share *aloha* (love or friendship) and *'ohana* (family). Hawai`i is a state of non-discrimination because it has always been a melting pot of culture from all over the world. Hawai`i does not discriminate against race, religion or sexual orientation."

Morehouse is speaking of the law. Housing laws, employment laws, federal laws are enforced and appreciated here, Morehouse says. Officially.

A young, slight, blond homosexual man tells another story. Walking along highways, he has twice been accosted by "locals" and beaten, he says.

Some good advice:

- **Know potential employers.** Gay and lesbian job hunters should "do their homework" before they disclose their status during a job interview, advises Morehouse. Try to ascertain the attitudes of people with whom you interview, or the reputation of the company with which you are considering a job. It's illegal to discriminate against homosexual workers, but some places can be more understanding and more pleasant to work in than others. "Whether or not you disclose that you are gay depends on the attitude of the business, of who you are interviewing with," he says.

- **Know the territory.** Some parks and beaches are "local" territory at night and they can be the same areas that are filled with tourists during the day. Stay off the beaches after dark until you learn which are safe. And avoid anyone who has been drinking excessively or appears argumentative.

- **Know your rights.** In 1997 Hawai`i was the first state to pass a law extending many marital rights to gay couples. Additional laws granting further rights and benefits under the Reciprocal Beneficiary Act were approved in 1999, and more may be added as time goes on. For Websites and more information, see the Romance section of this book.

A third time, he was followed into a men's room at a local bar and warned, "We don't need more fags here."

"Those times on the road, well, I couldn't help that," he says thoughtfully. "But I should have known better than to go to a local bar."

"You have to be careful," Morehouse says, "to judge wisely. It's not just a gay thing. You don't, as a single woman, walk out the door of a cocktail bar and walk down an alley late at night. You don't walk around wearing Versace clothes and carrying a gold bag and be surprised when you are mugged."

In recent years, being gay has become a national "in." Television shows and movies routinely feature gay men, although few, so far, feature lesbian women. But tolerance of homosexuals is more than a trend in the islands. Hawaiians have a long tradition of being tolerant of gays, recognizing homosexuality not as an aberration, but as natural. The Hawaiian word *mahu* refers to men who take on the role of women, cross-dressing and helping to raise children. There is no stigma to it, Morehouse says.

"Unfortunately, you may see cross-dressing guys working the street as prostitutes, and they are called mahu, but that is not the real meaning. It's a much gentler meaning," Morehouse adds.

Homosexual lifestyles are much more accepted here than in less-liberal areas of the country. Overall, if you are gay or lesbian and planning to move to the islands because you feel you can be more open here, you probably will not be disappointed. However, you might be more comfortable in O`ahu or Maui than on the more rural islands.

An effort to legalize homosexual marriages in Hawai`i failed in 1996, but not before it provoked anti-gay feelings. "With the gay marriage suit, some people who were not as prejudiced [became] more so…afraid we are going to take over the world and start with Hawai`i," Morehouse says. The fears do not seem to generate in any particular ethnic or age group. Some argue that homosexuals will flock here, somehow changing the ambiance of the islands; others say recognizing homosexual marriages will be a burden on taxpayers.

"I get along with everybody, but I've learned to get along," Morehouse offers. "Newcomers to the islands have to establish what a comfortable territory for them is and respect the local's territory. The culture, the traditions are very different here. It's America, but it's not the mainland. You need to respect that. You have an obligation to understand the environment."

Car bumper stickers say it all.

If you are going to live in Hawai`i, it is important to know that prejudice exists. But prejudice, its anticipation and its effects, are sometimes hard to gauge. What is real? What is imagined?

A little plastic bag...

A few years before I moved to the islands I was visiting my mother on O`ahu. We sat on a bench reading the Sunday newspaper, patiently waiting for a bus. It began to rain, but before we were really wet, the bus appeared.

We gathered up our papers clumsily, boarded the bus in noisy confusion, fumbled for our fares. We turned to find seats and looked into a silent sea of Asian faces — eyes staring at us resentfully, mouths pursed in disapproval. The rain pelted the darkened bus and I shuddered as we sat down in front of a middle-aged woman who seemed to be scowling.

My mother, who has been in love with Hawai`i for the 20 years she's lived here, chatted happily and seemed oblivious to all this. How can my mother live in this place? I wondered. So far from friends and family, so full of angry strangers.

The words of a Big Island missionary ran through my mind. "They love tourists, but they distrust *malihini*, people who move to the islands. Caucasians, after all, have taken the land that is theirs."

Just then, I felt a tapping on my shoulder.

I turned and the woman behind me, still scowling, was reaching into her purse. "Here," she said, pulling out a neatly folded plastic bag. "You take."

"What? I don't understand," I frowned, shaking my head.

"Give me," she said, taking my damp newspaper. She carefully refolded it and neatly put it into the bag. "Now stay dry. More better to read."

She gave the parcel back to me and said some words I could not translate. Finally she smiled slightly and nodded in a kind of short bow.

My mother nodded to the woman and smiled. Then she explained. "She says you must always carry a plastic bag in Hawai`i because you never know when it will rain. And she is giving you hers."

na kalani `aina

politics and issues

To understand modern life

in these islands you must know

at least a little of our history

Photo by G. Brad Lewis

Kaleiolani's story: White men working

Ten-year-old Kaleiolani was excited as the airplane landed at the San Francisco airport. It was August, 1956, and his family was moving from rural Niu Valley on O`ahu to Portland, Oregon, where Kaleiolani's father would attend college. As the family began a long Greyhound bus ride, the boy stared out the window in awe: such tall buildings, so many people, so many cars on wide highways.

The bus moved slowly through the traffic and Kaleiolani's eyes rested on some men digging a ditch along the highway. He blinked and looked again, amazed. The men were *haoles,* white. It was the first time Kaleiolani had ever seen white men working as laborers. Until then he had pictured Caucasians only as bosses, as people in charge.

Allen K. Hoe today

"All the mid-level managers at the plantations were always *haoles,*" he remembers.

Today, Kaleiolani is Allen K. Hoe, an O`ahu attorney in private practice, a Vietnam combat veteran, and a member of the Hawai`i Sovereignty Election Council. Over the past 140 years, land and the power to govern themselves have been taken from native Hawaiians. Now they seek restitution and self-government.

"For everyone who has come to Hawai`i, Hawai`i has represented a dream and an opportunity," Hoe says. "And everyone has come and used Hawai`i as a means to an end. The Hawaiians have always welcomed them and Hawaiians have paid the price."

The past

First, the ali`i

For about 800 years, between the time the first Tahitians sailed to the islands until Western missionaries arrived in 1820, Hawai`i was governed by *ali`i* (chiefs) and *kahuna*, religious leaders and experts who served as advisors to *ali`i*. Hawaiian society was governed under a system of taboos or *kapu*, which could mandate death for all classes, but which in everyday affairs bore most heavily on women and children. The penalty for walking on the same ground as *ali`i*, eating the same food as a chief, or crossing his shadow, could be death. Hawaiians were unfamiliar with the concept of land ownership, but they believed *ali`i* were caretakers of the land on behalf of the gods. Commoners planted, harvested and fished, and tithed to the *ali`i* a portion of their take, much as we support our religious leaders today.

Then, Captain Cook

English explorer Capt. James Cook was on his way to the Arctic to find a northwest passage between the Atlantic and Pacific Oceans when he sailed into Kaua`i's Waimea Bay in 1778. He arrived during the harvest celebration of *Makahiki*, and Hawaiians believed he was Lono, god of the harvest. They welcomed Cook and his men who brought both tools of construction — nails — and tools of destruction — guns — and traded them for yams and pork, as well as sexual favors from eager *wahine*, women. Aware that his men carried venereal disease and other illnesses to which Hawaiians had no immunity, Cook tried to limit contact. He failed.

Hawai`i's feudal past dictated its development, influences today's government, and overshadows our future.

The nails, much valued by natives, eventually led to Cook's downfall. On a later visit, a group of Hawaiians seeking more nails stole one of his ships. A fight ensued and Cook was injured. Seeing his blood, a sign of mortality, the Hawaiians were enraged that he had let them believe he was a god, and they killed him.

Kamehameha I unites the islands

Cook initiated change in the islands and, a few years later, in 1795, so did the Hawaiian warrior King Kamehameha I. Using weapons Kamehameha had seen Cook use and waging relentless war on rulers of the other islands, Kamehameha gained control of all the islands, gathering them for the first time under a centralized government. As he matured, Kamehameha I, from all historical accounts a warring and lusty king, grew to be a kind and wise monarch whose laws benefited his people, especially children and the elderly.

Eventually, Hawaiians, including the *kahuna* and *ali`i*, began to question the restrictive *kapu* system. Among other things, the *kapu* forbade men and women from dining together. Kamehameha II, known as Liholiho, succeeded his father. He shared power with the dowager queen, Ka`ahumanu. One day Ka`ahumanu and Liholiho's mother, Keopuolani, persuaded Liholiho to dine with them. The gods did not retaliate and the *kapu* system was broken, leaving Hawaiians divided over the issue. Though a civil war broke out, it was quickly put down.

Using weapons he had seen Captain Cook use, Kamehameha I gained control of the islands

Missionaries arrive

The first missionaries — nearly all idealistic young men under the age of 30 — were affiliated with the United Church of Christ. Since the American Board of Commissioners for Foreign Missions stipulated all missionaries must be married, several of them quickly found wives. They left Boston on Oct. 23, 1819, and after a long and grueling journey eventually arrived at the Puna side of the Big Island in 1820. It was a fortuitous time for them: *kapu* had been broken and Hawaiians were adrift in a rapidly changing world.

The missionaries were literally greeted with open arms by powerful *ali`i* and *kahuna*. Hawaiians saw the work of missionaries as being twofold: *pule* (worship) and *palapala* (learning). They dug coral and hewed wood to build churches and homes for the first missionaries, who were soon followed by missionaries from other sects, including Roman Catholic priests from France in 1827.

Whalers and traders had already begun to ply the islands. They too were welcomed by the natives: *kane* (men) shared food and knowledge; *wahine* (women) eagerly shared their bodies, much to the missionaries' horror. Missionaries discouraged Hawaiians from wasting time in games, *mele* (song) and dance. Eventually the *hula*, which they considered lascivious, was banned. They also urged *wahine* to cover their bodies, introducing the loose, modest *mu`umu`u*.

The missionaries were strict and puritanical, but they were also hard-working and, by most accounts, devoted to their converts. They eventually taught Hawaiians — a race without a written language — to speak, read and write in English. Meanwhile, they taught that salvation came through reading the Bible, and so they developed a written version of the Hawaiian language and translated the Bible. Many Hawaiians wanted to learn and study. The missionaries labored long and hard, fulfilling the role of minister, teacher, doctor and building contractor. Eventually, urged to do so by royalty, a few missionaries and many foreigners became active in island government.

The missionaries also started numerous schools, some still among the best private schools in Hawai`i. To educate their own children in English, they founded Punahou School on O`ahu in 1841. So great was the desire for education that when the last of the Kamehameha dynasty, Bernice Pauahi Bishop, died, she bequeathed her wealth — an inheritance of all the royal lands — to the establishment of the highly-regarded Kamehameha Schools, which gives preference to admitting children of Hawaiian blood. The holdings of Kamehameha Schools are estimated to be worth over $5 billion in today's market, making it one of the largest private charitable trusts in the United States.

The ahupua`a

In early Hawaiian times the islands were divided into *ahupua`a*, pie-shaped slices of land running from the top of a mountain to the sea. Ideally, an *ahupua`a*, could produce everything needed to sustain life. It included an ocean to fish, valleys in which to gather plants and food, and mountains from which waterfalls and streams ran.

Business takes over

By the 1850s, benefiting from a modern concept — being in the right place at the right time — descendants of missionaries (as well as other Caucasians) began to take advantage of the opportunities the islands afforded. They went into business, establishing first sugar, and then pineapple plantations. They controlled the commerce that followed: banking, shipping, retailing. Some of them married the offspring of *ali`i*.

Challenged by foreign sailors and growers who felt they were exempt from island law and who were attempting to claim the island chain for foreign powers, Kamehameha III in 1840 proclaimed the first constitution of the Kingdom of Hawai`i. From 1848 to 1852, his Great Mahele (land division) allowed first Hawaiians, then foreigners, to own land. But the concept of land ownership was unknown to Hawaiians, who had no money to buy anyway. So Westerners — including *haole* businessmen — bought up about 80 percent of the land that had been privatized, many in large estates. Disenfranchised Hawaiians worked virtually as landless proletariat on land they had for hundreds of years considered on loan from the gods. Some Hawaiians left the rural areas of the islands and went to work in towns, hoping to earn enough to buy their lands. Others gave up and left the islands to live elsewhere.

Author Robert Lewis Stevenson, left, dines with Lili`uokalani, fourth from left, and King Kalakaua.

But the greatest threat to the Hawaiian people was disease. Foreigners brought new illnesses — venereal disease, smallpox, measles and others — for which the biologically inexperienced Hawaiians had little resistance. Scholars debate the number of Hawaiians prior to contact with foreigners. Some estimates run as high as one million; others as low as 150,000. But by 1870, the Hawaiian population had dwindled to 60,000. Some historians say it was more than disease. Some say the communal Hawaiians, separated from their `aina and *mana* (land and spirit) and their `ohana (family), died of broken hearts.

There were too few Hawaiians to work the burgeoning plantations, so in the mid-1800s and for the next 70 years, thousands of plantation workers were imported, first from China, then from Japan and Portugal, and finally from the Philippines and other countries around the world. These immigrants would forever change the face of the islands, making Hawai`i today, in the words of historian and author Gavan Daws, "the most successful multi-cultural society in history."

The Hawaiian Islands grew more valuable as huge plantations prospered. For over one hundred years, a few companies — known as the Big Five — dominated commerce: Castle & Cooke, Alexander & Baldwin, American Factors (Amfac), Theo H. Davies, and C. Brewer Co. Three of these companies are still powerful today.

A queen imprisoned

Queen Lili`uokalani

In 1852, a new Constitution reduced the king's power and increased the power of an elected Legislature. And in 1887, King David Kalakaua was forced by a *hui* (group) of American businessmen and plantation owners to accept the Bayonet Constitution. It limited his power, as well as the voting power of Hawaiians and Asians. Kalakaua died in 1891 and his sister Lili`uokalani ascended to the throne. She retained control for two years, and in 1893 attempted to declare a new constitution which would return power to native Hawaiians and other voters. Plantation owners and businessmen eventually launched a coup, creating a provisional government. In 1894, they

Hawai`i State Archives

Hawai`i's Largest Landowners

In acres

Landowner	Landholdings
State of Hawai`i	1,202,900
Hawaiian Home Lands	190,290
Federal government	338,000
Major private landowners (greater than 5,000 acres)	1,566,037
Small private landowners (less than 5,000 acres)	813,740
Total land area of state	4,110,978

Source: Atlas of Hawaii, third edition.

declared the "Republic of Hawai`i" with Sanford Dole, an attorney who worked for the sugar industry "elite," as president.

Queen Lili`uokalani, much distressed, tried to regain political power for native Hawaiians in a brief, unsuccessful counter-revolt. In 1895, she was arrested and confined to her bedroom at Honolulu's `Iolani Palace for nine months. As her subjects kept vigil outside, Lili`uokalani sewed quilts, wrote beautiful songs (including the moving lament *"Aloha `Oe"*) and waited for U.S. President Grover Cleveland to send help. Cleveland expressed his support for the queen in a message to the U.S. Congress, but Congress did nothing. The annexationists simply waited until William McKinley was in office before successfully seeking annexation again in 1898. Two years later Congress adopted the Organic Act, creating the Territory of Hawai`i with Dole as governor. By 1902, Republicans (primarily wealthy and powerful businessmen and landowners) had taken control of the territorial Legislature.

The Democratic years

After World War II, returning veterans, especially young Japanese Americans, as well as sons and daughters of other plantation workers, began to unite, largely through the Democratic Party and the unions, which had started to organize plantation workers as early as 1910. In 1954 the Democrats gained control of the territory's Legislature in "The Democratic Revolution." No longer were large landowners in control of government; the new liberal government had as its goals democracy and equality for all, breaking the control of the Republicans, big business and the Caucasian-owned sugar and trading companies.

In 1959, Hawai`i became the 50th American state and a 30-year period of unparalleled prosperity began. With the advent of modern jet travel, tourists from around the world flocked to the islands. Land prices swirled upward in a climb that would peak in the late 1980s. Tax money rolled in.

The Democrats made great strides in fulfilling their goals: Hawai`i moved from a rural plantation society to an urban service society. Today, the state's biggest industry is tourism, not agriculture. Small business provides most jobs.

Sovereignty

Although President Cleveland sent no help to Lili`uokalani in 1893 or thereafter, he called her imprisonment and the overthrow of the monarchy "not merely wrong, but a disgrace." More than a hundred years later, the United States agreed the coup was illegal and President Clinton signed a formal Apology Bill. The bill did little *but* apologize; it specified no course of action to make amends. But Hawaiian activists hope the President's apology will serve as an acknowledgment of U.S. guilt and lead to an eventual rectification.

Over the years, the government has agreed to set some areas aside as Hawaiian Homelands, to give to those of native lineage a small part of the lands that were taken from them. In 1920, the U.S. Congress passed the Hawaiian Homes Commission Act, creating a homesteading program for Hawaiians. However, most of the land that was set aside was of poor quality, and Congress also specified that only Hawaiians of 50 percent or more native blood would qualify. Management of the program was returned to Hawai`i when it became a state.

Is aloha real? Ask a newcomer

Longtime residents sometimes ask if aloha, the loving spirit for which Hawai`i is famous, still exists, if it ever existed, or was just the figment of the tourist industry's imagination. But newcomers from less gentle parts of the world know the answer is yes, aloha is alive and well.

Shortly after Serge and Gloria King moved to Kaua`i, they went shopping in Lihu`e, about 40 miles from Princeville Resort. They bought several chairs and were trying to figure out how to get them into their car when a local man — dark-skinned and of mixed race — asked where they lived and offered to follow them home, carrying the chairs in his truck. When the caravan arrived in Princeville, the man helped unload the chairs and Serge offered him money for the delivery. The man declined, accepting only a beverage to quench his thirst, and said he had to be on his way back home.

"Where's that?" Serge asked. He assumed the man lived in his own neighborhood.

"Waimea," the man said, motioning back the way they had come. "Long way."

Serge was stunned. Waimea was across the island. "I thought he helped us because he lived on this end of the island... and here he had gone all that distance, altogether about 100 miles out of his way, to help, to make a newcomer, a haole, feel welcome!"

The unsolicited good deed put a happy tone to the Kings' transition to Kaua`i. They settled in easily. "Within two weeks on Kaua`i," says King, "we made more friends than in all our years in Malibu."

Many Hawaiians who qualify have been waiting for years for land of their own. Meanwhile, the program has been hampered by a documented history of mismanagement by federal and state governments, sporadic federal and state financial support and other problems. Some Hawaiians grow old and die, waiting. Meanwhile, Hawaiians continue to be displaced from land they consider their own, some of it having been in their families for generations.

Especially in the past twenty years, a quiet anger has smoldered among native Hawaiians. Bolstered by renewed interest and concern for true Hawaiian history, but often hampered by in-fighting, the Sovereignty Movement, a demand for self-government, has taken shape.

Four possible resolutions

Hawaiians are divided on the sovereignty issue, but at least four resolutions are possible.

• **The first,** considered very unlikely, is a totally independent Hawaiian nation. The Hawaiians would take back the islands, making the state of Hawai`i a separate nation.

• **The second,** more likely solution, is "nation within a nation" status, granted by the federal government, setting aside certain land as the Hawaiians' own, similar to American Indian reservations on the mainland. In that case, life could really change for Hawaiians and everyone in the islands. For instance, casino gambling, which is allowed on Indian land, would bring significant economic changes. Also, crimes committed on reservation lands, even by non-natives, would be subject to internal police and court systems.

• **The third** possibility is for the state, not the federal government, to grant some kind of sovereign status to Native Hawaiians. In that case, there might be little effect on life here.

• **The fourth** alternative, expected by many people, even as they read the headlines and watch television stories on Hawaiian issues, is that nothing at all will change.

U.S. Sen. Dan Inouye of Hawai`i has said Congress would most likely grant Hawaiians only the nation-within-a-nation status, similar to that of Native Americans on tribal lands. A controversial Federal Recognition Bill would create a process for Hawaiians to form their own sovereign government.

> 'They diminish Hawaiians and hold them down by making them wards of the state and treating them like children... '
>
> —Earl Arakaki

Commonly called the Akaka Bill for its sponsor, Sen. Daniel Akaka, D-Hawai`i, the bill has stalled in Congress since 2000, facing both support and opposition from native Hawaiian groups and the public. Some Hawaiian activists say the issue should be taken internationally. They advocate letting the world, not the U.S. government, decide.

"No one honestly believes that the state or the federal governments are going to, of their own good will, give back to the Hawaiian people what was illegally taken,"said Allen K. Hoe, Hawaiian affairs activist.

"But I think once the Hawaiian community rises up and expresses its will there will be a powerful alliance of governments within the international community that will compel that justice be done for Hawaiians."

Meanwhile, 15 state residents, including three people of Hawaiian ancestry, filed suit in 2002 to eliminate the Office of Hawaiian Affairs and the Hawaiian Homes Commission Act, charging they are racially discriminatory and "divide Hawai`i's people."

"They diminish Hawaiians and hold them down by making them wards of the state and treating them like children incapable of handling their own affairs," writes Earl Arakaki in an editorial in *The Honolulu Advertiser*. Arakaki is lead plaintiff.

A Big Island protester wears the image of Queen Lili`uokalani.

Those of us who have come late to Hawai`i tend to be split on the issue. Many of us sympathize and agree that some form of restitution is in order. Meanwhile, an O`ahu man sums up the feelings of those opposed to any form of resolution. He points out that throughout history countries have been conquered, most with war and loss of lives, and insists that Hawai`i's people have fared no worse.

The point could be made, however, that Hawaiians continue to suffer. Gilbert Githere, a Kenyan immigrant who lives in O`ahu and is active in African-American concerns, makes a strong assessment of the Hawaiian rights issue.

"[The Hawaiians are] facing a power, the biggest in the world. Even Colonialism in Africa never was as bad as it was here. Colonialism never killed a language," Githere says. "We are talking about the extinction of a people; their lives have become extinct."

Politics today

First Hawai`i was ruled by *ali`i*, then in effect, by plantation owners and businessmen. And despite the Democratic Revolution, vestiges of that paternalistic background remain. Hawai`i's government, strongly centralized, is the most powerful state government in the country.

A sit-in at the State Capitol building includes hula, ancient chants and an all-night vigil.

The state collects the bulk of tax monies and decides how they will be allotted and spent, including funding for public education. It has almost total control of all the state's schools; it issues most business and professional licenses. Some allotment of power seems blurred — while the individual island counties can issue traffic citations, the money collected goes to the state.

Now, Hawai`i remains one of the most liberal, most spending and most taxing states. And, perhaps thanks to our indentured past, one of the most docile. With a constant influx of new residents, times are changing, but both longtime residents and starry-eyed newcomers seem reluctant to rock the boat. Here, speaking ill of someone, creating bad *mana*, is still frowned upon, is taboo. That easy-going peacefulness is part of Hawai`i's charm.

When the economy flourished, as it did during the 1970s and 1980s, money poured into the state coffers. It was easy to pay for the good life:

State Government Expenditures
In thousands of dollars

Function	2005	2006	2007	2008
Total expenditures	6,399,696	7,062,832	7,888,242	8,220,571
Current	6,077,748	6,615,255	7,385,509	7,741,836
General government	508,154	493,301	458,236	537,541
Public safety	291,369	322,578	376,032	411,152
Highways	301,784	267,213	337,862	406,795
Conservation of natural resources	74,188	86,628	107,578	103,596
Health	564,807	685,679	832,333	863,914
Welfare	1,614,559	1,709,810	1,770,707	1,857,473
Lower education	1,798,208	1,984,129	2,305,280	2,201,901
Higher education	559,379	678,338	759,777	815,116
Other education	19,667	19,183	20,122	23,206
Culture and recreation	73,774	87,478	92,574	110,404
Urban redevelopment & housing	52,698	60,725	170,614	255,783
Economic devel. & assistance	214,377	215,559	147,146	149,075
Other	4,784	4,634	7,248	5,880
Debt service	321,948	447,577	502,733	478,735
Principal	128,378	247,935	271,010	231,478
Interest and others	193,570	199,642	231,723	247,257

Source: Hawaii State Department of Accounting and General Services, Comprehensive Annual Financial Report For The Fiscal Year Ended June 30, 2008, p. 151

liberal perks for residents and government (federal and state) workers, who make up 10 percent of the workforce. The Gulf War and world economic difficulties brought a halt to that prosperity. During the 1990s and early 2000s Hawai`i treaded water, "getting by" and holding costs.

Development vs. conservation

In Hawai`i, development, conservation and the economy form a peculiar *ménage à trois*. Development — the building of homes, apartments and condominiums on former sugar lands — provides sorely needed jobs and lures tourists, who have become the lifeblood of these islands. Yet overpopulation and over-development on some islands are already detracting from the natural beauty that draws visitors.

As development explodes, so have battles over conservation. How much land will be used for development? How will the land be treated? Where will the infrastructure come from to support new development? How will water be supplied to all those condominiums, all those golf courses, all those people?

On O`ahu and Maui, water is becoming scarce as housing developments are built. Aquifers in the O`ahu mountains pour water into a new community and restrict its flow to an old one. Desalination of ocean waters is being considered. Maui's mayor institutes a freeze on new water meters reservations and is criticized by developers and business people who say the action will cause Maui's skyrocketing real estate prices to escalate even more. The mayor begins to back off from the threat, to find ways to work around it.

Cultural issues abound. The H-3 freeway through O`ahu's Ko`olau Mountains comes under fire from Hawaiians because it disturbs a *heiau*, or temple. At the State Capitol, Hawaiians march for gathering rights — legal permission to enter properties to collect traditional food and flowers for *lei*. Their protests, as benefits these gentle islands, include *mele* (song) and *hula* (dance).

The problem, says one conservationist, is that these islands are a democracy and anyone who wants to move here may. If people would just visit and go back home instead of moving here, we'd have fewer problems.

Become *kama`aina*. Make a difference.

On small islands, it is very easy to have a voice, to make a difference. Here's how:

• **Become involved.** Become active in the issues you feel strongest about. Or help govern these islands by becoming involved in politics. In addition to the traditional ways — calling party headquarters and volunteering or attending fund-raising functions — you can call the mayors' offices directly. Volunteer to serve on boards and commissions for which you have expertise.

• **Immerse yourself** in real Hawaiian culture through books, classes such as language, dance and song, or in local sports such as canoe paddling. Become acquainted with the Hawaiian community and its traditions and beliefs. Newcomers may feel they are intruding by joining in such activities, but Hawaiians interviewed for this book, including activist Allan K. Hoe, welcomed newcomers' interest. Another suggestion from Hoe: "The first place they go after getting off the airplane should be Bishop Museum [in Honolulu]" to begin to study island history and culture.

And environmental issues are especially important in a land so beautiful. A developer's plan to uproot a banyan tree for a two-tower O`ahu housing complex is protested by an environmental group that includes mostly *haoles*. On Kamehameha Highway in O`ahu, conservationists protest the installation of tall aluminum lighting poles that detract from nature's beauty and the state spends thousands to remove them, halfway through the project. In Hawai`i Kai, residents fight to keep the last bit of farm-like land free from developers.

In South Maui, pristine snorkeling sites are threatened by overuse, movie actors' mansions loom over once-sheltered beaches. And conservationists fight to keep beachfront vistas open.

On Moloka`i, development faces stiff opposition from Hawaiians who want to retain the remnants of an old lifestyle — living off the land that belonged to their ancestors. Protesters stave off visits by massive cruise ships that might despoil the fragile ocean and consider compromises — tourists brought in from the ships on smaller boats. But finally, the cruise line capitulates and sinks plans to stop at the quiet island.

On the Big Island, protesters halt the lease of former sugar lands for eucalyptus forests by a Japanese paper company, and environmentalists oppose construction of a radiation facility to sterilize produce so that it can be sent to world markets.

The problem, one conservationist says, is that these islands are a democracy and anyone who wants to move here may. If people would just visit and go back home instead, we'd have fewer problems, she asserts.

It is, in effect, the islands' beauty that feeds us by luring tourists — and is destroying us by attracting new residents.

Taxes: the good, bad and in-between

While you are lolling in one of Hawai`i's many beach parks, admiring Honolulu's carefully cared-for old government buildings, driving O`ahu's breathtaking Pali Highway, ask yourself this: How much is all this worth to you?

The average Hawai`i family pays about 42 percent of its income in state and federal taxes, statistics from the Tax Foundation of Hawai`i show. Persons or families who earn $50,000 have on the average only $29,000 to spend on necessities like food, shelter and transportation. In fact, in 2000 Hawai`i had the eleventh highest state taxes and fees in the United States. Alaska led the nation, followed by Washington, D.C., and New York.

"By several measures, Hawai`i has a relatively high rate of taxation...," a website of the state Department of Business, Economic Development and Tourism admits. However, "the relative burden on a family of four is distinctly lower... because the calculation applies to a family and thereby excludes the significant portion of taxes borne by non-residents."

For details — and a defense — of Hawaii's general excise tax go to www.state.hi.us/tax/

In other words, Hawai`i's tax system is set up so tourists and temporary residents share the costs of government.

Our real estate taxes are low and our state income tax is moderate, but our general excise tax is extremely high and pervasive. And each year at budget time, tax increases of all kinds are considered. So far, the Legislature has steered clear of a rise in the state's most controversial and costly levy: the excise tax.

The excise tax

A four percent excise, collected on virtually every purchase made by the state's 1.2 million residents and nearly 7 million annual visitors, provides the elephant's share of state general fund revenues, about 48 percent. Designed in part to make sure tourists help pay for parks and roads, the tax eats relentlessly at the pockets of residents who must purchase food, services and medical supplies.

It is not a sales tax; it is a "transaction" tax, the state maintains. By any name, the tax is assessed over and over again along the production and wholesale chain (sometimes at a lower rate at the manufacturing stage). By the time everyone down the line pays, Hawai`i's excise tax equals a 16 percent actual sales tax, some economists maintain.

The excise tax is regressive, says Lowell L. Kalapa, president of the Tax Foundation of Hawai`i, because it hits hardest at those earning the least. The poor spend a larger share of their money on taxed necessities like food and rent. The wealthy spend less of their income on necessities.

The excise tax is regressive, says Lowell L. Kalapa, president of the Tax Foundation of Hawai`i, because it hits hardest at those earning the least. The poor spend a larger share of their money on taxed necessities like food and rent. The wealthy spend less of their income on necessities, as little as 30 percent, investing or saving the rest. Even nursing homes pay the excise tax, tacking it on to their elderly clients' bills.

In 1998, bowing to constituent protests, the state Legislature declined to raise the excise tax, as recommended by the governor-appointed Task Force on Economic Development. But by 2004, an additional island-administered excise tax was being considered. The County Sales Tax bill would allow each county to levy a sales tax of up to one percent on the cost of all goods and services, in addition to the 4 percent state tax already collected. That plan did not come to fruition in 2004, but could in future years.

Real estate taxes

The counties (islands) administer and collect real estate taxes. Property is assessed at 100 percent of its "fair market value." Hawai`i has unusually low real estate taxes, among the lowest in the nation, because county government here has fewer functions than in other locations.

Our real estate taxes may be low, but our assessed property values are very high. In addition to low real estate taxes, people who reside in their homes are also entitled to homeowner's exemptions. Exemptions vary by county, from $40,000 to $80,000. For example, if your house is assessed at $400,000, you might be taxed on only $360,000. As you grow older the exemption increases, in most counties, peaking at $100,000 or $120,000 (Honolulu) when you reach 70 years of age.

RESOURCES

ISSUES

- **For a more detailed look** at Hawai`i's taxes, visit the Tax Foundation of Hawai`i website at www.tfHawaii.org
- **To compare Hawai`i's taxes** to the rest of the nation, visit www.retirementliving.com
- **For a chart of all state taxes,** go to www.state.hi.us/tax/pubs/09outline.pdf
- **For additional tax information:** www.state.hi.us/tax

State income tax

A very high state income tax has for years provided one-third of state general fund revenues. Hawai`i income tax is collected at a graduating rate to a maximum of 8.25 percent. The top income brackets for joint returns and "head of household" kick in when income reaches $80,000 and $60,000 respectively.

Tourist taxes

Hawai`i has a couple of extra levies designed to cash in on the tourist business. The nearly 7 million visitors pay $3 each day for every car they rent; they also pay 7.25 percent on every room they rent. And that is in addition to the 4 percent general excise tax on that same room rental. Tour vans pay $60 a month for vehicles seating 26 or more passengers; $15 per month for vehicles seating 8 to 25 persons.

Hotels, inns, "bed and breakfasts," timeshare condominiums and all short term rentals pay a transient accommodations tax of 7.25 percent of rents collected.

continued on page 56

War rooms in Paradise

Currently, America's war is being fought in Iraq, but many of its weapons and its warriors are trained in Hawai`i, especially on the beautiful island of Kaua`i. The nation's high-tech, sea-based, anti-missile defensive and offensive systems are tested at the U.S. Navy's Pacific Missile Range Facility at Barking Sands in western Kaua`i.

Among that island's war arsenals: the Theater High Altitude Defense System (THAAS). Kaua`i's *Garden Island* newspaper calls THAAS "a war room in paradise," a secret, guarded room so technologically equipped that much of the world can be viewed on wall-sized electronic screens. At THAAS, military and civilian signal callers can literally conduct a world war from the middle of the Pacific Ocean, directing planes, ships, ground troops and other forms of weaponry.

Photo courtesy of United States Army

Northrup Grumman, the world's foremost shipbuilder and number-two defense contractor (behind Lockheed Martin) wants to refurbish Kaua`i's sleepy Koke`e Air Force Station with high-technology sensors, radars and other devices, turning the station into a warfare integration laboratory.

Critics of the missile testing cite economic and ecological concerns. Dropping missiles, exploding bombs and practicing war in Hawai`i's beautiful terrain damages the environment and can endanger residents too. Hikers and homeowners on the Big Island and O`ahu occasionally find bombs and shrapnel. They come from tests and practice maneuvers dating back to World War II and continuing to this day. The U.S. Army Corps of Engineers will spend $50 million over the next few years to remove World War II ordnance from nearly 123,000 acres on the Big Island. And concerns about unexploded ordnance keep firefighters from brush fires near Waikoloa, a major Big Island housing development.

In the mid-1990s, millions of dollars were allotted by the federal government to partially clear the island of Kaho`olawe of shells and bombs after decades of weapons testing after World War II and continuing through the 1980s. The cleanup was abandoned in 2004 when money ran out.

Meanwhile, military training continues and expands in the Makua Valley of O`ahu, within earshot of residents.

Critics say such activity is hardly compatible with visits by seven million tourists annually and question whether the threat of attack to the U.S. is sufficient to justify the financial and ecological expense.

No one — not ecologists, scientists, politicians or the military — mentions another quiet concern occasionally voiced by residents: could such military activity, especially high-tech weapons development and training, make the islands a prime terrorism target? Could THAAS's high-tech facilities and the work underway in Kaua`i make it the Pearl Harbor of the 21st century?

Where does it go?

The state general treasury operating budget is over $12 billion a year. Where does all that money go?

About $2.4 billion goes to teach Hawai`i's children.

About $69.2 million is spent on tourism promotion. A 1998 increase in hotel room tax goes directly to promotional spending, deemed extremely important to Hawai`i's future. However, in recent years the state legislature has skimmed funds formerly dedicated to tourism promotion to fund state park and trails maintenance. By 2010 the tourism industry is expected to account for 1 in every 2.6 jobs in this state.

Hawai`i also supports a high, but not unusually high, number of public employees for its population size. Legislators have made attempts in recent years to cut costs and employees, but Hawai`i's strong labor unions fight privatization and job cutbacks that could save money.

What does it mean for you?

What does Hawai`i tax situation mean to you? Depending on where you live now, it means you may be paying hundreds and perhaps thousands of dollars more on every dollar you earn and every purchase you spend.

Is paradise worth the price?

Go, listen and learn

Neighborhood board meetings, at which residents have an opportunity to voice comments, are held regularly throughout the islands and some meetings are broadcast on community television channels. Watch for announcements of meetings in newspapers or call your island's city hall to find out when your neighborhood board meets. A good idea: attend a neighborhood meeting BEFORE you purchase a home in that area, so you'll be familiar with issues concerning residents.

VOTER INFORMATION

(800) 442-VOTE (8683)
or (808) 453-8683
http://hawaii.gov/elections

- **The Green Party,** Honolulu (877) 324-7336
- **The Democratic Party** (808) 596-2980
- **The Republican Party** (808) 593-8180

Your elected representatives:

U.S. SENATORS
(6-year term)

Daniel K. Inouye
300 Ala Moana Boulevard #7325
Honolulu, HI 96850-4975
(808) 541-2542

Daniel K. Akaka
PO. Box 50144
Honolulu, HI 96850
(808) 522-8970

chapter 3

Ka hana

work

Are you

willing to

change

occupations?

Photo by G. Brad Lewis

Daryl's story: He's successful

In some places in the world, a college graduate who has been a bellhop for over 20 years might consider himself a failure. Not in Hawai`i. Not Daryl Davis.

Daryl, polished, polite and professional, beams as he pushes a brass luggage trolley through the lobby of the Renaissance Wailea Beach Resort in Maui.

"The rest of the world might think of this as a low-paying job," Daryl, 55, says. "But things are different here. Here it doesn't matter what you do. It's who you are and what you contribute to society, to your community."

To survive in Hawai`i's fluctuating job market, you have to be flexible, and Daryl has certainly been that. A Vietnam veteran raised on the islands, he taught school in California for a while, then returned to Honolulu in 1974. No teaching positions were available, so he took a job as a parking lot attendant at a Waikiki hotel.

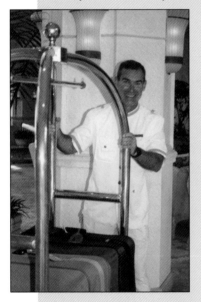

A year later, he moved to Maui and became swimming pool manager at a resort, then a bellhop. It was supposed to be a temporary job, but Daryl quickly learned "I could make as much as a bellhop for 40 hours as I could working as a teacher for 100 hours." That was 20 years ago; now he's looking toward retirement, planning to take advantage of perks like discounted rooms at his hotel chain's resorts around the world.

In his spare time, Daryl started two taxi cab companies, a jeep rental company, a wedding service and a bicycle tour company. He sold all of the businesses, which still function. Meanwhile, a friend helped him build several homes which he rents out.

Daryl's story illustrates an important point echoed by job specialists interviewed for this book: to prosper in Hawai`i you must be flexible and open-minded, ready to accept a job that pays less than you are earning now or willing to accept a position in a totally different field. You must be ready to start at the bottom and work up, clever enough to find an additional source of income, or able to live happily with the fact that you may never progress financially.

You may be able find a job...

Cyclical. That's a term kama'aina use to describe Hawai`i's economy. Since this book was first printed in 1999, Hawaii has endured a financial bust, enjoyed an incredibly high financial boom, and now (in 2010), like the rest of the country, hopes the next couple of years will bring recovery from a deep recession.

At this writing tourism, which provides the bulk of jobs, is down about 30 percent.

Finding "work" in your field depends on your experience, education and skills. Your best bet is to access job websites (page 79), talk to people in your field and weigh carefully your decision.

You can probably find a job in Hawaii, but depending on your field, the job may be part time and you may need an additional job or two to support yourself.

...but will it be the job you want?

In addition, the same consolidations and downsizing that affect jobs on the mainland claim a toll here. For example, a major Hawai`i bank recently began "outsourcing" its computer work to the mainland, cutting costs and putting about 200 Hawai`i residents out of work.

So where do you fit into the picture? Workers are needed, but more importantly, the right workers are needed, with skills to fill specific jobs. If you have experience in those areas, you should be able to find a position. Whether the job will pay what you are accustomed to, or be quite what you expected, is another question.

Trained workers are needed

The five fastest-growing occupations with the highest number of annual job openings are:

- **Healthcare practitioners** and healthcare support workers.
- **Construction workers** of all kinds, including supervisors.

Hawai`i's minimum wage is $7.25 an hour, the same as the federal minimum wage. However, in deference to our high costs of living, it is common for Hawai'i employers to pay more. Usually $8 to $10 an hour.

- **Teachers**, especially science, math and special education teachers.
- **Protective-service workers**, such as police and both private and public (airlines) security personnel.
- **High-tech industry workers**.

Those five occupational groups are expected to generate nearly 5,000 openings a year statewide through the rest of the decade. Of that number, nearly half will be new jobs, as opposed to job openings created through attrition, according to the state Department of Labor and Industrial Relations.

'Don't think an employer will pay your way out here'

Hawai`i needs, and will continue to need, workers. But that does not mean that you can easily get hired from the mainland and expect a company to pay the cost of you and your possessions getting here.

So, you're moving here without a job. The economy is so good here, you are confidant you'll find a job and you've already bought a ticket to Hawai`i. OK, says one local headhunter, but be careful. Bring enough money to support yourself for a minimum of three months, and ideally six months if you can afford it. Don't wait too long to find the "perfect" job. Be ready to accept a job that pays less than you made on the mainland for the same work. And remember: your cost of living may be 30 to 40 percent greater here.

"We get a lot of calls from the Mainland," Hank Sotelo, a recruiter for Dunhill Search of Hawai`i says. "I'm very truthful. First of all, I tell them if there is an equally experienced or talented person here on the islands, preference will be given to that person."

Some things have changed since 1999, when we talked to Sotelo for the first edition of *So You Want to Live in Hawai`i*. Sotelo gets more e-mails now than he does phone calls, but his advice is the same: "Don't think an employer is going to pay your way out here."

The high turnover of residents here is partially responsible, he says. Many recruits stay just a year or less, and contract "rock fever," grow tired of living on a small island, and leave their jobs just as they are becoming most valuable to their employers.

Maybe we should all work 'ukupau'

Ukupau philosophy is an interesting concept, popular on these islands, but not unique to them. *Ukupau* is a Hawaiian word meaning "finished pay." An ukupau system allows workers to complete the task assigned for that day and go home — no matter how short or long it takes.

According to A Newcomer's Guide to Hawaii: The *ukupau* attitude can be traced back to ancient Hawai`i when clock time did not exist, only work to be performed. Later, some plantations allowed workers to do an expected amount of work no matter how long or short it took. *Ukupau* also carried connotations of pitching in, working together to accomplish something that needs doing.

Today, *ukupau* is just about *pau*, gone, although a few offices and delivery services still use the concept; so do refuse collectors in Hawai`i and some mainland cities and towns. Hawai`i's refuse collectors finish their day in about three or four hours, a county personnel manager says.

Ukupau may be almost *pau*, but its attitude remains. On these islands, where an ocean and warm breezes beckon, work is secondary to play.

Sound connected, committed

"We still have a situation where companies are nervous about hiring people who are just coming from the mainland, who have not made a real commitment to the islands," says Nita Williams, co-owner of HR Pacific, another Honolulu recruiting firm that specializes in executive help. "Companies are still much more interested in meeting people who are already here," she says.

At the time of our interview, Williams was attempting to fill positions for upper-level accountants and CFOs (chief financial officers) for banks. She was also seeking applicants for management-level jobs for an anticipated coming construction boom: professional engineers, project managers and project coordinators.

"These are not temporary jobs," she said. She expects the jobs to last "a good 20 years or more."

Williams advises newcomers and would-be newcomers to do their homework; read about island culture, stay connected to resident friends. In an interview, sound as though you are sure Hawai`i is the place you want to live, work, raise your family, and stay forever.

Some jobs

need workers

A good bartender can usually find employment, at least part time. Tour boat workers, especially those speaking German or Japanese, should be able to secure work. Positions in the Honolulu police force are usually available and you need not be a Hawai`i resident to apply.

Where the jobs are

Here are 19 occupations in search of workers. You may fit into one of them. For further information and job listing sites, see the Resource page that follows this story.

Advertising

It has been said that Hawai`i has the largest collection of free curbside literature in the nation. Tourist-oriented brochures and publications overflow racks throughout the islands, most designed by graphic artists and written by copywriters, usually freelancers. Honolulu's many advertising agencies employ account executives and periodicals hire ad salespeople. Nationwide, the advertising field has been flooded with newcomers in the last decade, and competition for these jobs is as stiff here as elsewhere. But a graphic artist with sophisticated technical skills — computer design and Internet skills or an artist who can follow an assignment through from design to printing — is ahead of the game. So are creative writers willing to research. And sales professionals can usually find good jobs anywhere. Pay is commensurate with ability, experience and reputation.

The best employment advice? Before you decide to move, talk to people in your field here in Hawai`i. Talk to bosses and workers, says a placement specialist. Sound sure of yourself and definite about your move when you talk to employers; sound less certain when you talk to people at your professional level. Give them a chance to tell you both the negatives and positives.

Arts and crafts

Two things draw artists to Hawai`i: the natural beauty and the 6 million to 7 million tourists who come each year, eager to take home reminders of their visit. Painters, sculptors, carvers and craftspeople ply their trades in home studios throughout the islands and peddle their products at a galaxy of galleries and shops, via Internet sites and at weekly arts and crafts shows. Some artists, like internationally known Christian Riese Lassen, own their own galleries. Maui is touted as this nation's second-largest fine art market (behind New York City). But, be warned: only the best artists and craftsmen or those with exceptional marketing savvy make a substantial living. Others settle for a pleasant, pressure-free lifestyle, or let their arts and crafts supplement income from other jobs.

Computer industry

There's a need for workers in the computer industry, says Harry Winfield, manager of Honolulu Workforce Development for the Hawai`i Department of Labor, but it's far from the data entry jobs once associated with the computer industry. Needed now and in the future are highly specialized technicians who can deal with the constantly changing industry and latest developments such as nano-technology.

Construction

The construction industry remains optimistic and relatively busy both in private and military building. Large housing developments and new communities are planned on O'ahu and Maui. For job openings, be sure to check newspapers and state employment offices in addition to websites.

Dock and cargo workers

Since about 95 percent of material goods used in Hawai`i come through ports in Honolulu, you'd expect dock jobs to be available. But on the days we called the employment lines listed below, few positions of any kind were open. However, human resource professionals urged jobseekers to keep trying. More ships and bigger ships are expected in the near future. And rapid business growth, spurred by an economic boom, could mean a shortage of labor and resulting wait time for consumers, according to Pacific Business News. The shipping industry is organized by the International Longshore and Warehouse Union, dba Hawai`i Stevedores, Inc. Harry Winfield, manager of Honolulu Workforce Development for the Hawai`i Department of Labor, says the maritime industry also needs at least 200 hands a year for supply ships in Hawaiian waters. These are not cruise boats, but merchant marine and supply vessels bringing goods to military ships.

- McCabe, Hamilton & Renny Co., Ltd. supplies union workers to some shippers, including Matson Navigation Company: **(808) 524-3255**
- Horizon Lines, human resources: **(808) 842-1515**
- Young Brothers Ltd.: **(808) 543-9486**
- Matson Navigation Company: **(808) 525-6642**. (Supervisory positions only. McCabe, above, provides dockworkers.)

Farming

The national trend toward organic foods and Hawai'i's efforts to make the islands more self-sufficient could eventually mean more jobs in farming. Large sugar plantations are shutting down. If the land doesn't all go to housing development, that may open more ground to small farming. The need for soil and plant and environmental scientists here is also predicted.

Government, civil service

Government budget decreases mean civil service jobs have been cut in recent years, but cities, counties and the state continuously recruit for many positions, especially in the police and fire departments. Highly unionized, Hawai`i's state, city and county pay poorly when the cost of living is taken into account, but benefits are substantial, including paid vacations, health care, sick leave and generous retirement plans. The 24-hour job lines below describe available civil service positions. Some applicants claim you must live on the islands for generations or "know somebody" to get hired in state or county positions, but persistence pays here. Some newcomers get these jobs, too. A state human resources spokesperson says you do not have to be a resident for state or federal jobs, but you must be a resident for city and county jobs. The exception is police departments, which are continually in search of recruits. Also see Police, below.

- State employment: **(808) 587-0977**
  www.ehawaiigov.org/statejobs
- Honolulu City and County jobs: **(808) 523-4301**
  www.co.honolulu.hi.us/hr
- Federal Job Information Center: **(703) 724-1850**
  www.usajobs.opm.gov
- For individual counties, see the Resources section of this chapter.

Jobs with a Future
Number of workers needed

Industry	2007	2015	2025	2035
Agriculture	7,321	7,490	7,770	8,020
Mining and construction	40,341	42,200	46,530	50,250
Food processing	6,321	6,390	6,570	6,700
Other manufacturing	9,120	9,350	9,720	9,960
Transportation	30,576	32,790	35,900	38,890
Information	10,786	11,270	12,090	12,870
Utilities	3,031	3,180	3,450	3,700
Wholesale trade	18,737	19,870	21,690	23,460
Retail trade	72,478	77,080	83,980	90,080
Finance and insurance	17,515	18,280	19,850	21,290
Real estate and rentals	13,587	13,940	14,620	15,180
Professional services	25,934	27,510	30,410	33,370
Business services	51,854	54,640	59,970	65,090
Educational services	15,213	16,580	18,310	20,050
Health services	62,375	70,010	82,410	95,860
Arts and entertainment	12,657	13,460	14,770	16,130
Hotels	39,697	42,370	46,210	49,410
Eating and drinking	59,357	62,600	68,120	73,270
Other services	32,295	34,310	37,600	40,730
Government	131,917	138,690	149,820	159,790
Total Wage & Salary Employment	**661,112**	**701,990**	**769,790**	**834,090**
Self-employed Workers	168,297	178,990	25,600	26,300
Total Civilian Jobs	**482,400**	**502,900**	**197,540**	**215,570**

Source: DBEDT -"Population & Economic Projections For State of Hawaii to 2035"

"Green" technology

Like the rest of the nation, Hawai`i is going green. Windmills spin on mountain tops, photovoltaic panels flash across island roofs and Hawai'i is the first state to require solar water heaters in new homes. This state relies on imported fossil fuels more than any other state, with about 90 percent of its energy sources coming from foreign countries, according to state data. Look for sales, technology, research positions and new businesses in the future.

Grocery stores

Forty to fifty people each month leave positions as grocery store cashiers, clerks, meat cutters and wrappers and delicatessen workers, and new workers take their place, says Pat Loo, president of the United Food & Commercial Workers Union, Local 480. The union represents workers on all islands in the state's largest markets: Foodland, Star, Safeway and Sack-N-Save. Several smaller chains and markets tend to hire more frequently, but pay slightly less, Loo says. If you are currently working in the grocery industry, you may be able to transfer to a position here, he adds. For job openings, apply directly at the store or visit the union at 2305 South Beretania Street, Honolulu.

* United Food and Commercial Workers Union: **(808) 942-7778**
  www.ufcw480.org

Healthcare

Hawai`i ranks high in quality of healthcare. People are constantly being sought to fill a variety of positions: nurses, case managers, physicians' assistants, advanced-care nurses, physical therapists and entry-level clerical workers. Kathy Newkirk, president of Kahu Malama Nurses, Inc., a statewide medical recruiting firm, says jobs are available for nurses on all islands. At the time of our interview, the company was seeking critical care and emergency room nurses for O`ahu. Permanent jobs are more scarce on the outer islands, but temporary nursing positions are usually available, she said. Traveling nurses, who spend at least three months on a job, receive reimbursement for housing and expenses. At LAM

Associates, a physicians recruiting firm, Patricia Lam says she always has *locum tenens* (temporary) as well as permanent positions available. Also needed in the medical field: highly skilled technicians who can care for today's sophisticated healthcare equipment.

- Kahu Malama: **(808) 951-0111** or **(800) 773-9021**
- Hawai`i Pacific Health. Handles human resources for Straub Clinic & Hospital, Inc. (O`ahu), Kapi`olani Women's and Children's Hospital (O`ahu) and Wilcox Memorial Hospital (Kaua`i), as well as other health care providers:
  (800) 578-7282 or **(808) 535-7555** or www.hawaiipacifichealth.org
- Kaiser Permanente, Human Resources office: **(808) 432-4900**. Job hotline **(808) 432-4944** or www.kaiserpermanentejobs.org
- Queens Medical Center, O`ahu: **(808) 547-4355** or www.queensmedicalcenter.net
- Maui Memorial Medical Center: Human resources: **(808) 242-2251** or www.hhsc.org or mmmc.hhsc.org
- Kona Community Hospital: **(808) 322-9311** or www.kch.hhsc.org
- Hilo Medical Center: **(808) 974-4700**
- North Hawai`i Community Hospital: **(808) 885-4444** or www.northhawaiicommunityhospital.org
- LAM Associates: **(808) 947-9815** or **(800) 258-4526** or www.mdopenings.com or e-mail lamdocs@aol.com

High-technology

Hawai`i's hopes for job diversification hang on high-tech industries such as telecommunications, advanced computer applications and multi-media production. High-tech companies get a boost from the state's technology investment and research tax credits. Some of the employers in those fields say it is hard to keep talent in Hawai`i because jobs elsewhere pay more. Businesses tend to develop here, only to move away to locations where the cost of doing business is less. However, positions are available for highly skilled programmers, analysts and designers, recruiters say. The key word is "skilled"— recruits must match specific employer needs exactly. Some entry-level jobs may also be available.

- Try www.techjobshawaii.org

Photography

Hawai`i not only provides wonderful scenery for photographers — it also provides jobs. Commercial photographers are hired by local resorts, magazines and ad agencies, and the best photographers and photojournalists also sell to national and international markets. There's plenty of work, but also much competition. Novice photographers usually shoot *lu`au* and weddings, and work their way up to more lucrative assignments. The best photographers build portfolios of scenic, sports action and other photographs to sell worldwide.

Police

Honolulu police department jobs were once plentiful. As of this writing, they are harder to come by. That's probably because the $51,000 recruits earn (plus generous benefits) is enticing in a down economy. You do not have to be a Hawai'i resident to apply for a police recruit or dispatch position. Testings for new recruits are held periodically. Very thorough information, answers to questions and applications at:

Hoping for civil service job?
Go to page 79 for information on all counties.

• www.honolulupd.org

Real estate sales

Real estate is one of the few professions where successful people can earn more here than on the mainland. "It's not a situation of who you know here, but what you know," says one leading broker. "Success is based on how hard you work, your aptitude for sales." You are, in effect, starting your own business, he points out, and the start-up costs are very low compared to most other businesses. But, if you are a newcomer, be warned: The hours are long. Hawai`i's real estate laws and requirements are complex. And you may be dealing with foreign investors, requiring special knowledge and skills. For more information on licensing:

• Hawai`i Association of Realtors (O`ahu): **(808) 935-0827**
• Maui Board of Realtors: **(808) 873-8585**
• Hilo Board of Realtors: **(808) 935-0827**
• Kona Board of Realtors: **(808) 329-4874**
• Kaua`i Board of Realtors: **(808) 245-4049**
• Moloka`i Board of Realtors: **(808) 553-9009**

Retail sales

Well-groomed, friendly people can usually find jobs in retail sales, including management and assistant management positions in boutiques, dress shops, gift shops and art galleries. The pay may be low (see charts) and hours part-time. Managers or salespeople who work on commission can usually earn more than those receiving hourly wages. Shops in tourist areas prefer clerks who can speak at least some Japanese, but often have to accept workers who don't. Art galleries and tourist activity booths throughout the islands also hire frequently; pay is usually based on commission.

Resort positions

Once it was relatively easy to pick up a job as a waiter or waitress, cook or busperson, maid or maintenance worker almost anywhere in Hawai`i. That's not necessarily true today. This is a tourist economy and the need for people to fill these jobs can vary throughout the year. (Busiest seasons are from Christmas to the end of March and summer months when families with children travel.) Pay is slightly higher than on the mainland, however, and many positions include hospitalization and other benefits. See the Classified section of newspapers, or call the resort directly to inquire about jobs.

Teaching

A high turnover of public school teachers means positions are often available, especially in rural areas on neighbor islands. The average new teacher stays on the job two years, says Ray Hart, past president of the Hawai`i State Teachers Association on Maui. Only ten percent of Hawai`i's teachers have been in their jobs longer than ten years. There are fourteen steps on the salary scale negotiated by the Hawai`i State Teachers' Association. Wages are in the medium range of national averages, but that ranking does not take into account the high cost of living here.

   Substitute teachers are usually in demand. They must have Bachelor's degree and complete a State-Approved Teacher Education (SATE) program. Some island newcomers take the necessary courses and become substitute teachers temporarily until they find positions in their specialties. The numerous island private schools also hire teachers and newcomers, typically paying less than the D.O.E. The job market for elementary teachers varies from year to year, says Ellen Okamoto, a personnel specialist with the D.O.E. As a rule, more jobs are available in rural areas, but Okamoto offers a warning to recruits.

"Many (recruits) say they want to be in a remote area. But, when they think of rural, they expect an area where you can drive three miles and be in a less remote area," she says. "I have to remind them that Hawai`i's remote is very remote (for example, Moloka`i or Lana`i).

Teachers interested in working in this state can call the recruitment office toll-free during Hawai`i business hours. Also read the Children (Education) chapter of this book.

- Hawai`i State Teachers Association: **(808) 833-2711**
  Website: www.hsta.org
- Department of Education job availability all islands: **(800) 305-5104** (toll free) or **(808) 586-3420**. The URL www.doe.k12.hi.us will eventually take you to a job website and application forms. Or write: Personnel Management, Department of Education, Certificates Section, P.O. Box 2360, Honolulu, HI 96804

Tour operators, divers, sales

Newspaper classified sections are dotted with jobs for dive instructors, tour van drivers and tour boat operators. Tour employees we talked to reported earning $40,000 to $60,000 a year; most had full benefits because the work includes an element of risk. All seemed happy with their work, possibly because they are outdoors doing what they enjoy. One commented, "Some tourists can be a pain, but most are having a good time, and so my job is like going to a party every day." Another said he appreciated the fact that his clients "change daily, so you are always dealing with new people. There's no baggage to deal with." Being multi-lingual is a major advantage — and often a requirement in this line of work — noted a dive instructor who minored in Japanese and German at college. He said he is constantly getting job offers. Most of these positions require certification or additional licensing. See the classified section of your island's newspaper.

Truck drivers, delivery persons, warehouse workers

Licensed commercial drivers are needed, a state job counselor says, but stresses that truck driving and warehouse jobs on an island are very different from those on the mainland. Short distances and small companies mean a driver must be willing to load and unload goods as well as drive; warehouse workers often must have a commercial driver's license. A job recruiter commented, "Drivers say to me, 'Well, I just want to drive' and I say, 'Where are you going to drive to? The island's only 50 miles wide!'" Most companies are so small they have only two or three trucks. Even sales representatives must sometimes make deliveries.

See the classified section of your island's newspaper or apply at the local state employment office.

Kirk Lee Aeder, Imoco Media, courtesy of the Big Island Visitors Bureau

A horse-drawn wagon takes tourists through Hawi on the Big Island. Van and tour guides with perfect driving records can easily find jobs on most islands.

Average Hourly Pay Rates

In dollars.

Job classification	2004	2005	2006	2007	2008
Clerk, entry level	11.33	10.84	11.15	11.25	11.90
Secretary	14.97	15.80	16.02	16.39	17.53
Communications operator	12.99	15.26	14.79	15.44	15.95
Bookkeeper, full-charge	17.67	18.10	19.13	18.00	20.42
Cashier	14.72	14.91	15.48	16.26	16.90
Engineering drafting Technician	26.38	28.14	21.86	27.35	30.48
Housekeeper	12.40	13.07	13.60	13.82	14.35
Cook, general	15.51	15.48	17.15	16.08	16.64
Wait help	6.94	6.85	7.57	8.50	7.97
Laborer, light	11.60	9.55	10.87	10.12	10.68
Carpenter, maintenance	19.45	20.61	21.35	23.12	21.05
Electrician, maintenance	23.11	24.13	24.33	29.68	28.80
Automotive mechanic	19.81	23.47	24.55	23.71	24.69
Truck driver (trailer)	14.07	15.79	17.43	17.26	16.71

Source: Hawai`i Employers Council, Pay Rates in Hawai`i (annual), and calculations by Hawai`i State Department of Business, Economic Development & Tourism.

JOBS

Executives come and go here

We see it often in the islands. A top-notch mainland executive is summoned here to run a business, a company, a college or a non-profit institution. He or she did a great job performing a similar task in Topeka or L.A., Chicago or New York.

But once in Hawai`i, the exec starts to falter. His or her business savvy just doesn't seem to gel. People are pleasant, but they don't call back or respond the way the exec expects. Tactics that worked on the mainland are failing.

In a year or two, the exec is gone. Sometimes, it's his or her choice. Sometimes, it's the decision of his boss or his board of directors.

So, what went wrong? What is so different about business relationships here? The *Honolulu Star Bulletin* attempted to answer that question by talking to some long-time Hawai`i business people. Here's what they said:

• **We're less verbal.** "People on the mainland tend to be more verbal," a bank executive said. "Hawai`i people are just as capable (as those elsewhere), " maintained BancWest Chairman and CEO Walter Dods in the *Star Bulletin* story, "but because of their culture they tend not to be as verbal."

That can be confusing to a transplanted executive. If people don't talk a lot, don't verbalize, it is difficult to judge reactions. You can come right out and ask, but you may get only a polite, noncommital answer. Or you may just get a smile or a nod.

• **We're more laid back.** The pace of deals in Hawai`i is generally less frenetic than on the mainland, says a Honolulu corporate attorney. We don't like deadlines.

"(On the mainland) timelines are often shorter," Dave Banks told the *Star Bulletin*. "And the expectation is that everyone will work around the clock on the deal until it is completed."

Here, our priorities are well in place. Work is work and family is family. Work gets done within working hours, even if that means it takes days, or even weeks longer.

- **We're small town.** "It's a relatively small place, where everyone knows everyone," said Michael O'Neill, former chairman and CEO of Bankoh. "A lot of people are related. So what goes around, comes around. I think you need to be conscious of that."

  In other words, you can talk stink about your competitor, and find out the person to whom you are speaking is his nephew.

- **We're on to you.** It's not smart to talk down to locals, or anyone, or try to "make sneaky" or be dishonest.

  "I will say this about the people in Hawai`i," Dods said. "Because of their multicultural experiences, they have great B.S. detectors, and they can spot a fast-talking person pretty quickly."

- **"Localness" is important.** When the University of Hawai`i paid a mainland firm big bucks to design a logo, the school got plenty of criticism, and finally re-bid the job to local companies. "Local" suggests a way of knowing, sharing with, and respecting one's neighbors that seems particularly strong in island cultures. It is pride, seasoned with humility, another paper, *The Honolulu Advertiser*, editorialized.)

Consider condo cleaning. Many professional cleaners do well in our tourist environment. "The trick," says one cleaning lady, "is to work several apartments on the same floor and do all the dusting at once, all the tubs and tile, like that." She says she is paid very well per condo, and the work can take less than 30 minutes. Apply at condo management companies.

Women in Hawai`i on average, working full-time, year-round earn 79% of what men earn, according to a study by the National Women's Law Center.

About 3,000 young, educated workers leave Hawai`i each year to work on the mainland, where they feel job prospects are better and the cost of living is less.

Ray's story: he works "side jobs"

Construction workers are needed in Hawai`i and joining a union is the usual procedure, but at least one journeyman carpenter, a member of the carpenter's union, is sticking to smaller, private "side jobs."

Ray (not his real name) came to the islands six years ago, easily found work laying floors and building walls in the numerous low-to-middle-income houses in O`ahu's rapidly growing Kunia and Mililani areas and he was paid about $48 an hour. After deductions for taxes, union fees and a union pension plan, he took home just under $32 an hour. The money is good, he says, on par with what he received at mainland jobs. But there's a difference working in Hawai`i, he maintains.

"You work harder here," Ray says. "More is expected of you."

On the mainland, carpenters who work quickly sometimes do piecework, that is get paid for the amount of work they do. They are reimbursed for fast work. Here, he says, piecework quotas are set and become the standard for workers; workers are expected to fill the high quotas and there is no extra pay for working quickly. "The bosses are on top of you," Ray says. "You work much faster here."

Ray still works union projects, but occasionally takes on smaller, private jobs, where he can work at his own pace or take a day or two off when he wants to. He earns somewhat less, about $35 an hour, but feels more comfortable and less stressed.

**Hawai`i has the second highest union membership** in the country, with 25.2 percent of workers belonging to a union. Only New York at 26.4 percent has a higher membership. In Hawai`i, the rate of unionized government workers has held steady since 1983; the rate for private industry has fallen by nearly half, following trends on the mainland.

Ray's experience — working harder than he has in the past — isn't unusual, and it isn't limited to construction, says a government employment specialist.

"Everyone's working harder these days," he says. "On the mainland, and in Hawai`i too. Employers (in every field) are trying to do more with less. It has to do with attrition. In other words, to save money, jobs are not necessarily refilled when workers leave. Instead, other workers take up the slack."

Job hunting, sort of, on vacation? Some tips.

You're in Hawai`i on vacation, like it a lot, and are sure you'd love to live here. So, you figure you might as well do some investigating. Stop in for a few job interviews, see what's available in your field. Who knows? Maybe you'll strike it lucky.

Well, okay, go ahead, but beware: Hawai`i's managers, executives and employment agencies may give you less than a warm welcome.

It's just that so many people have the same idea — they decide to spend a couple of days or a few hours job-hunting while they're here. They fill out time-consuming resumes, tie up busy middle-managers, and then go back to Michigan or Montreal, never to be heard from again. In other words, they waste the time of employers and agencies.

If you're on vacation and determined to job-hunt, here are some tips from island head-hunters:

- **Dress the part.** Don't wear a tank top and shorts. "You don't need to wear a suit or jacket, but maybe a good aloha shirt and long pants or a skirt," says Nita Williams, co-owner of HR Pacific, a recruiting agency. In other words, look professional and downplay the "I'm a tourist" bit.

- **Bring a resume.** Talk is cheap. A thorough, neat, professional resume shows you put some thought into the interview or application. And a good resume helps would-be employers remember you after you've gone back home. If you have not brought your resume with you, visit Kinko's or a similar copy shop, and create one.

- **Follow up.** Send a thank-you note immediately, then follow up with a phone call as soon as you get home. Be friendly, not pushy. But also be definite in your desire for the job.

- **Stress your island connections.** Do you have relatives, friends, a college connection here? Mention it. "Any contact that shows you have ties here, have a real interest in the islands, that you've done your homework," Williams says.

- **Follow up again.** Call the potential employer back in two or three weeks and reiterate your determination to come to the islands, to work for the company. Keep in touch.

Erica: A few words made a big difference

When Erica Maluski, 24, graduated with a master's degree in Art Therapy, she knew one thing for sure: she wanted to travel away from busy New York City to some place exotic. She wanted an adventure. Hawai`i sounded just right, so she scoured CareerBuilder, an Internet web site that functions in conjunction with newspapers around the country, and for several weeks she responded to ads, sending out about five applications a week.

She described her qualifications and her ambitions. She wrote about wanting to come live in Hawai`i. She sent out at least 20 letters. And she got no responses.

Still, Erica was determined to live and work in the islands, so she bought herself a one-way plane ticket to paradise.

She kept sending out job letters, but now they read more assertively, sounded more definite.

"I am coming to live in Hawai`i," she wrote. "I have purchased a ticket and I will be in O`ahu and available for an interview on June 20."

Suddenly, like magic, Erica began to get responses to her queries.

"Having a ticket. Being definite. Stating that I'm coming for sure…that made all the difference," she says.

The day of her graduation, she came home to find a response from Kahi Mohala ("place to blossom"), a psychiatric hospital in leeward O`ahu. After two telephone interviews, Erica was hired to be one of only ten art therapists in the state. At $37,500 a year or about $18 an hour, she is earning about the same as she would in the New York area, she says.

A rephrasing of a few words, sounding definite about coming, helped Erica fulfill her dream. She had just three weeks to pack up her life and begin her great adventure.

Erica's story continues in the Necessities *chapter.*

Job hunt via your telephone and computer

With Internet, it's easy to organize a job hunt from anywhere in the world. But be warned: many Hawai`i employers prefer people who already live on the islands.

www.doe.k12.hi.us
State Department of Education, all islands:
(800) 305-5104 or **(808) 586-3420**

www.ehawaiigov.org/statejobs
State employment: **(808) 587-0977**

www.honolulu.gov/HR
City and County of Honolulu
Department of Human Resources
715 South King Street, Suite 550
Honolulu, Hawai`i 96813
(808) 523-4301 (24-hour Job Information Line)

All kinds of civil service jobs
http://agency.governmentjobs.com/hawaii

www.co.hawaii.hi.us/directory/dir_civserv.htm
County of Hawai`i
Department of Civil Service
101 Aupuni Street, Suite 133
Hilo, Hawai`i 96720
(808) 961-8361
(808) 961-8618 (Job Hotline)

Applying via the Internet? Unless the job posting says otherwise, follow up within two days with a polite

www.co.maui.hi.us/jobs.aspx
County of Maui
Department of Personnel Services
200 South High Street
Wailuku, Hawai`i 96793
(808) 270-7850

www.kauai.gov/personnel
County of Kaua`i
Department of Personnel Services
4444 Rice Street, Suite 140
Lihu`e, Hawai`i 96766
(808) 241-6595

www.career.uhh.Hawaii.edu
Employers from throughout Hawai`i post job openings on a site run by the Career Center at the University of Hawai`i-Hilo.
(808) 974-7687

www.HonoluluAdvertiser.com
Go to the careerbuilder icon for hundreds of jobs that have been listed in the *Honolulu Advertiser* newspaper.

www.kaiserpermanentejobs.org
Kaiser Permanente Human Resources office: **(808) 432-4900** or job hotline **(808) 432-4944**

www.usajobs.opm.gov
Federal Job Information Center: **(703) 724-1850**

www.hawaiiorganicfarmers.org
Find out more about organic farming, a growing business in Hawai`i

www.ctahr.hawaii.edu/GMO
University of Hawai`i College of Tropical Agriculture

www.hawaiipacifichealth.org
Hawai`i Pacific Health Human Resources
Employment at Kapi`olani HealthHawaii (O`ahu), Straub Hospital (O`ahu) and Wilcox Memorial Hospital (Kaua`i)
(808) 535-7555

www.TopUSAJobs.com

www.htdc.org
www.techjobshawaii.org
High-tech jobs in Hawai`i

Considering Kaua`i? WorkWise Kauai has the largest jobs database in the state. www.workwisekauai.com/about/partners.asp

www.ncl.com
Norwegian Cruise Line employment

www.Kamaainajobs.com
Find jobs throughout the islands

e kūkalu ma kou
no`eau pono`ī

– *"build upon your own skill"*

bring your own **business**

It's not easy but,

the rewards

are great

Photo by Toni Polancy

Jerri and Bob: They listened to the tourists

To succeed in business in Hawai`i you need the qualities most entrepreneurs possess — wits, daring, drive and creativity — plus an extra dose of perseverance. Bob Jasper and Jerri Wassink have that. When they came to Kaua`i 16 years ago, Bob became a photographer, taking souvenir photos of macaws sitting on tourists' shoulders, but...

"Nobody wanted pictures; they wanted to buy our birds," Bob says. So they opened a shop and sold exotic birds. That business was fine until Hurricane Iniki struck Kaua`i in 1992, demolishing homes, hotels, and wiping out nearly all island business. Bob and Jerri moved to Maui for a few years, then returned to Kaua`i in

Photo courtesy of Hawai`i Movie Tours

1996. Business was slow, but one day Bob realized that tourists kept asking the same questions: Where's that hotel from the Elvis Presley movie *Blue Hawai`i*? Which cliff did *King Kong* climb? Which beach did Mitzi Gaynor use to wash that man right out of her hair in *South Pacific*?

He had an idea. Why not take tourists on a tour of Kaua`i's famous movie locations? Jerri and Bob spent two years researching locations, getting studio approval to show movies, and obtaining landowners' permission to enter properties. Then they bought a funky old jeep used in the movie *Jurassic Park* and started Hawai`i Movie Tours. By 2004 they had several vans and buses transporting tourists around the island, planned a movie museum in Kapa`a, and had licensed similar tours in Monterey and San Francisco and Washington, D.C.

"We've found business in Hawai`i very cyclical," Bob says. "We are so dependent on air travel. Outside events like 9-11, the Iraq war, the SARS scare affect us as opposed to mainland tourist destinations where people have no qualms about driving. And, of course, Mother Nature. We really found out about that. But doing business here is also very rewarding. It's a unique place on earth. We and other businesses have made it through all these events."

B.Y.O.B.

(Bring Your Own Business)

There's one way to make sure you have a job in Hawai`i: bring your own. You will read in this chapter many of the dis-incentives for starting a business here. Be aware of these negatives, but not necessarily dissuaded by them. For many reasons, Hawai`i blooms with opportunity. Small businesses are started in Hawai`i almost daily, some by people bringing new ideas from other parts of the world, and many of those businesses succeed. Choose your business and its location carefully, bring plenty of start-up money, and plan to work very hard for several years.

The advantages

Entrepreneurs in Hawai`i have some unique advantages.

- **The state is at least two years behind the mainland** in business trends and on some islands that time lapse can be as much as four or five years or more. An entrepreneur has the opportunity to create a business today with the knowledge of yesterday. There is no excuse for saying, "If I'd only known then what I know now." Things that happened years ago, opportunities missed, are occurring here, now.

- **The islands are still growing and developing.** New towns are being established; old ones are increasing in size and changing character. Businesses are needed. A successful graphic designer insists he has a list of "at least 100 businesses I could go into right now, any one of which would succeed." (He declines to share the list.)

- **State enticements, tax credits.** Like many states, Hawai`i encourages new endeavors with tax incentives. For example, the Act 221 technology tax credit program

Here's help

Considering a business in Hawai`i? The Department of Business, Economic Development & Tourism offers helpful information both before and after you make your decision, including a feasibility plan. Call (808) 586-2545, fax (808) 586-2544 or visit www.Hawaii.gov/dbedt

provides a 100 percent state income tax break for qualifying technology investments. It has lured investors, but has been criticized for being applied outside the strict "technology" definition, for example, to film making.

- **Competition may be relaxed.** The key to his own success, says the young artist, has been applying mainland concepts surprisingly rare on the islands: serious work and regular hours. Many people move here with the idea that they will work less; many others have been raised here without entrepreneurial backgrounds. "A savvy person willing to put the time in will succeed here," the artist says. And several other business owners agree.

- **Hawai`i's exotic appeal**, and the 6 to 7 million people from around the world who visit annually, provide special opportunities for small business people. For example, Hawai`i is probably one of the few places in the United States where:
  - Little-known artists and craftspeople can make a living selling their wares.
  - New products can find a worldwide market without leaving home.
  - Many resorts and lounges employ entertainers. Talent is encouraged and nourished.

The problems

Don't expect establishing a new business to be easy. Hawai`i is the most expensive state in the country in which to do business, according to a survey by Regional Financial Associates in Pennsylvania, with the highest labor and energy expenses in the nation and the second highest state and local taxes (behind Alaska).

The Washington-based Small Business Survival Index is a concise measurement of just how difficult it is to do business here. The index ranks Hawai`i at the bottom for small businesses. It scores the islands as having the highest excise (sales) tax, highest electricity cost and highest gasoline tax. It says the state has the fifth-highest workers' compensation rates, fifth most-costly unemployment insurance, sixth-highest personal income tax and tenth-highest capital gains tax.

Hawai`i also has a higher-than-average failure rate for new business. Bob Johnson, formerly president and chief executive officer of the Maui

Economic Development Board, Inc., in a *Maui News* article, provides a reason for these failures.

"Many [people] come here to visit, have liked it here, and without a great deal of research and analysis, start a business," he says. "They run into trouble.

"The plan may have worked somewhere else, but if it fails to consider the state's tax structure, the legislation affecting workers and the permitting process, it likely will [not succeed]."

The Maui Economic Development Board refers entrepreneurs to information and research sources, so they can make a wise decision before starting a business.

Sam Slom, state senator and president and executive director of Small Business Hawai`i, a private organization of 3,000 business owners, cites several disincentives for business. Most begin with Hawai`i's centralized state government, which wields extremely strong powers.

The counties have strict ordinances controlling size and locations of signage. Business owners sometimes turn trucks into signs and park them in busy locations. Jeffry Hansen, owner of the Eskimo Candy seafood market on Maui, says he was told this truck could stay, but he had to remove the arrow pointing to his business.

Disincentives include:

• **Mandated employee benefits** such as heath care, worker compensation, unemployment compensation and temporary disability insurance. Coupled with federally-mandated employee costs, they add 35 to 40 percent to the cost of hiring employees.

"A worker who complains he's only getting $7 an hour, is in fact earning $10 or $11 in actual compensation," Slom points out. And the cost of benefits increases as the pay goes up. A person earning $12 an hour costs his employer at least $16 an hour. The result can be disadvantageous for both employers and employees, as it keeps wages low and the actual cost of employment high. Many small businesses hire fill-in or temporary employees rather than pay the high cost of permanent, full-time employees.

There is some good news: worker compensation rates are coming down. They have been cut drastically in the past few years, saving business about $100 million.

Our 'casual' employees

The cost of hiring employees is very high in Hawai`i. Altogether, health insurance, worker's compensation and the employer's share of social security, as well as other expenses, may add as much as 40 percent to the price of hiring a fulltime employee. For that reason, many jobs in Hawai`i tend to be part time and "casual." And many people hold two or three such jobs to earn a living.

The Prepaid Health Care Act of 1974, the only state law of its kind in the nation, requires employers to provide health insurance coverage and pay the bulk of the premiums for employees who work more than 20 hours a week. An employer can ask the employee to pay one-half of the premiums, or 1.5 percent of their wages, whichever is less. The law, hailed throughout the nation when it took effect in the 70s, has led to a spurt in part-time employment. From 1990 to 2000, the number of part-time workers in Hawai`i increased 44 percent, from 79,000 to 114,000. The number of full-time workers increased only 2.5 percent, from 445,000 to 456,000.

According to the Medical Expenditure Panel Survey, which tracks healthcare costs across the country, Hawai`i employers pay the highest percentage of health insurance premium costs in the nation.

- **High costs for commercial space.** All rents are high in Hawai`i compared to many places on the mainland, but the cost of commercial space, especially in high traffic areas, is particuely dear. Meanwhile, the price of land and construction makes owning your own business property impossible for many small businesses. Most islands have an "industrial area," where warehouse and commercial space is available at somewhat lower rates.

- **High freight and import costs.** If your business requires material from the mainland or another country, freight costs by sea or air can cut steeply into profits. They can even lead to a business failure.

- **Excessive taxes.** The 4.166 percent state excise tax (at the retail level) and .05 percent tax (at the wholesale level) is collected over and over again from businesses at various stages of production and service, and 4.166 percent is also charged on rents. The tax is collected so often that some economists say it amounts to an actual (sales) tax of 16 to 18 percent. For example, construction contractors, restaurants and real estate agents are licensed by the state. Like all businesses, they must pay excise tax. If they fail to do so, their business licenses can be withheld. Since the strong state government administers this tax, there is little or no recourse, no way to argue disputes or correct errors.

- **Scarcity of employes.** In some businesses, finding and keeping good employees is a problem. A former car rental agent tells about being solicited almost daily by other car rental companies seeking employees. "They would come over and say, 'We'll give you $2 an hour more'... and some people would just quit and walk over to the other company." Island unemployment rates are already among the lowest in the nation and a shortage of workers in some positions is predicted. (See the Working chapter.)

- **Liberal laws.** "I can't grow my business," says a Hawai`i dress shop owner. "I'm scared to death to hire employees because they have so many rights."

The state Supreme Court ruled in 1997 that employees who suffer stress as a result of disciplinary action could collect worker's compensation benefits. Since almost any employee is disciplined at some point, and any discipline is stressful for employees and employers, the law is frightening for employers.

"Lawmakers must correct that provision. If the employee deserved to be disciplined, he should not receive compensation for stress," the *Honolulu Star-Bulletin* has editorialized.

Other considerations:

- **Our vulnerability.** We are a string of tiny islands, isolated in the ocean, dependent on tourism. We rely on the world's mood for our sustenance. A war on the other side of the world, an economic downturn in a country two oceans away, can affect our economy here. We are also dependent on imports for about 95 percent of our goods, including gasoline to run our cars. We are at the mercy of terrorist acts, adverse weather, airline and dock strikes, all of which can affect our supplies of either tourists or material goods. And that means they can affect our business.

- **Time differences.** Business owners also mention another setback. Hawai'i's isolated location is far from other markets. And the time difference means, says one, "You must start your day at four a.m. if you do business on the mainland. If you sleep in until six, you miss people who are out to lunch, and their business day is half over."

Tourism and your trinket

How important is the tourism industry to Hawai'i? Visitors bring $10.3 billion into the state annually.

Waikiki attracts 72,000 visitors on any given day, or 44 percent of all tourists present in the state. The area accounts for eight percent of the state's total economic output, and ten percent of its private-sector jobs — a payroll of $800 million in 2000, according to the Department of Business, Economic Development & Tourism.

However, don't bank on producing and marketing the perfect tourist knick-knack and making an easy buck. Shelf space on Waikiki's bustling Kalakaua Avenue is hard to come by, and dominated by a few stores and few distributors.

If you plan to market a tourist-related item, you may have to start by showcasing it at weekly swap-meets, out-of-the-way boutiques and on the Internet. In recent years, Chinatown, near the center of Honolulu's business district, has enjoyed a resurgence of tourism. Rental space and shelf space in established stores is somewhat easier to come by there. Neighbor islands also have regularly-scheduled craft meets.

For example, the book you are holding...

This book has sold over 75,000 copies. That's well over $1 million gross.

Where did all that money go and why does so little of it show up as net profit? Although publishing is a notoriously unprofitable venture, the answer points up the extra costs related to conducting business in the Hawaiian Islands.

Here is a breakdown of who gets how much for each book, which at the retail level costs $19.95. We'll simplify it to $20.

- Cost of printing: $3 per book
- Cost of shipping from California printer to Honolulu warehouse: 50 cents per book.
- Cost of warehousing product: About 5 cents per book, per month
- Bookstore's profit for selling book: $8
- Distributor's profit for taking book to store: $3.60.
- Profit per book to publisher: $4. But wait, from that $4 deduct the cost of a writer, a designer and a photographer. Subtract advertising and we are down to about $2 per book profit. Also deduct .05 percent for state G.E.T. on wholesale sales made inside Hawai`i.

Meanwhile, if the book is not sold or gets dirty in the bookstore coffee shop, it is returned to the publisher, who pays the return freight:
- deduct 50 cents per book again.

That brings the average net profit down to as low as $1 to $1.50 per book. Not a very big margin.

You can expect your own business to be a bit more lucrative than publishing, but you will still bear many of those extra costs: shipping to Hawai`i, storing, and reshipping if you sell to a neighbor island or outside Hawai`i.

Honolulu Freight Service

CERTIFIED FREIGHT FORWARDER ICC-FF 267   See back for REM

Deliver To:
PARTNERS BOOK DIST WEST I
1901 RAYMOND SW STE C
RENTON, WA 98055

Bill To:
BAREFOOT PUBLISHING INC
32 UILANI ROAD
KIHEI, HI 96753

Vessel & Voyage		Contr# - B/L Date	From - To
		MATU245466	HNL
KAUAI 56A		07/08/03	SEA

Pieces	Unit	Commodity Description
12	CS	E/B REGULAR CARGO
		STC BOOKS
		POA 425-227-8486
		ADVANCE PU/MARW/MARTIN
		WAREHOUSING
		ISLAND FUEL MARTIN
		C VANCE RENTON DELT

Tom and Jody: From tragedy to triumph

Sometimes it takes a tragedy to make a dream come true.

For 16 years, Jody and Tom van Aalst had a love affair with Maui. For 16 years, they came to the island from Portland, Oregon for long vacations. They loved the islands so much they wrote a book, *Maui Made Affordable*, and maintained a mail-order bookstore, The Island Bookshelf, specializing in island products. They planned in the future, when Tom retired from his job as production manager at a manufacturing company, to retire to the islands. For 16 years it was something to look forward to, a dream for *someday*.

The longtime companions married in April of 2001 and four months later, their peaceful life and dreams for the future were shattered. Tom, 59, suffered a brain aneurysm. In a coma, he fought for his life. When he awoke four weeks later, much of his memory was gone, wiped away.

Tom would spend a month in a nursing home, two weeks in in-patient rehabilitation and three months in out-patient rehab. Little by little, his memory began to return. He went back to his job, but could not handle the work, and was finally terminated by the company that had stood by him during the hospitalizations.

Toni Polancy

"Every day, bits of the old Tom, parts of his personality, returned," Jody remembers. "But it was a very slow process and it was just too soon for him to go back to work."

Tom was 59 and unemployed. He would have a difficult time finding another job on two counts: his age and his illness. In his position, a less determined person might give up, feeling his financially productive years were over. Not Tom. Instead, the van Aalsts decided this was the time to fulfill their Hawai`i dream.

"Why wait? For what? Life is short," Jody says, having just been reminded by Tom's illness.

So Tom and Jody said goodbye to friends and family, sold the house he had owned for 22 years, and moved to O`ahu, where Jody, 56, had many contacts in the publishing industry and hoped to find a good job. People were helpful, friendly, but the only position she secured after four months was as a bookstore salesclerk.

"Minimum wage that did not make it worth the trip (to Honolulu) from Ewa Beach," she says.

Hawai`i was expensive. The move to the islands, including shipping a car, had cost them $5,000; their cat's one-month quarantine was another $865, and their two-bedroom Ewa Beach apartment cost $1,000 per month. The money from the sale of their house was draining fast, things were a bit glum, but the van Aalsts are not the kind of people who look back. They came up with a plan. Before his illness, Tom had always enjoyed working around his home and had developed the many talents needed to renovate houses. "I'd been doing that stuff since I was a kid and I didn't seem to have lost any of those skills," he says.

Hawai`i real estate was booming. Why not use the funds left from the house sale to put the down payment on a "fixer-upper"? Renovate a house and sell it, hopefully for a profit. And as long as they had a choice of islands, why not go to Maui?

"Our dream was always Maui. If I couldn't get the job I wanted on O`ahu, why not go to Maui? I could be just as unemployed on Maui as on O`ahu," Jody jokes.

On Maui, after several weeks of intense searching, they found a dilapidated house in the county seat, the quaint old town of Wailuku. They spent the next seven months renovating the 65-year-old building. They hired help for the most difficult work, like replacing termite-eaten beams. Meanwhile, Tom replumbed and rewired, put in new floors, replaced windows and sills, installed a new kitchen and two new baths, replaced lighting fixtures. Jody spent much of the seven months in paint-splattered coveralls, sanding woodwork, painting walls and hauling shrubs. The couple worked six days a week and rested on the seventh day. Seven months after they began, they put the house on the market. It sold in 19 days.

The profit was considerable (a "wage" of about $20,000 a month, Tom points out). But even better was the knowledge that despite his illness he could take charge again, find work he enjoyed, and be successful in a place the couple loves.

It was much more than money, Tom insists. "The thing that felt good was people looking at the house and saying 'You did a fine job.'"

State Business Tax Climate Index

The higher the score, the more favorable the state's tax system is for business. Rankings do not average across to total.

Location	Total Score	Overall Rank	Corporate Tax Index Rank	Individual Income Tax Index Rank	Sales Tax Index Rank	Unemployment Insurance Tax Index Rank	Property Index Rank
U.S.	5.00						
Alabama	5.19	19	23	18	25	16	17
Alaska	7.38	3	26	1	5	29	15
Arizona	5.01	28	22	24	46	2	4
Arkansas	4.61	40	39	35	43	17	20
California	3.89	48	34	48	48	14	13
Colorado	5.63	13	12	16	31	20	6
Connecticut	4.72	38	18	25	27	34	48
Delaware	5.98	8	49	36	1	13	7
District of Columbia	4.72						
Florida	6.62	5	15	1	32	3	22
Georgia	5.01	29	8	31	23	22	36
Hawaii	5.05	24	10	44	11	12	8
Idaho	5.21	18	17	30	12	48	3
Illinois	5.01	30	27	10	41	46	39
Indiana	5.67	12	21	11	20	11	12
Iowa	4.23	46	45	42	33	33	31
Kansas	4.93	32	40	22	24	6	32
Kentucky	5.18	20	42	33	7	36	19
Louisiana	4.74	35	19	26	47	8	24
Maine	4.83	34	43	17	6	40	41
Maryland	4.26	45	14	49	10	37	38
Massachusetts	4.73	36	47	14	26	49	45
Michigan	5.35	17	48	15	9	45	33
Minnesota	4.44	43	44	38	40	38	16
Mississippi	5.16	21	13	19	35	4	23
Missouri	5.37	16	5	28	16	7	18
Montana	6.32	6	16	23	3	21	10
Nebraska	4.88	33	35	32	17	15	34
Nevada	7.05	4	3	1	44	42	14
New Hampshire	6.25	7	50	9	2	39	40
New Jersey	3.60	50	41	47	38	25	50
New Mexico	5.06	23	32	20	42	19	1
New York	3.66	49	20	50	36	47	43
North Carolina	4.66	39	25	37	34	5	37
North Dakota	5.04	25	30	34	21	28	5
Ohio	4.04	47	38	46	37	10	49
Oklahoma	4.97	31	7	27	45	1	27
Oregon	5.59	14	31	45	4	30	9
Pennsylvania	5.03	27	37	13	29	41	42
Rhode Island	4.33	44	36	39	13	50	47
South Carolina	5.03	26	9	29	18	43	26
South Dakota	7.42	1	1	1	30	35	11
Tennessee	5.10	22	11	8	49	32	46
Texas	5.70	11	46	7	39	9	30
Utah	5.80	10	6	12	28	24	2
Vermont	4.56	41	28	41	14	18	44
Virginia	5.53	15	4	21	8	44	29
Washington	5.81	9	33	1	50	26	21
West Virginia	4.73	37	24	40	22	31	28
Wisconsin	5.54	42	29	43	19	23	25
Wyoming	7.38	2	1	1	15	27	35

Source: Tax Foundation, Background Paper, "2010 State Business Tax Climate Index" (September 2009)

Entrepreneurial opportunities

Weddings

The wedding business is vast and lucrative in Hawai`i. In a three-month period, 51,288 of 1.6 million visitors came here to get married, said the state Department of Business, Economic Development & Tourism. Of that number, 39,943 came from Japan and 11,345 came from the mainland. And that does not even include local weddings. The wedding business benefits photographers, singers, musicians, limousine companies, caterers, florists, gown suppliers and freelance ministers as well as wedding planners, hotels and places of worship. The latest trend: small, private "boutique" hotels where the happy couple, and friends and relatives, can reside and celebrate.

High-Tech

There are an estimated 600 high-tech enterprises in Hawai`i with 18,000 employees producing about $2 billion a year in revenues. About 10 percent of it feeds off a 100 percent technology tax credit. Controversial Act 221 works like this: a Hawai`i taxpayer (individual, company or business) invests in a high-tech business such as computer software, biotechnology, ocean sciences, astronomy, alternative energy or performing arts. The investor can receive a tax credit equal to 100 percent of his investment over a five-year period, or up to $2 million per year per company. The effectiveness of Act 221 in creating jobs has been difficult to measure.

Eco-Tours

Hawai`i's scenic beauty makes it a natural for eco-tourism, currently experiencing a boom throughout the world. Within the past few years, hiking, biking, and various other tours, including a rope ride on Haleakala mountain, have come into being. The state is spending $2 million to upgrade its 52 parks with an eye to attracting more eco-tourists and eco-tour businesses. If you find a new way to let visitors enjoy the great outdoors, and can make it educational to boot, you may have yourself a new business.

Service industries

These days, it seems, nobody wants to get his hands dirty — that is, physically work. In a state that cleans thousands of hotel rooms every day, in a state where residents cherish their gardens, there's plenty of need for people who will do the dirty work. Landscapers, housekeepers, small-job maintenance people are much appreciated. And some entrepreneurs make a business of supplying such workers to residents and businesses.

Healthcare, elderly care

Any business that can reduce the cost of healthcare will be greatly appreciated in coming years, a Hawai`i labor specialist predicts. That can be any kind of business, from training and providing qualified healthcare workers, to servicing highly technical pieces of equipment, to providing licensed care homes.

One-of-a-kind businesses

Because the islands are small and the cost of doing business is great, there are numerous one-of-a-kind businesses functioning throughout the state, with little or no competition. Can you provide competition? Can you do the job better than it's already being done?

Consider a national franchise

Look for a franchise that is popular on the mainland. Would it work in Hawai`i? Talk to the franchisee, the parent company. Chances are they have already considered Hawai`i and may be looking for the right individual to bring their product or service to the islands.

The Pacific Business News' Book of Lists is a great reference guide for entreprenuers. see www.bizjournals.com/bookoflists

Starting a business? Here's some advice

➤ **TIP**: **Keep it small.** Leroy Laney, chief economist at First Hawaiian Bank, has advised that to survive in Hawai`i businesses must be either very small or very large. A small business can avoid much of the overhead, such as the cost of employees and commercial buildings. A very large business has the resources to survive them.

A Maui accountant agrees, "Keep your business small, with just yourself or family as employees. Keep it in your home. That way you avoid some of the overhead and the extra costs of doing business."

"There's a huge amount of underground business being done on these islands," he adds. "Employees being paid under the table. People working from their homes despite zoning restrictions, people trading goods for services or services for services; anything to avoid the high cost of doing business here. And you can't blame them. I never advise my clients to cheat, but sometimes it's the only way to stay in business."

➤ **TIP**: **Know your island.** Be sure you understand the island on which your business will be located. Each island's economy and business climate is unique and offers its own problems and opportunities. It might be very difficult to maintain a business on Lana`i or in rural Hana, Maui, due to the small populations. And it would be difficult on Moloka`i for two reasons: many of its 7,000 people are jobless, plus residents often fight development. But there are no absolutes. A charming restaurant/gift shop/vacation rental business in isolated Hana thrives; so does a bakery/restaurant/general store (offering a variety of needed goods) in tiny Kaunakakai, Moloka`i. A hardware store opened recently on Lana`i. These are carefully chosen businesses serving specific needs.

➤ **TIP**: **Look for business opportunities when you first visit** the islands, while new experiences make the greatest impression. What service or product did you enjoy in your country, state, or hometown that is not available here? Would it succeed here? Get some opinions from accountants, bank advisors and other business people.

➤ **TIP**: **Buy an existing business.** Business owners sell out here for all the same reasons they do on the mainland, plus an added one. Some owners get "island fever" — they grow tired of being in slow-paced paradise and are anxious to sell and return to the mainland.

BUSINESS

➤ TIP: **Get in the business business.** If you have a strong track record of building successful businesses, consider starting businesses here and selling them. Many people want to move to Hawai`i, and most of them are looking for ways to earn a living. Some brokers specialize in selling currently operating businesses to foreign investors, especially those who want to move to the United States. Specific regulations and requirements apply; be sure to get full details and work with a reputable business broker knowledgeable in this field.

➤ TIP: **Read** *Pacific Business News*, a weekly newspaper. It includes lists of business bankruptcies and foreclosures statewide. If you spot a bankruptcy in a business similar to the one you are considering, attempt to talk to the owner. What went wrong? What went right? What is their advice for you? (Subscriptions: P.O. Box 833, Honolulu, HI 96808).

➤ TIP: **Network with other businesspeople.** Join your local Chamber of Commerce, Small Business Hawai`i, or other group. You'll learn about island business practices and you'll also tune into the "coconut wireless" — the gossip/news of the islands. Here, as in any business climate, *who* you know matters as much as *what* you know. See the resource page of this section for organizations and a list of Chambers of Commerce.

➤ TIP: **Obtain education, advice.** Many of the business world's top people retire or visit here; some of them volunteer services through agencies like SCORE. In addition, most islands have business development centers. Start with the resources at the end of this chapter. Also, take at least two courses in running a small business in Hawai`i, which are offered regularly through local Chambers of Commerce and community colleges.

➤ TIP: **Bring enough money** to keep your business afloat for four years. Expect to be in the red your first year or two, and then break even for another year or two before making a profit. This is typical for a new business. Many new businesses fail because they do not have enough resources to survive this period.

Photo courtesy of the Powells

Jim and Deb: Re-routing a dream

When Jim and Debra Powell moved to Hawai`i a few years ago, they left their business in Los Angeles. Sort of.

Their company, Logistics Training, educates airline personnel, packers and shippers in the transport of hazardous materials. It's a serious, demanding business that takes Deb and Jim around the world. But each time they returned to L.A. from some faraway place, Jim would crawl into his hot tub, light a cigar, close his eyes, and be... well, less than totally content. He and Debra had an unfulfilled dream. They wanted to live in the place they loved best: Maui. The problem? Jim felt they could not operate a legitimate, international business from an island famous for its laid-back lifestyle and surfing mentality.

"The biggest problem with setting up a consulting business in Maui and catering to mainland clients is their impression that if they hired a consultant from Maui, I'd somehow show up in an aloha shirt carrying a tiki torch!" Jim says.

One day Jim returned from a teaching trip and was soaking in his hot tub when the phone rang. It was a telephone company solicitor. Just as Jim was about to slam the phone down he heard her say, "Would you be interested in a call-forwarding service where you can have a Los Angeles phone number, but it will ring anywhere you want?"

Jim put the phone back to his ear, took the cigar from his mouth, and listened.

"For 12 dollars a month you can have a local number in Los Angeles, or New York, or anywhere," the phone solicitor said.

"So, you mean, I could get an L.A. phone number and have it ring, say, in Maui?" Jim asked.

"Sure."

"So, you mean, I could get an L.A. phone number and have it ring, say, in Maui?" Jim asked.

The Powells conduct training classes at clients' offices or at nearby hotels. They have no business location, just phone lines into their home. And clients never visit. If business calls could be routed through L.A., there was no reason clients had to know, or care, where they lived. The business could, in effect, remain in California and the Powells could move to Maui.

"I'll take two of those numbers," Jim said. "One for my phone and one for my fax."

Thus, Jim made an instant decision that was to forever change his and Deb's life. The Powells opened an account at Mailboxes Etc. in L.A., set it up to forward their mail, and moved to Maui.

That was several years ago. Their business calls, placed to a Los Angeles number, are flawlessly routed to Hawai`i. And their business, conducted from the middle of an ocean, continues to grow. In fact, the island location has been a boon. Over the past couple of years they've added clients in Guam, Micronesia, Samoa and Hong Kong.

Starting a business in Hawai`i? Here's help.

- **Hawai`i Business Action Center**
  Information on starting a business here: licenses, permits, forms
  www.Hawaii.gov/dbedt/bac/business.html
  Phone (808) 586-2423

- **Hawai`i Business Resource Center**
  Economic, statistical information about the state
  www.hawaii.gov/dbedt
  Phone (808) 586-2423
  Fax (808) 587-2790

- **Hawai`i Department of Business, Economic Development & Tourism**
  All kinds of information, statistics on Hawai`i. Applications for doing business here
  www.hawaii.gov/dbedt
  Phone (808) 586-2423
  For a free workbook "Starting a Business in Hawai`i" call the
  Business Action Center, (808) 586-2545
  This branch of the Hawai`i Department of Business, Economic Development & Tourism provides entrepreneurs with information, business forms, licenses and permits

- **High-Tech Development Corporation**
  Incentives, encouragement and networking. High-tech business directory
  www.htdc.org
  Phone (808) 539-3806
  Fax (808) 539-3611

- **O`ahu Small Business Development Center**
  Counseling, information
  Phone (808) 522-8131
  Fax (808) 522-8135

- **SCORE**
  (Service Corps of Retired Executives)
  Advice and help in the start up and growth process
  Resource of the U.S. Small Business Administration,
  www.score.org
  Phone (808) 522-8132

- **Small Business Hawai`i**
  Organization of small business owners works for better laws, taxes, conditions. Offers information and resources, as well as group savings plans
  www.smallbusinesshawaii.com
  Phone (808) 396-1724
  Fax (808) 396-1726
  E-mail: sbh@lava.net

BUSINESS

- **U.S. Small Business Administration**
  www.sba.gov

- **Professional and Vocational Licensing Division**
  Department of Commerce and
  Consumer Affairs, State of Hawai`i,
  pvl.eHawaii.gov/pvl
  (808) 586-3000

- **State Department of Labor and Industrial Relations, Workforce Development**
  (808) 984-2091

MAUI

- **Small Business Development Center**
  and
  The Business Information Center
  590 Lipoa Parkway
  Kihei, HI 96753
  www.hbrl-sbdc.org
  (808) 875-2400
  E-mail: hbrl@hbrl-sbdc.org

For the negative and the positive aspects of doing business in Hawai`i, visit this website:

www.smallbusinesshawaii.com

- **Maui Chamber of Commerce**
  www.mauichamber.com
  (808) 871-7711

KAUA`I

- **State Department of Labor and Industrial Relations, Workforce Development**
  3100 Kuhio Highway, Suite C-9
  Lihu`e, HI 96766
  dlir.state.hi.us/wdd/lihue
  Phone (808) 274-3056
  Fax (808) 274-3059

HAWAI`I

- **Hawai`i Island Economic Development**
  www.hiedb.org
  (808) 966-5416

- **Research and Development**
  www.hawaii-county.com/directory/dir_research.htm
  (808) 961-8366

- **Kona-Kohala Chamber of Commerce**
  www.kona-kohala.com
  (808) 329-1758

- **Hawai`i Island Chamber of Commerce**
  (808) 935-7178

chapter 5

ke kumu
ku`ai
necessities

Photo by Toni Polancy

Can you

afford

paradise?

Marty-Jean's story: A *kama`aina* shops

"When I lived in California," says Marty-Jean Bender, a 20-year Hawai`i resident, "I would sit down, decide what to have for dinner for the upcoming week, make out a grocery list, and go shopping.

"Here, I see what's on sale, and that's what we'll have to eat. I'll buy whatever vegetable or fruit is in season. If something's really a bargain — say ground round at $1.99 a pound — we'll have it maybe three or four times in a week. You have to shop like that here. It's the only way to feed a family."

Marty-Jean is the sole support of herself and her teenage daughter. A part-time teacher at a private school, she also tutors children after school. To meet the mortgage payments on the $340,000 home she bought in 1992, Marty-Jean rents an apartment on the first level and occasionally rents the extra bedrooms in her home.

For "serious grocery shopping — stocking up" she shops at the two discount warehouses on Maui, Costco and V.I.P. Food is sold in large amounts, but an early modification on her garage included a pantry and room for a second refrigerator/freezer to store the extras. She shops carefully for everything, occasionally visiting weekend garage and moving sales, and perusing thrift stores for clothing. Among her favorites is Savers, a chain operated for the non-profit Big Brothers, Big Sisters. From stores on O`ahu and Maui, Savers sells used and new clothing and household goods, including donations from retail stores like Sears and Ross.

Marty-Jean's social life is active, but relatively inexpensive: Wednesday evening dance lessons ($25 for 3 months), game nights and buffet suppers with friends, church-sponsored boat trips, camp-outs and whale watches. She splurges occasionally to attend a concert of her favorite Hawaiian musicians and catches their acts when they promote new releases at free events and at the Maui Arts and Cultural Center.

Toni Polancy

Marty-Jean Bender and daughter, Makana

Surviving Hawai`i prices

Hawai`i has long had a reputation for being costly. Yet most newcomers — and even some residents — don't realize just how much more expensive island life is compared to the mainland U.S.A. Tally up the prices of rent, food, taxes and gasoline, and the cost of living in Hawai`i can be well over the 35 percent figure usually quoted. Depending on which part of the world or the mainland you come from, the additional costs can range from as little as 10 percent (California) to about 65 percent (rural Southern U.S.).

"You can tell people about the high costs here, but they just don't believe it," says a Honolulu businessman. "People moving here are caught up in a kind of excitement. It's like being in love. The hormones are kicking in. They hear about Hawai`i's high costs and they tell themselves, 'That's okay. I'll live in (a smaller) house; I won't eat as much' or 'I'll work hard; I'll make myself succeed.' And some of them do, but it's much, much harder than anyone can imagine while they are caught up in the throes of love."

Food

"Guess what I had to give up when I moved here?" a long-time resident laughs. "Cucumbers! They just cost so much and I never get over that when I go to the market. My boyfriend offered to gift wrap one and give it to me for my birthday."

Most major food markets say their profit margins are about 1.3 percent, the same as mainland markets. Yet, food costs are typically 35 percent higher here. Markets maintain that the extra cost is due to freight charges incurred shipping the food to the islands. Food prices are greater on neighbor islands, reflecting additional shipping charges.

Unfortunately, family necessities like bread, milk and cereal seem to bear the

One of the greatest contributors to the high cost of feeding a Hawai`i family is the state excise tax (4.167 percent at this writing and legislators occasionally consider increases). In most states, food is exempt from sales tax or it is applied only to luxury items like liquor and candies. Hawai`i's tax is assessed on all groceries, even those necessary to sustain life and nourish children: milk, vegetables, cereals, everything.

When supplies are threatened....

What one product do Hawai`i residents seem to value above all else? When a dock strike or hurricane, or anything else threatens to cut off our supplies, what product do residents run to markets, Longs drug stores and Costco warehouses to stock up on?

Is it Spam? Fish? Saimin? Some other life-sustaining food?

No.

Batteries? Candles? Gasoline?

Hardly.

It's toilet paper.

More than 90 percent of consumer goods are shipped to Hawai`i via ocean carriers and every so often something threatens to cut off our lifeline. In the early 1990s, it was hurricanes. In 2001, the impending war. In 2004, and other times in the past decade, dock and shipping strikes loomed.

We residents hurry to stock up on things like batteries, flashlights, and food. But, most of all, to buy plenty of toilet paper.

The run on one of life's most-important luxuries is understandable. If a disaster did cut off our supplies, necessities would probably soon be airlifted to us. But toilet paper would not be considered a necessity...and it might be difficult to come by.

brunt of high food costs. Although bargains can be found, milk can cost over $7 a gallon in convenience stores and the price fluctuates greatly in supermarkets. One week, it's a "loss leader" item offered at $4.50 a gallon, a bargain designed to bring in shoppers; the next week it's back up to $6. Bread usually costs at least $5 a loaf. Costco shopping club, with stores on O`ahu, Maui and the Big Island, is a popular place to "stock up" on groceries, because it retains consistently low prices on necessities like bread and milk.

Fruits and vegetables are very costly and sold by the pound instead of by the dozen as in mainland markets. Most produce is flown in at considerable cost — consider how bulky and heavy apples and oranges are and how perishable lettuce is. This travel time affects the quality and freshness of our fruits and vegetables. You'll get used to buying head lettuce that is browning at its edges (imported from California), grapes that are either unripe (so they can

You *can* save money on food

You don't have much control over how much you'll spend for necessities like housing and gasoline, but on most islands you can choose to spend less on food. These tips should help.

- **Make smart choices**. Forgo expensive packaged cereals and prepared foods for bulk items, available at some markets and at island health food stores. Watch for weekly farmers' markets and swap meets where seasonal vegetables and fruits are sold for as low as one-third of grocery store prices. On most islands you can buy in bulk at warehouses or wholesale "clubs" such as Costco and Sam's Club. If buying bulk means buying more food than you can use, consider sharing costs and quantities with a neighbor or friend.

- **Avoid small markets in tourist areas.** Prices for staple items tend to be higher in markets near hotels and tourist centers.

- **Know your roadside stands.** In Hawai`i, some roadside stands cater to tourists and prices can be high. (For example, an editor of this book commented that she knows a man who buys pineapples at Costco and resells them at a small roadside stand.)

- **Go to the source for your food.** Talk to friends and neighbors who hunt, fish and garden. Ask them to sell you their surplus.

- **Grow some of your own produce,** especially if you live in an area where it rains frequently. Even a small garden here produces abundantly because the growing season is constant. Be sure to take a class in gardening before you begin. Hawai`i's garden insects and unique conditions can be a challenge.

- **Watch for free fruit sources.** Even on these rapidly developing islands, many Hawai`i parks and forests contain fruit-bearing plants and trees that no one harvests. Learn to recognize island fruits like liliko`i, mango, guava, breadfruit.

travel longer) or a bit soft (having traveled too long), meat from unknown origins that should be carefully sniffed for freshness before being eaten.

Locally grown produce and locally produced meat and eggs are available on most islands, but are usually costly and are often sold to high-end restaurants. Hawai`i's scarce land and high labor and utility prices are usually blamed for high locally-produced food prices.

FOOD

Food costs 11 to 32% more — plus tax

How much more you'll pay for groceries in Hawai`i depends on where you live now. Shoppers on four Hawaiian islands and in several cities across the United States and one city in Canada were asked to compare costs for the same grocery list. Hawai`i's shopping list averaged $41.72. That was 32 percent higher than Pennsylvania's, but only 11 percent higher than Chicago's. The 4.167 percent excise tax is figured into Hawai`i's totals.

To assure accurate comparisons each shopper bought the same brands and sizes or as close as they could find. They disregarded sale or "club" prices and used costs usually charged by the stores. Here's the list:

- lettuce from general display, not gourmet;
- least expensive 16 oz. loaf of white bread;
- Miracle Whip Light salad dressing, 32 oz. size;
- one pound ground beef, not more than 30% fat;
- Gerbers baby carrots, 2.5 oz.
- one dozen large eggs;
- one gallon whole milk, least expensive;
- one can Campbell's tomato soup, 10-3/4 oz.;
- Mrs. Smith's Pumpkin Custard Pie, 1 lb. 10 oz.;
- Taster's Choice instant coffee, 4 oz.;
- 12-pack Coca Cola Classic.

in Hawai`i:

Safeway
Kihei, Maui

Lettuce (lb.)	1.29
Bread	2.99
Salad dressing	5.19
Ground beef	3.69
Gerbers carrots	.80
Dozen eggs (18)	3.79
Gallon milk	3.50
Tomato soup	1.39
Pumpkin pie	9.59*
Instant coffee	4.99
6-pack Coke	3.50
Total	**39.45**
State tax	**1.64**
Total	**41.09**

* Pumpkin not available. Price is for Mrs. Smith's frozen cream pies.

Foodland
Princeville, Kaua`i

Lettuce	1.39
Bread	2.89
Salad dressing	3.99
Ground beef	3.39
Gerbers carrots	.69
Dozen eggs	2.99
Gallon milk	6.59
Tomato soup	1.59
Pumpkin pie	6.25*
Instant coffee	5.39
12-pack Coke	4.99
Total	**40.15**
State tax	**1.67**
Total	**41.82**

* Pumpkin not available. Price is for Mrs. Smith's frozen cream pies.

KTA Superstores
Hilo, The Big Island

Lettuce	1.39
Bread	2.09
Salad dressing	5.39
Ground beef	2.57
Gerbers carrots	.89
Dozen eggs	1.91
Gallon milk	3.79
Tomato soup	1.49
Pumpkin pie	6.83*
Instant coffee	3.89
12-pack Coke	8.39
Total	**38.63**
State tax	**1.61**
Total	**40.24**

* Pumpkin not available. Price is for Mrs. Smith's frozen cream pies.

Foodland
La`ie, O`ahu

Lettuce (lb.)	1.49
Bread	2.39
Salad dressing	4.85
Ground beef	1.29
Gerbers carrots	.79
Dozen eggs	2.99
Gallon milk	7.99
Tomato soup	1.29
Pumpkin pie	6.37*
Instant coffee	6.85
12-pack Coke	4.99
Total	**42.03**
State tax	**1.73**
Total	**43.76**

* Pumpkin not available. Price is for Mrs. Smith's frozen fruit pies.

on the Mainland:

Dominicks
Chicago , Illinois

Lettuce	1.49
Bread	2.79
Salad dressing	3.39
Ground beef	4.43
Gerbers carrots	.50
Dozen eggs	1.79
Gallon milk	3.29
Tomato soup	1.09
Pumpkin pie	3.29
Instant coffee	6.49
12-pack Coke	3.99
Total	**37.24**

Safeway
Walnut Creek,
California

Lettuce	1.49
Bread	.99
Salad dressing	4.39
Ground beef	4.29
Gerbers carrots	.47
Dozen eggs	2.99
Gallon milk	3.99
Tomato soup	.99
Pumpkin pie	5.49*
Instant coffee	6.59
12-pack Coke	4.99
Total	**36.67**

* Pumpkin not available.
   Price is for Mrs. Smith's
   fruit cobbler.

Safeway
Calgary, Alberta,
Canada

Lettuce	1.69
Bread	1.99
Salad dressing	3.25
Ground beef	1.65
Gerbers carrots	.59
Dozen eggs	2.99
4 liter milk	3.61
Tomato soup	.75
Pumpkin pie	5.40
Instant coffee	6.39
12-pack Coke	8.49
Total	**36.80**

Publix
Delray, Florida

Lettuce	1.28
Bread	1.89
Salad dressing	1.12
Ground beef	1.29
Gerbers carrots	.42
Dozen eggs	1.57
Gallon milk	2.99
Tomato soup	.79
Pumpkin pie	4.49*
Instant coffee	5.99
6-pack Coke	3.97
Total	**25.80**

* Pumpkin not available.
   Price is for Mrs. Smith's
   frozen cream pies.

Giant Eagle
Erie, Pennsylvania

Lettuce	1.29
Bread	.79
Salad dressing	2.79
Ground beef	1.99
Gerbers carrots	.49
Dozen eggs	1.55
Gallon milk	3.01
Tomato soup	.60
Pumpkin pie	6.99*
Instant coffee	6.19
6-pack Coke	2.50
Total	**28.20**
State tax	**.15**
Total	**28.35**

* Pumpkin not available.
   Price is for Mrs. Smith's
   frozen cream pies.

Super Fresh
Trenton, New Jersey

Lettuce	1.49
Bread	1.50
Salad dressing	3.49
Ground beef	3.19
Gerbers carrots	2/.89
Dozen eggs	1.89
Gallon milk	3.19
Tomato soup	.99
Pumpkin pie	5.49*
Instant coffee	6.29
6-pack Coke	2.99
Total	**30.96**
State tax	**1.86**
Total	**31.82**

* Pumpkin not available.
   Price is for Mrs. Smith's
   frozen cream pies.

Prices reflect days shopped and are
for comparison only — the price
may change weekly or daily

Shopping...

If you are one of those people for whom shopping is a relaxing hobby, think twice about moving to neighbor islands like Maui, Kaua`i and the Big Island. Each has just one or two major department stores, one discount clothing store, one warehouse shopping club, and numerous tourist boutiques mostly offering bathing suits or t-shirts. It's not difficult to find the clothes or items you need because you don't need much here; it's a matter of not being able to shop as often as you might like or have the variety you might be used to.

Nearly everything, even most Hawaiian souvenirs, is imported. Residents of all islands quickly learn a little rule: if you see something you want, buy it now. It could be sold out by the time you make up your mind, and waiting for more to arrive via barge may be futile.

for clothing

Hawai`i's lifestyle is very casual, which keeps clothing costs down. For nearly all professions and occasions, slacks and good-quality "aloha" shirts suffice for men. Women's clothing tends to be simple and colorful, in cool fabrics like washable rayons and cottons. Unfortunately, *mu`umu`u*, the traditional loose dress, is seen less frequently than it used to be, even on Aloha Fridays when employees are encouraged to dress "island style." Honolulu is dressier than the neighbor islands.

Each of the major outer islands has at least one shopping center with the usual chain clothing stores such as The Gap and Banana Republic. For many years, locally-owned Liberty House was the only upscale department store offering popular designer items. A few years ago, Liberty House, a subsidiary of Amfac, one of Hawai`i's original Big Five companies, was purchased by the huge Macy's chain, which continues to expand here. Sears also has stores on all major islands, although its Kaua`i store does not offer clothing.

Most resorts and hotels include boutiques geared to tourists, and their markup is high. Residents usually visit such boutiques only during annual sales.

on O`ahu

For the cost of *kama`aina* airfare (at this point, about $200 round-trip), outer islanders can fly to shopping heaven. Honolulu's Ala Moana Center is one of the largest shopping malls in the nation. It includes several American department stores and an interesting Japanese department store, Shirokiya. Ala Moana also has almost every mainland chain store — The Gap, Laura Ashley, Ann Klein, Banana Republic, etc. — plus some expensive shops such as Chanel and Gucci, the upscale Neiman-Marcus department store, and a sprinkling of touristy island boutiques and specialty stores.

O`ahu also has discount and outlet shopping. Waikele Center in western O`ahu offers 20 to 50 percent discounts in a few outlet stores including Saks "Off Fifth" Avenue.

In the past few years, discounters like WalMart and Kmart have established O`ahu and neighbor island stores, promising to sell at mainland prices. When Kmart opened near downtown Honolulu a few years ago, eager shoppers created traffic jams on busy Nimitz Highway. Costco shopping club, featuring everything from cauliflowers to computers, also debuted to big crowds and thousands of memberships. Here, as on the mainland, the arrival of big discount stores has been a mixed blessing. The discounters have forced the closing or retrenching of some small businesses, but they have also reduced living costs here. There is no Costco on Lana`i or Moloka`i.

for furnishings

Furniture in most households is simple and easy to clean. Light colors are popular, but not always practical. The islands' famous red dirt makes it difficult to keep upholstered furniture and carpeting fresh. For the same reason, fewer knickknacks and small collectibles are seen in the average home.

Buy 'used'

Many people move from the islands, so household and "moving" sales abound on weekends. The numerous thrift stores and consignment shops include interesting furniture and clothing from all over the world at big savings.

Shopping on O`ahu?

Ask for free shipping. Some Honolulu stores will pack and deliver large items, without cost, to the Honolulu wharfs to be carried interisland by Young Brothers. (A large couch costs about $100 to ship from Honolulu to Kaua`i.)

Mail order shopping? Watch those shipping and handling charges

Because of our island location, a large percentage of our shopping tends to be done from catalogues and on the Internet. That means we pay extra to get the item to our home or business. You should be aware of shipping charges and watch out for companies that make a profit on shipping and handling.

Honolulu Advertiser columnist Deb Adamson shopped for a diamond bracelet on the Web and found shipping and handling charges ranged from $5 to $60 for the $299 bracelet. Some retailers based fees on a percentage of the total cost. Her findings:

- **J.C. Penney charged $60**
- **Amazon.com charged $16**
- **Target charged just $5.**

A better shipping bargain: the bracelet could have been mailed in a Priority U.S. post office envelope and shipped for $3.85, usually arriving within a few days.

(Some retailers profit from high shipping charge, *Honolulu Advertiser*, August 1, 2004.)

Much furniture is traded via household and garage sales or used furniture stores. There is also a preponderance of inexpensive boxed furniture such as that sold by Kmart and WalMart.

Upscale furniture on the neighbor islands is usually purchased through interior decorators, although two or three small furniture stores operate on Maui, the Big Island and Kaua`i. People who are serious about furnishing or renovating high-end homes usually travel to Honolulu to choose supplies, or hire an interior decorator.

for 'hardware'

Luckily for Hawai`i's numerous hardware stores, residents and workers like to have paint supplies, glue guns, garden equipment, etc. close to where they live. Most islands are blessed with an abundance of hardware stores.

As on the mainland, Lowes and Home Depot compete, usually within a few miles of each other. And smaller and individually owned hardware stores such as Ace Hardware remain popular and busy. Kilgo's, on Sand Island in O`ahu, is especially popular with contractors. And O`ahu's City Mill chain of neighborhood hardware stores puts the emphasis on service.

Transportation

If you live in Waikiki, downtown O`ahu, or some of its nearby suburbs, you may be able to save a lot of money by NOT having a car. O`ahu is the only island with regular, dependable bus service. TheBus travels all over the island and most routes are serviced every half hour. Fares are reasonable at $2.25 per ride, and student and elderly passes make it less expensive. While buses tend to be crowded — standing room only during rush hour — they are cool, well-maintained and a real bargain versus the cost of maintaining a car.

But beware: bus rides are slow and time-consuming with frequent stops. They can add hours to your "work" day. See Erica's story, this chapter.

If you live on a neighbor island, you will need a car. Outer islands have no dependable means of convenient mass transportation, or are struggling with developing reliable service. At this writing, the Big Island has once-a-day bus service across the island; Kaua`i has subsidized van service in operation regularly, but it is in danger of running out of funding; Maui has various shuttles and a new service, but it runs infrequently; Lana`i has shuttle service every half hour from its two major hotels to Lana`i City, but it's geared towards tourists; and Moloka`i has no service at all.

Autos

Honolulu is the eleventh most expensive metropolitan area in the nation in which to use an automobile. On the average, it costs $7,100 per year to drive a car in Honolulu. Gasoline, maintenance and insurance, as well as license, registration fees and annual depreciation were calculated in 80 cities by the management consulting firm Renzheimer International.

Too much driving?

If you're moving from busy traffic areas like New York City or Los Angeles, you may not find the relief you seek in Hawai`i. Hawai`i has the 11th-longest one-way commute time in the nation, a survey by the Census Bureau showed. The average Hawai`i resident spends 25.4 minutes traveling to work. Commuting time was highest in New York, at 31 minutes, followed by Maryland, New Jersey, Illinois and California, according to the Associated Press. If you're tired of driving, try moving to South Dakota. South Dakotans spent the least time, about 15.5 minutes.

Matthew Thayer

Rush hour in downtown Honolulu.

Their analysis was based on a midsize car driven 15,000 miles a year within a 50-mile radius of a city and traded in after four years. (Los Angeles at $8,762 was the most expensive city and Sioux Falls, S.D., was the least costly at $5,710).

Cheaper on O`ahu?

Talk to automobile salespeople and you will hear several stories about how much island living adds to the purchase price of a new car. Some sellers say there is no difference, since all autos must usually be shipped to dealerships anyway; others say their markup from the MSRP (manufacturer's suggested retail price) differs from mainland dealers only by the cost of freight to ship cars to Hawai`i. Still other dealers blatantly tack on a "dealer markup" that can be several thousands of dollars.

And they quickly point out that if you bought a car on the mainland and shipped it yourself, the freight cost would be higher. Shipping an auto from California, Washington state or Oregon costs around $1,000. (See the Moving chapter of this book.)

Are autos less expensive on busy O`ahu than on the neighbor islands? At some dealerships, yes. Honolulu dealerships are larger, sell more autos, and their overhead is therefore spread over more sales.

If you live on a neighbor island, would you save some money by traveling to O`ahu to buy a car? Not necessarily. Most of the car dealerships on all islands are owned by the same few companies. However, dealers will negotiate their prices with savvy buyers, several Honolulu auto salesmen say.

Consider a "Hawai`i cruiser"

"Hawai`i cruisers" are used cars, usually showing a bit of wear, and selling for less than half new car costs. You don't have to buy an old car, but here are four good reasons to consider buying a used car:

1. Cars depreciate quickly from the ocean salt and your new car is likely to take on an old patina soon anyway.

2. An older, less attractive car is less appetizing to thieves and is less likely to be broken into or stolen, common problems on these islands.

3. People leaving the islands sometimes don't want to take their cars with them, so used car bargains abound.

4. Life is laid back here. You don't need to impress anyone with a fancy car.

"The dealer may not (negotiate) if you are looking at a real popular car, in great demand, and he doesn't have enough of them. But for other cars, we negotiate," commented one of the salesmen.

It costs about $150 to send an average-sized auto from Honolulu to another island by Young Brothers, the primary interisland shipper.

Here, from salespeople, are tips for smart island car shopping.

- **Shop with information in hand.** Refer to consumer books and magazines or the Internet for suggested prices and markups. Visit various dealerships with information in hand and try to negotiate a price. Intellichoice.com is one of many Internet sites that contain helpful auto-buying information.

- **Get quotes in writing.** If you call an O`ahu dealership from a neighbor island to inquire about car costs, you are sure to be quoted a very low price, said one neighbor island salesman. But be sure to get that quote in writing before you travel to O`ahu to buy the car, he advised, or you may find that particular car sold when you arrive at the dealership.

- **You don't have to travel to O`ahu to buy your auto.** If you know exactly what you want, the transaction can be completed via phone, fax and mail. The dealer will arrange for the car to be shipped to your island.

- **Negotiate inter-island shipping.** Two O`ahu auto salesmen offered this tip: Most O`ahu auto dealers will pay the inter-island freight cost as part of price negotiations.

A van, for free

Imagine getting a free van just for picking up a few people on your way to work every day and taking them back home at night. In a program aimed at cutting the number of autos using Hawai`i's busy highways, Vanpool Hawai`i offers drivers full-time use of new Ford Windstars, Dodge Caravans and Chevrolet Astros, among other vans.

The program works like this: Several commuters agree to travel together, choose a driver and share parking and gasoline costs. Vanpool supplies the van and collects from $150 to $300 a month from the group. Riders and driver share the cost. The more people who ride, the less the cost and the driver can also drive the van for personal use. Vans carry seven to fifteen passengers.

The program is run by a private business, VPSI, Inc. in Troy, Michigan, and is federally subsidized with tax dollars, according to Teresa Whitfield, account executive. Call (808) 596-8267

➤ **TIP: Ask Vanpool to give you** the names of two or three drivers who have been operating a pool for at least six months. Ask the drivers for any suggestions they may have to make your group function more smoothly and ask how they handled problems like commuters who show up late or are delinquent paying. That way, you can structure your group to avoid problems.

Gasoline prices

Hawai`i has the highest gasoline prices in the nation. Oil refineries and gasoline dealers are reluctant to compare costs, but gasoline usually costs about 30 to 35 percent more on O`ahu than on the mainland U.S. and an additional 10 to 15 percent on neighbor islands.

The islands are too young to have natural deposits of crude oil, so Hawai`i is 90 percent dependent upon imported oil to provide its energy, more than any other state. On the mainland, many refineries are connected to their crude sources by underground pipelines, but here all crude oil and refined products must be imported by tanker.

Hawai`i has two main oil refiners, Tesoro Hawai`i and Chevron USA. Gasoline products are manufactured and stored on O`ahu, then transported via barge to outer islands. Stafford Kiguchi of Tesoro cites another reason for our high gasoline costs: we have fewer roads and limited opportunity for travel, so fixed costs (such as stations, pumps, employees) must be spread over fewer actual gallons of gasoline sold.

State legislators have passed a cap on gasoline prices, but face arguments that price controls would lead to shortages and higher prices, and it may never take affect. While the debate rages, a Hawai`i Toyota dealership has a six-month-long waiting list for the hybrid Prius which burns about half the gasoline of traditional cars.

Auto insurance

Hawai`i's automobile insurance rates are the second highest in the nation (New Jersey's are higher) and have long been the topic of heated debate among both legislators and constituents. The average insurance rate on the islands, two agents confirmed, is about $600 every six months — or $1,200 a year. That can be as much as twice what you are paying now, depending on where you live. Why so high? It's easy to blame no-fault insurance laws but Hawai`i set a record in 1997 for the highest profits on auto insurance in any state during this decade, and it takes the number one spot in the nation for overall auto insurance profitability. The figures came from the Auto Insurance Report, a California-based auto insurance industry publication.

But agents insist there's more to the story. Insurance is also costly because these islands have one of the highest auto accident rates in the nation. And we also have very high medical and litigation costs.

Auto insurance rates vary, not only from state to state, but also from county to county. Here's the comparison for a family (two drivers with clean records) owning two vehicles, a 2002 Volkswagen and a 1997 Honda. The liability and physical damage coverage is the same. There were differences among medical coverage required for each state, according to Mike Takahara, sales manager at Liberty Mutual insurance company in Honolulu.

Portland, OR	$1325
San Jose, CA	$1459
Seattle, WA	$1943
Ewa Beach, O`ahu	**$1423**
Topeka, KS	$1425

(2005 rates)

Keeping in touch

"I spend $4,000 to $8,000 a year on travel," says a successful O'ahu businesswoman in her forties. "I either visit my family on the mainland or help them come here. This is money that should be going into a retirement fund. But I figure, what the heck, you only live once and family is important to me."

When you are calculating expenses, be sure to add the cost of keeping in touch. If you can afford it, you'll probably travel often to see mainland friends and relatives and to assuage "rock fever" — a confined feeling some people experience from living on a small island.

You are also apt to be visited by many friends and relatives during your first few years here. If you can afford it, a guest room or guest cottage is convenient. At the least, a "pullout" couch bed or futon is necessary.

Many *malihini* interviewed for this book echoed this comment: "I really felt the distance evenings, when my day was ended. I'd get lonesome and want to call home, but by then it was midnight back in New York. Too late to call. I felt so alone."

Since there is such a time difference between Hawai'i and just about anywhere, you'll want to keep apprised of lowest rates and bargains on cell phone "anytime" minutes.

Here are a few tips on keeping in touch:

- **Since it is earlier in Hawai'i**, ask mainland contacts to call you late evenings their time, when rates are lower for them. This has two advantages. You won't wake them. And they'll pay less for "late night" phone rates.

- **Get a cell phone plan with "anytime minutes"** that let you call the mainland without long-distance charges.

- **Cell phone and long distance phone** plans can vary widely. You'll need to watch advertisements. And don't just quit your current phone company to switch to another; discuss your rate with a company sales representative. Often your current long distance provider will try to meet a competitor's rates. That saves the inconvenience of switching accounts.

- **Watch your phone bills carefully.** Once you've switched to the least expensive provider, make sure your bill is calculated at the rate you expect. Inter-office miscommunications can cost you big bucks.
- **Email is great** for communicating with friends and relatives faraway because it is non-intrusive, no ringing telephones.
- **Track airline costs.** Since flights to some parts of the U.S. can range from a few hundred dollars to well over a thousand, depending on time of year and "specials," you'll want to keep tabs on rates. Ask a friendly travel agent to keep you advised of airline specials. Or search the Internet for travel bargains. Try Travelocity.com.
- **Book flights for the Christmas holidays** at least four months in advance for best rates.

Prepaid phone cards

are a great way to save money. Costco offers a card that costs as little as 3 cents a minute for interisland or mainland calls

Interisland flights among most expensive, per mile, in nation

"Because Hawai`i is an archipelago, transportation within the state has always been expensive. Air flights are frequent and convenient, but comparatively expensive. Three of the ten most expensive airfares per mile in the United States are the connections between Honolulu and Maui, Honolulu and Kona, and Honolulu and Kaua`i."

That information appears in the *Atlas of Hawai`i.*

In recent years, the cost of flying inter-island has, well, taken off. Many island residents count on free airline "miles" accumulated through credit card use. But cashing in those miles can be a frustrating experience, with few flights available.

Another way to save on interisland flight costs: Watch for airlines' special offerings, like coupon books of six flights at a discounted cost. At this writing they can be under $100 a flight.

(Atlas of Hawai`i, *third edition, University of Hawai`i Press, Honolulu.*)

Honolulu has the highest percentage

of Internet users with broadband connections of 75 metro cities. About 52 percent of Internet users here have broadband connection compared with 33 percent in the rest of the nation. Hawai`i's location and time difference play a part in the high usage, making it more convenient to communicate via computer than by phone.

A 2005 study by Scarborough Research, New York City.

Water is a concern, now and for the future

The title of this chapter is "Necessities" and nothing is more necessary, more vital to our lives, than the water we drink. The islands are surrounded by water yet, like many parts of the country, we face a major problem. Our fresh water supplies are limited. In 2004, the federal General Accounting Office predicted that in the next 10 years a majority of states will experience significant water shortages. Hawai`i is among those states.

Already Maui's main source of water, `Iao aquifer, is pumping at capacity. Water meter reservations for Central and South Maui were halted in 2003, slowing only slightly permits for new developments. Upcountry residents look down on the sleek green lawns and golf courses of South Maui's resorts, built on deserts, and shake their heads. *They are taking our water.*

In an article in *Hawaii Business* magazine (Water Shortages Demand Stewardship, October 2003) former governor George R. Ariyoshi explains the water situation in Hawai`i.

"If we are short of water now, what will the situation be for our children and grandchildren?" he asks.

"(A recent) call for short-term water conservation made banner headlines, but the most disturbing report did not make the front pages. It was about increased salinity in some of the wells that provide us water.

"If we think of our island as a porous rock that seeps with water, the base is salt water from the ocean. Floating on top is a lens-shaped underground reserve of slightly lighter fresh water, accumulating from rainfall. Between the salt and fresh water is a zone of mixing.

"Although conditions vary from place to place, typically there is a 40-foot base of fresh water below sea level for every foot of fresh water above sea level. When the fresh water above sea level drops one foot, the freshwater base below sea level diminishes forty feet, with a corresponding 40-foot rise in the saltwater level.

"We should hold this image clearly in our minds and teach it to our children," Ariyoshi writes. "It allows us to better understand that our water supply is fragile. Consuming more water than nature supplies results in mining the water supply. Like gold or coal, fresh water can disappear When the more saline water rises, wells are in danger of being fouled."

What can we do about it?

"Stewardship is about keeping our resource base in balance," Ariyoshi writes. "If we do not have the answers to questions about water, we should restrain development, particularly in dry areas that require an extra-ordinary amount of water, such as Ko Olina (a resort development in arid leeward Oahu)." Ariyoshi cites the importance of education on this issue and the vital need for reforesta-tion and forest manage-ment. Among the long-term solutions suggested both by Ariyoshi and Maui's mayor Alan Arakawa, is desalina-tion of ocean waters. It would be, at this time, a very costly solution.

Should Hawai'i's cur-rent and future water problems keep you from moving to the islands? No. We will solve the problem because we must, even if it means an extremely high water cost in the future. But you must know that, like the place from which you are coming, Paradise faces problems and this is a serious one.

(George R. Ariyoshi, governor of Hawai'i from 1973 to 1986, is an attorney. He was the first Japanese American to be elected governor in the United States.)

And then there's electricity: twice the nation's average cost

The average cost for a kilowatt-hour of residential use in 2006 was 20.06 cents compared to a national average of 11.4 cents, according to figures from Hawaiian Electric Company.

"Many have come to accept that reliable electrical power in a place as small and isolated as Hawai'i means they're stuck having to pay more than the residents of any others state. In most cases, far more," writes Jan TenBruggencate in the *Honolulu Advertiser*.

Nuclear, coal and natural gas generate electricity for most of the rest of the nation. Most of Hawai'i's electricity is generated via petroleum. Hawai'i relies on diesel and fuel oil, easier to transport to a far-away island.

Costs are particularly high on neighbor islands. In 2005, the average cost for a residential consumer in Maui was $167.95 per month, Kaua'i's was $171.00 and O'ahu's $120.54. O'ahu's Hawaiian Electric Co. uses primarily low-sulfur residual fuel oil which has not risen in price as much as other types of fuel, an electric company spokesperson said.

Erica's story: Starting from scratch

When Erica Maluski arrived on O`ahu to begin a job as art therapist at Kahi Mohala, a leeward psychiatric hospital, she was starting from scratch.

"I packed up my life in two large suitcases and two duffel bags; mostly books, clothes, knickknacks that meant something to me," she says.

From New York, via the Internet, Erica booked an inexpensive hotel, hoping to enjoy the busy Waikiki area for a few weeks before finding a permanent apartment. She had been on a "high," looking forward to the exotic adventure of Hawai`i, imagining herself on a hotel lanai, ocean breezes ruffling her hair. But as she lugged her bags up to a shabby room and stared out the window at a building jammed next to the hotel, she felt lonely and scared. At 24, she was, for the first time, thousands of miles from the family she loved.

"What am I doing in this crappy hotel? What am I doing in Hawai`i?" she asked herself and broke into tears.

'What am I doing in this crappy hotel? What am I doing in Hawai`i?'

Things weren't much better the next day. Erica's mother had given her a copy of the first edition of this book. In it Erica read about O`ahu's efficient bus service and she assumed she would not need a car. Ewa Beach was only about 40 miles from Waikiki; she could easily ride TheBus.

But Erica was late for work her first day on the job. The bus, which stopped often to load and unload passengers, took two hours to travel to the leeward coast. Back and forth, that was four hours out of Erica's day, worse than most New York-to-suburbs commutes.

And as the bus headed up the O`ahu coast, Hawai`i looked less and less like the posh resorts and lush green postcards that had lured her here. To be sure, there's an azure ocean on one side, but in the summer the leeward coast can be brown and dry. Farrington Highway is loaded with bumper-to-bumper traffic, dotted with dusty towns and rusty shacks. This is the low-income side of O`ahu, a world away from enticing tourist brochures.

Things improved as soon as Erica saw the hospital where she would work and met her supervisor Joe Yoshida. The Kahi Mohala campus, spread over 14 acres, is more like a resort than a hospital. Erica would be working with behavioral health patients from as young as three to as old as seventy-three. It was exactly the job for which she had hoped and trained. After showing Erica around the hospital, Joe took her on a tour of Ewa Beach and suggested she make her life easier by renting an apartment in one of the many modern complexes close to her job. Answering newspaper ads, Erica found an unfurnished studio and moved in within a few days of her arrival. At $775 plus utilities, the 415-square-foot apartment, with lanai and full kitchen, cost "about half what I'd pay in the New York area," she says.

Now, she figured, she could easily bike the four miles to work. Erica slept on the floor of her apartment with just a sheet, pillow and her teddy bear for a few nights until she had a day off to shop for furniture. She rode TheBus to

A surfboard, a plant and her teddy bear make Erica's apartment a home.

WalMart to buy $1,000 worth of assemble-it-yourself furniture and took a cab back to her apartment. The cab driver kept the clock running as he helped lug the boxes up to her second-floor apartment.

"Just like a New York cabbie would," she jokes.

She tried the same approach to stock up on groceries. She couldn't carry much on her bike, so she took a bus to a Waipahu market, several miles away, filled her shopping cart with staples, and called a cab to take her home.

"In New York or just about any place, you can just do that. Call a cab and they come," she says. But she was told all the taxis were booked and none could be sent for hours.

"I went back into the store and told them," she said, "and I wasn't exactly overwhelmed with aloha spirit. The clerks just stared at me."

"I went back into the store and told them," she said, "and I wasn't exactly overwhelmed with aloha spirit. The clerks just stared at me."

So Erica returned all the groceries and rode TheBus back home, empty-handed. At that point, she decided, "The bike thing just wasn't working. Okay, I need a car."

By the way, there's one group of people who treat newcomers very well in Hawai`i, Erica comments. Bus drivers.

"Bus drivers are very nice to you. In New York if you don't know where you're going, the attitude is it's your fault. Here, drivers go out of their way to help."

She rode TheBus into town one Saturday and shopped from 8 a.m. to 8 p.m., purchasing a new car with $800 down.

"My first real big purchase as a grown-up," she laughs ruefully.

But nothing comes easy. She was shocked to learn of the number of car thefts in peaceful Hawai`i and bought a "club" for her car, a safety device to thwart burglars.

"So, within a week I had my apartment, and within a month I had furniture and a car and a safety device for my car. Pretty much everything you need... whether you are in New York or in Hawai`i."

She had everything, in fact. Except friends.

Erica's story continues in the Other Considerations *chapter.*

$1,000,000
Leasehold
Fee Available

OCEAN FRONT

kahi e noho ai

a place to live

Will you rent or buy?

A house or an apartment?

Photo by Toni Polancy

Matthew Thayer

In paradise, many of us aspire to a condominium penthouse near the ocean. But high prices put us in small houses on "flag" lots, tucked behind other small houses on small lots.

Matthew Thayer

Housing

Tourism may be Hawai`i's lifeblood, but real estate is one of its most vital concerns. Next to the weather, and the number of visiting tourists, the price of housing is the state's most passionately-discussed topic. Whether you rent or buy, the cost of real estate affects your pocketbook and your lifestyle.

Just how prohibitive you will find Hawai`i's home prices depends on where you live now. If you are coming from a pricey area — New York, Boston, California — you may hardly notice a difference. If you are moving from a region where prices are low, you will feel as though you've been hit by a tsunami.

Picture the Koolaus on O'ahu. Real estate values here are like those sharply ridged mountains. A few years ago prices climbed to one of those peaks and it looked as though housing costs would leap up into the stars. Today some home prices are down in one of those valleys.

Depending on location, the slide can be from 10 to 40 percent.

My gardener has been on the islands for 30 years. He has seen three peaks and three valleys. He says there is another peak ahead.

This is, some people say, a good time to buy real estate. "Entry level" condominiums (on the low end of cost and appealing to first-time buyers or as rental investments) are down from the high-$300,000s to about $200,000. That's a bargain... even counting the $400 monthly maintenance.

But will prices climb that ridge again? Maybe.

Higher priced apartments and houses ($1 million plus) have experienced a less dramatic decline. Here, as in the rest of the country, it's all about location, location, location.

Rents, meanwhile, have dropped in price a bit, especially in large low-and medium-income complexes. So...

Will you rent or buy? A house or a condo?

Renting

Compared to buying a house, renting is a bargain — usually much less than mortgage payments would be for the home if it were purchased with a 10 or 20 percent down payment.

Depending on your needs (children? pets? yard? condo? house?), you may be able to find a rental property quickly, or you may have a long, difficult hunt. Not surprisingly, the more you are willing to pay for a rental, the easier your search will be. This state has the highest rents in the nation, according to the 2000 U.S. Census. Renters here pay just over 27.2 percent of their earnings for rent and utilities. Only renters in California and Florida pay a higher percentage. (Gross rent is the monthly amount of rent plus the estimated average cost of utilities.)

Searching for apartment rentals in Hawai`i is further complicated by the fact that apartments within most complexes are owned by individuals rather than one large corporation. That means to find apartments or homes for rent, you'll search daily newspaper classified ads and talk to several individual owners instead of one building manager. This can also complicate keeping a rental, since individual owners tend to change their situations more often; for example, deciding to sell or occupy the property themselves.

Know your rental rights

Landlord and tenant issues are handled by the Office of Consumer Protection, part of the state Department of Commerce and Consumer Affairs.

- **Visit** the agency Web site, which includes links to the landlord-tenant handbook, the state landlord-tenant code, and answers to frequently asked questions: hawaii.gov/dcca/ocp/landlord_tenant

If you have a problem or question:

- **Call** the Residential Landlord-Tenant hotline on O`ahu, 8 a.m. to noon weekdays: (808) 586-2634.

Craigslist.org

This popular website includes rentals and sales on all islands. It's a great place to start your search.

Townhouse complexes like this one dot the islands. Aimed at the local market, they provide reasonably-priced housing, by Hawai`i standards. At this time, a two-bedroom apartment would cost about $300,000 to $400,000 fee simple, depending on location on the island. These are also popular moderately-priced rentals.

If you are hunting for a rental on O`ahu, a twice-monthly magazine, *Rentals Illustrated*, may help. Available at markets and shopping centers, it showcases both homes and apartments for rent on O`ahu, mostly from private owners. However, if the advertised apartment or home is reasonably-priced and desirable, it may be rented before the magazine hits newsstands.

In general, expect to pay a minimum of $800 a month for a studio apartment (usually one large room), $1,000 a month for a one-bedroom apartment and at least $1,200 for a two-bedroom on the outer islands or in an O`ahu suburb. You may pay more in Waikiki and downtown Honolulu. Those prices would be for a small apartment, unfurnished or partly furnished, usually including stove and refrigerator, and without an ocean view. You'll pay much more for penthouse apartments or apartments on the ocean. Completely furnished apartments usually cost at least $200 more. Because many apartments are rented on a short-term basis to visitors, they may come completely furnished down to cutlery and pans.

On any island, renting a house will cost from about $1,500 (and way up) per month. And you will need a security deposit, usually amounting to one month's rent. Most homes are unfurnished, but include appliances.

Seeking a place to live? Some tips:

- **Plan to rent during your first year here**, while you get to know the islands. That will give you time to decide whether you will remain in Hawai`i, stay on the island you've chosen, and which part of the island you prefer.

- **Before bringing your pet to Hawai`i,** consider that few apartment complexes allow pets and even fewer landlords welcome them. If you plan to rent, it may be wiser to leave your dog or cat on the mainland and have it shipped here later, after you've settled in and have secured suitable housing.

- **Leases tend to be shorter here** than on the mainland. Ask for a six-month or month-by-month lease while you search for more permanent living arrangements or while you decide on which part of the island you want to live.

- **Don't bring more than you need.** Most apartments are rented either fully or partially furnished. Partial usually includes kitchen appliances: stove, refrigerator, dishwasher. Fully furnished means just that, often down to such details as silverware, can openers, and pots and pans.

- **Quiet-by-day** can be less-than-peaceful by night when residents are home from work and school. Visit the apartment or home you are considering at various times of day and night so you'll have no surprises after you move in.

- **Avoid houses or apartments that are for sale.** Most real estate is selling quickly now and you may be moving out shortly after you've moved in. And how will you feel about potential buyers traipsing through your home? Or being forced to move within 45 days? (State law says your landlord must give you at least that much notice, but you can request 60 or 90 days in your lease, thereby giving yourself at least some stability.)

2 Sources

www.apartments.com

Rentals Illustrated magazine
(808) 949-3686
www.rentalsillustrated.com

Buying a home

Here's another overheard conversation — this one from a tourist on a Kaua`i beach:

"I bought a farm (in Montana). It is 60 acres and cost $300,000 and I thought that was a lot of money. But you can't even buy a little house for that here. How do families manage to live here?"

Good question. We manage by working two or three jobs, by cutting back the size of our dream and settling for less, by living with relatives, if we are lucky enough to have relatives nearby. Some of us — not the trust babies or movie stars that have made the islands famous for costly homes — but those of us who simply live our lives here, afford a mortgage by slicing our homes into ohanas (studios) and renting them to help pay the mortgages. Surveys say Hawai`i has the most crowded living spaces in the nation. Look at the number of cars and trucks parked in driveways, on lawns and on streets at night in moderate and lower income neighborhoods.

As we write this in 2010, housing prices have been falling somewhat for the past few years and foreclosures are almost as common on the islands as in the rest of the United States. It may be a good time to buy, says one local Realtor. "But," she asks, "will prices ever reach the high of 2005?"

It's a gamble:

In one Maui complex, condominiums that sold for over $300,000 four years ago can be purchased on short sale for as little as $135,000. But there's a catch: maintenance fees that are not collected for troubled units can be added to other condo owners' fees. At this complex fees have reached $400 a month. At posh condos, monthly fees can top $1,000.

Leasehold or fee simple?

Homes, condominiums and commercial property on the Hawaiian islands are sold as fee simple or leasehold. Fee simple means you own the land on which the home or condominium is built. In a leasehold situation, you usually own the building, but rent the land on which it stands. Some of O'ahu land is leasehold; relatively little of the outer islands' property is leasehold.

Among Hawai'i's controversial issues is leasehold conversion — the court-mandated sale of land that has been leased to homeowners for decades. From about 1930, private residences, condominiums and commercial buildings were constructed on leased land, usually owned by the large estates. This made homes and buildings less expensive, but inevitably led to disputes as lease agreements ended or lease fees were renegotiated and raised.

In recent years, the state had stepped in, forcing some lessors to sell, at market value, land on which private homes are built. In 2005, forced sales of leased land were halted.

Still, if you are considering buying property, you should either:

1) Stay away from leasehold property entirely, or

2) Consult an attorney; learn about leasehold laws. Most real estate agents will also answer your questions honestly, if you know which question to ask. At the least, inquire:

  • How much the lease costs each month;

  • When the lease is due to be renegotiated. Your lease fee could go up dramatically;

  • Whether it is possible to purchase the land now;

  • Whether any of the owners (in a neighborhood or condominium) have been able to purchase their land. (Usually, once a land owner sells to one tenant in a project, he must be willing to sell to all.)

Lucky you own? Yes, but...

With real estate prices rising, it would seem that people already settled into homes are fortunate. But spiraling real estate prices are a double-edged sword for homeowners, potentially driving some from their dwellings. As the perceived value of a home increases, so do taxes. Some homeowners, especially those on fixed incomes or families that have inherited a house to live in, say they cannot afford the ever-rising property taxes. On Kaua`i, Ohana Kaua`i, a property owners' group, seeks a county charter amendment that would roll property taxes back to 1998–1999 levels and put a 2 percent annual cap on future taxes.

The problem is not that our property taxes are high. It's just that as our home and land values increase, so do the taxes. Actually, Hawai`i's real estate tax rates are low compared to many places in the nation, and residents and people over the age of 60 qualify for additional tax breaks.

So much development

So much home building, so much development, is visible on most islands. Will inventory catch up with demand? Housing specialists say that may happen on O`ahu, where the military is putting billions of dollars into upgrading its family housing, but it is unlikely to happen on neighbor islands. The attempt to build new homes is often stymied by efforts to protect the environment, preserve sacred Hawaiian land, and secure safe and abundant water to new and existing developments. Permits can take years, and developers are sometimes ordered to halt projects already under way.

"On one hand," says a Realtor, "I'm all for building and developing. It's my livelihood. On the other hand, I know that if we build too much, become too crowded, too developed, we are destroying Hawai`i, the reason people come here and love it here. It's tough to be in the middle of this."

One person per room?

U.S. Census Bureau statistics show 15.9 percent of all homes in Hawai`i are officially classified as "crowded," or having more than one person per room. Nationwide, the average new house has more than 1,920 square feet; the average new single family home on O`ahu has only 1,342 square feet. Average condo living space here is just 711 square feet.

Ask for "comps"

Computers put information at your real estate agent's fingertips that can help you ascertain the value of your purchase. Ask your agent to pull a list of comparable homes for sale in the neighborhood and also a list of homes recently sold, including both the prices at which they were listed and the prices at which they actually sold. If you are considering a condominium, ask to see a list of all the condominiums for sale in the complex, so you can compare prices, and also ask for a list of all the sold apartments, with their final sales prices, going back two years. That information should give you a good base for an offer on the property.

An *ohana* helps…

…with the mortgage. Many island homes include an *ohana* (family) unit, small attached studio or cottage for elderly parents to live near their children, according to Hawaiian and Asian custom. Such two-or three-unit properties are available on most islands starting at about $600,000 and they can be a smart buy for first-time homeowners, providing extra income to help with mortgage payments. So many people and their cars on small lots make for crowded neighborhoods, but shop around. Some multi-unit properties are well positioned and landscaped for privacy. "When we build a multi-unit property, we consider privacy. We never build with windows facing windows or doors facing doors," a contractor says.

Homeowners tax relief

Most islands offer tax reductions to owners who live in their homes. Be sure to inquire about the tax break and submit necessary forms at your county tax office.

Landscaping

You probably appreciate the islands' lush tropical greenery, flowering shrubs and stately palm trees. That beauty is expensive. In dry (leeward) parts of

continued on page 133

Get the facts on home insurance

Homeowners insurance rates are about the same as the rest of the nation, unless your mortgagor requires you to carry additional hurricane risk coverage and/or flood insurance. Either can almost double the cost of your insurance coverage. Be sure to ascertain, BEFORE you agree to buy a home, if you must have either coverage. It can be a hefty addition to your monthly mortgage payment.

the islands lawns and shrubs must be watered. In wet areas (like Princeville and Kilauea on Kaua`i) vegetation grows quickly and must be regularly cut, trimmed and protected from fungi and insects.

You may be able to maintain a yard yourself, but if you are elderly or expect to be working a great deal, don't count on it. Count instead on adding at least $100 per month to your bills for gardening and $30 or $40 a month for watering.

In addition to routine gardening, palms trees must be trimmed regularly, usually by islanders highly skilled at climbing the slender, swaying towers and whacking off coconuts and old fronds for $20 to $100 a tree. Figure on trimming each palm twice a year. It's a must if your trees are near walkways; a falling coconut or frond could mean a lawsuit.

Some advice:

- **Be sure to get several estimates** for gardening. Price, experience, quality and follow-through can vary greatly by company or individual.

- **You don't need a costly garden** and a large lawn to enjoy Hawai`i's spectacular flowering trees and shrubs. They are everywhere. Live in a condo or a house on a small lot, take a walk and enjoy someone else's gardening efforts.

Matt Thayer

Add the price of termite treatment to the cost of owning a home. Most bug gurus recommend tenting a home every five years. An odorless gas kills all insects, leaving no residue. Tenting for a plain 2,000-square-foot home costs about $1400 at this time.

Kihei, Maui, $1.1 million

Olinda, Maui, $889,000

Homes:

Half a million dollars is 'affordable' — if you can find one that low.

Hawai`i Kai, O`ahu, $645,000

Punchbowl area, Honolulu condominium, $445,0000

Makiki, Honolulu, O`ahu, $3.2 million

Photos courtesy of participating real estate agents and *Homes and Land* magazines.

Hilo, Big Island, $130,000

*Kohala,
Big Island,
$7.3 million*

Kailua-Kona, Big Island, $665,000

All prices are fee simple.
The land is sold with the house.

Princeville, Kaua`i, $1,350,000

Kapa`a, Kaua`i, $435,000

My story: A home of your own, somehow

Life came cheap in Erie, Pennsylvania, my hometown. When I moved to Maui in 1991, years ago, I looked at the high housing prices, easily six times what they are in Erie, and said, "Well, I'll probably never own a home again." I had used all my savings to purchase the franchise for a new business and I arrived with just $10,000 in my pocket.

I rented apartments while I built the business, a real estate magazine. I lived in the first apartment ($800 a month) four months before it went up for sheriff's sale. I had to vacate the second apartment ($1,200) after a year, when the owner decided to move back in.

By then I really wanted a place to settle, a home of my own, but my business was just beginning to make a profit, and I had very little money for a down payment. I house-hunted half-heartedly, thinking I'd probably have to rent again, when a one-story wooden house came on the market for $279,000 — a low price in Maui even in 1993. The interior walls were dark green, dirty bamboo shades hung cock-eyed at the windows, the carpeting smelled of too many barefooted people, a bug zapper in the kitchen called attention to torn window screens. Fallen roof shingles hid in the overgrown shrubs around the house. A big swimming pool dominated the narrow backyard, but chips of pool liner were floating in its stagnant water.

Okay. The house *was* a mess, but I liked it. It included an *ohana*, a studio that could help pay the mortgage, and the yard was a big quarter-acre, so secluded you could swim in the buff. And six tall palm trees waved out front.

So, I made an offer of $230,000, which the owner eventually accepted. I figured I would live in the house a few years, fix it up a little each year, and when I could afford better, I'd sell it and move.

Ah, but my friendly neighborhood bank wasn't so cooperative. As a self-employed owner of a new business, I was a financial risk. My 25 years as journalist, my perfect credit record, and the eight properties I had successfully restored and sold on the mainland, counted for little here. Mortgage allowances are based on income, *current* income, and I didn't have a lot of that to show. The bank eventually agreed to a mortgage on the property, but I would need 20 percent down, not 10 percent as I'd hoped. I emptied out all that was left of my IRAs and savings, collected all of my business accounts payable, and I was still $17,000 short for the down payment.

I was sad, then angry, and finally just plain determined to find a way. So I made of list of clients who seemed happy with my magazine and had indicated they would be advertising steadily. I decided to visit each of them, tell them my plight, and plead with each to loan me a portion of the down payment, to be paid back by future advertising. The first client I visited listened sympathetically. Then he took out his checkbook and a pen.

"How much do you need?" he asked.

"Oh, whatever you can afford to loan me," I answered.

"I mean, how much do you need, altogether?"

I told him and watched in stunned silence as he wrote a check for the entire amount, $17,000.

Toni Polancy

The first morning in my new home, a Saturday, I awoke to a Tongan minister preaching (loudly) across the street, to a Mexican family holding a fiesta/yard sale on the corner, to a neighbor chatting in a Portuguese accent. I smiled. The sounds of the islands were drifting in through *my* windows, from *my* neighbors.

In the past 11 years, I have painted the house inside and out, put on a new roof, refurbished the pool, renovated the kitchen and baths, tiled every bit of floor. The bank says the house is worth at least $650,000 now. I think it's worth $5 million.

My story illustrates two important facts about life here. First, when you move to Hawai`i, you are truly starting over. Whatever you did, whoever you were in your past life, is *pau*. Gone. Over. You are starting at square one.

And second, if you want a home of your own badly enough, and most of us do, you will find a way. You'll downgrade your dreams, you'll renovate a condo, you'll work and beg, like I did, and even share a house if you have to. Then you'll let the natural (or, in Hawai`i, the *unnatural*) escalation of real estate prices sweep you along, catch you up. You will "build equity," until house prices don't sound quite so scary.

Your first home, here or wherever you are, is the hardest.

Visitors to Oʻahu's stunning Pali Lookout are greeted by great views — and some important warnings. Watch out for bees and thieves.

Toni Polancy

chapter 7

iki kumu

general information

A guide to health,

religion, culture

and entertainment

Bali Hai, Bloody Mary and the $7.95 lunch

We are sitting at the restaurant at the **Princeville Health Club and Spa**, a health/workout center created in glass and stone with marble staircases and brass railings. Its windows look out at ribbons of waterfalls streaming into glistening Hanalei Bay. Bali Hai, the seductive "island" Bloody Mary sang about in the movie *South Pacific*, floats in a misty background.

"Where else," asks Serge King spreading his arms, "can you enjoy all this for a $7.95 lunch?"

Serge writes and lectures all over the world on the Hawaiian philosophy of *huna*, which he describes as teaching people how to think positively in regard to mind, body and relationships. Fifteen years ago he and Gloria, his wife, were sitting on an ocean bluff, watching the sunset, and lamenting the end of one of their frequent vacations to Kaua`i. Suddenly they realized that their two sons were grown and Serge's occupation (and avocation) allows them to live anywhere they choose. They moved to Kaua`i a few months later.

One of the benefits of living in Hawai`i, Serge says, is that *kama`aina* can enjoy, on a regular basis and sometimes at reduced rates, those amenities for which tourists travel thousands of miles: lush island scenery, top-notch restaurants, posh hotels and outdoor activities. This inexpensive lunch, designed to generate business, is a good example.

Hawai`i residents do a lot of the same things tourists do — enjoy facials and massages, dine, dance, shop, snorkel, tour, visit hotels — sometimes at discounted *kama`aina* rates, anywhere from 10 to 50 percent below what tourists pay. Many businesses, restaurants, tours and activities offer discounts for people who can show a Hawai`i driver's license or other proof of Hawai`i residency. In addition, some well-to-do residents take advantage of annual sales at tourist boutiques, held during tourism's short "off" seasons.

(Note: The cost of lunch has risen to $9.50)

Arts and culture

If you are ever bored in Hawai`i, it's your own fault. There is plenty to do every weekend on most islands. Hawai`i's rich ethnic mix means there is an occasion to party almost every weekend. Some celebrations propagate traditions: Hawaiian *hula* competitions; Filipino *barrio fiestas* (parties); Mexican *Cinco de Mayo* celebrations and *fiestas*; Chinese dragon dances; Buddhist *o-bon* dances. For example:

The International Festival of the Pacific on the Big Island in July includes costumes and dances of Japan, China, Korea, Portugal, Tahiti, New Zealand and the Philippines. On O`ahu in March the **Honolulu Festival** features a traditional ancient Japanese custom. Warriors on horseback thunder down a sand track on a Honolulu street, shooting arrows.

Buddhists launch candlelit lanterns, bearing prayers for the dearly departed, and let the softly glowing bits of love drift on waters during *o-bon* season in July and August each year, when ancestors are paid homage. **Shinnyo-En Hawaii**, a Buddhist order with a temple in Mo`ili`ili on O`ahu, performs the ritual at Ala Moana Park on Memorial Day, beautifully blending Buddhist and American cultures.

Flowers play a major part in Asian culture. The **Narcissus Festival** in Honolulu welcomes the Chinese New Year with a Chinatown open house, lion dances, firecrackers, food booths and art and crafts. The **Cherry Blossom Festival** honors Japanese culture with crafts, drummers and dancers, games, tea ceremonies and *mochi* (a rice flour used to make candy and pudding) pounding in Waikiki's Kapi`olani Park. The **Okinawan Festival** is held in the same park in September and also includes dances, arts and crafts.

You'll have abundant opportunities to learn... from Hawai`i's mix of cultures. One issue of *Honolulu Weekly*, a popular alternative newspaper, offers Tai Chi lectures, Western square dance classes and Scandinavian folk dance exhibits, as well as classes in Hebrew language and American jazz. The Honolulu Weekly is free and available at locations throughout Waikiki and downtown Honolulu.

Establish residency

Establish residency as soon as you can to take advantage of *kama`aina* discounts, to make check cashing easier, and just to feel more at home in the islands. The most accepted proof of residency is a Hawai`i driver's license or a state identification card.

Driver's license: If you have a current driver's license from another state and you want to get a Hawai`i license, you don't have to take a driving test, but you must pass a written test, which is relatively easy. Buy a copy of the Hawai`i Drivers' Manual at a book store, drug store or convenience store and study for the test. Satellite offices of the state Motor Vehicle & Licensing Division are conveniently located throughout the islands. See the front of the manual or the county government section of your phone book for the closest office. No appointment is necessary, but expect to wait an hour or longer.

State ID card: This card is primarily identity for those who don't drive. To obtain this official state card, you'll need a certified copy of your birth certificate, your social security card, and, if you are married, a certified copy of your marriage certificate. On O`ahu, call **(808) 587-3112** for information; Maui, Lana`i and Moloka`i, **(808) 270-7840**; Kaua`i, **(808) 274-3100**; Hilo, Big Island **(808) 974-6265;** Kona, Big Island, **(808) 327-4953**.

On Kaua`i, the Garden Island Arts Council stages **E Kanikapila Kakou,** during which the audience participates in Hawaiian music and dance. And the **Mokihana Festival** in late September is a week-long celebration of Kaua`i composers, *lei* makers, slack key guitar players, *hula* dancers, and other Hawaiian artists.

The Hawaiian renaissance

Since the mid-1970s, Hawai`i has enjoyed a renaissance in Hawaiian and Polynesian cultures: no longer the glittery plastic-grass-skirted Hollywood version, but authentic chants, dances, *mele* (songs) and stories. Libraries, schools, resorts and cultural centers host *hula halau* (schools) that perform traditional chants and *mele*, as well as *kupuna* (grandparents or elderly people) telling stories of Polynesian history.

Hawai`i has its own modern music too, created and performed by musicians and writers like **Keali`i Reichel**, the late **Israel Kamakawiwo`ole** and others who have promoted interest in the native language and culture around the world. Reichel, a *kumu hula* (teacher), chanter, songwriter and singer, has performed in New York's Carnegie Hall. Songwriter and singer Kamakawiwo`ole, a gentle giant at over 700 pounds when he died in 1997, had come to represent the downtrodden Hawaiian who succeeds.

An array of concerts and gatherings, like the **Gabby Pahinui/Atta Isaacs Slack Key Guitar Festival** at Honolulu's Waterfront Park in August and the **Ukulele Festival** at the Kapiolani Park bandstand in July, allow music and musicians to shine. And events like the **Brown Bag to Stardom** at Kaua`i War Memorial Convention Center in January give amateurs their time in the spotlight.

The Big Island reigns when it comes to *hula*, hosting the famous week-long **Merrie Monarch Festival** in the spring and the **World Invitational Hula Festival** for three days in November.

Holidays

Every American holiday is celebrated here, as well as every Hawaiian holiday, like **Prince Kuhio Day** in March; **Lei Day**, May 1; **Kamehameha Day** in June; and **Admission Day** in August.

Add days of celebration from other ethnic groups, for example, Japan's "**Girl's Day**" in March and "**Boy's Day**" in May, and you have a very full calendar. Until recently, businesses and banks, but not the U.S. post office, celebrated the Hawaiian holidays as well as American ones. In recent years, banks stopped closing on Hawaiian holidays. However, it is still common for newcomers to find a business unexpectedly shut in honor of some special occasion. One transplanted businessman was surprised when his local staff did not show up for work. They simply assumed the business would be closed on (King) **Kamehameha Day**

Paintings, sculptures, crafts

It has been said that the historic whaling village of **Lahaina, Maui**, is the third largest art sales center in the world, behind only Paris and New York. Three or four galleries per block line eight-block-long Front Street. On Fridays, world-famous painters and sculptors visit "Art Night in Lahaina" where they share opinions and glasses of wine with visitors.

It's more than removing your shoes...

It's wise to keep abreast of Hawai'i's many ethnic holidays and customs; you could "lose face" by not knowing how to respond. Chinese celebrate the new year at the end of January with dragon dances. Costumed dancers parade from door-to-door or store-to-store. Chinese custom calls for monetary gifts, preferably in little red envelopes that bring good luck. The money usually goes to charity.

Steve Strand

One of the neat things about Hawai'i

Opt for loafers, sandals or zories, those little rubber soles with just one toe strap. You'll be removing your shoes often to comply with one of Hawai'i's unwritten laws of courtesy: *Remove your shoes before you enter a home.* Don't disregard the custom. Many people here take it very seriously and failing to remove your shoes can be a major breach of etiquette, showing disrespect for your host. The custom comes from Japan, but it makes great sense in Hawai'i, which can be very dusty or muddy. Going shoeless also provides a treat for tired feet: cool tile floors feel soothing.

Matthew Thayer

Tip: Get a local calendar that includes Hawaiian holidays as well as American ones. A few banks give them away at the beginning of the year and bookstores usually carry them year-round. Talk to people and businesses you deal with to see how they are celebrating. When you register your children for school, be sure to get a list of days off.

Makahiki

In ancient Hawai`i, four months each year were set aside for the observance of *Makahiki*, a time of thanksgiving and peace, from late October to February. *Makahiki* commenced on the day when the star group Pleiades, the constellation the ancients followed to Hawai`i, appeared on the Eastern horizon at sunset. This was the time of freedom from labor and war, when no large projects could be undertaken. Taxes of food were collected, displayed before the gods, and then distributed among *ali`i* (chiefs). In modern times, *Makahiki* begins with the eerily beautiful full moon in November and ends with closing ceremonies during the full moon in March. Only in very recent years have others than Hawaiians been invited to participate in a few traditional observances, but the sharing spirit of *Makahiki* is quietly honored by everyone in Hawai`i.

FUN

Big Island Hawai`i Visitor's Bureau, Bob Abraham

Commercial art galleries dot all the islands; some of them staffed with high-powered salespeople. More interesting are the quiet co-op galleries where artists take turns at floor duty and converse pleasantly with browsers. The Big Island has two such galleries: at the **Keauhou Hotel** near Kailua-Kona and at the restored **Waimea Fire Station**. Among Maui's most interesting galleries are co-ops in upcountry **Makawao**, the crafts guild located in a rustic old store in the town of **Pai`a**, and the **Hui No`eau Visual Art Center** on an old estate between the two towns.

On Kaua`i, several interesting shops and galleries offering local arts and crafts are located at Hanalei, south at Hanapepe, and centrally at **Kilohana Plantation**, an estate near Lihu`e. The **Kaua`i Society of Artists** presents three exhibitions a year, including a six-week event at the State Building each spring and a juried show in the fall.

Little Lana`i has a nameless downtown shop where artisans work and sell. On Moloka`i, artists and craftsmen gather at the Moloka`i Ranch town of **Maunaloa** on the far western part of the island.

On O`ahu, numerous shops and galleries feature local artists and craftspeople. Among the many: **The Contemporary Museum** in Makiki Heights, the **Honolulu Academy of Arts** on Beretania Street, and **Native Books & Beautiful Things** at Ward Warehouse, Honolulu.

Another way to get your fill of artistic offering, and good food, is **First Friday** night in Honolulu's **Chinatown**. Boutiques and galleries such as **Mark's Garage** stay open late, enticing residents and visitors with *pu`u pu`u* (hors d`oeuves).

Music, mele, talk story

The islands are small; but there is no shortage of top-notch entertainment, from rock groups like the Rolling Stones to Broadway shows to world-renowned musicians and dancers. Honolulu's **Neal Blaisdell Concert Hall** and the **Hawai`i Theater** glow with special events several times a month. Some of the famous performers extend their island stays by jetting over to the **Maui Arts and Cultural Center**. The center includes an art gallery and several auditoriums and also holds concerts and Friday night *pau hana* (done working) parties in its outdoor courtyard.

Internationally acclaimed artists from all over the world assemble to perform chamber music at the **Kapalua Bay Hotel**, Maui, during the **Kapalua Music Festival** in June. And the **Kaua`i Concert Association** hosts internationally acclaimed performers.

**The Lodge at Ko`ele** on Lana`i hosts creative people from around the world, like humor columnist Dave Barry, Pulitzer prize-winner Jane Smiley, and chef Emeril Lagasse. Their appearances are open to all Lana`i residents and visitors without charge.

Museums

Hawai`i's most famous museum is the **Bishop Museum**, off H-1 near the Pali Highway in Honolulu, endowed through the will of Charles Reed Bishop to honor his wife Bernice Pauahi Bishop, a descendant of Hawaiian royalty. The museum is devoted to Hawaiian history and contains many artifacts from the days when kings and *ali`i* ruled. The Bishop Museum is so revered it seems sacrilegious to say that despite its beautiful mansion-like buildings, display space is small and disappointing. However, the museum is well known for research facilities and is a good starting point for learning about island history and natural history.

A mile or so up Pali Highway sits a cozy museum that is a true gem: **Queen Emma's Summer Palace**. This modest home exhibits the very personal side of Hawaiian royal life, humble by mainland standards, and quaint.

`Iolani Palace** in downtown Honolulu is a grander look at royal living. It is said that Hawai`i's last king, Kalakaua, had `Iolani Palace built to prove to the world that Hawaiians were not savages. In a bedroom of this palace Queen Lili`uokalani was imprisoned when American businessmen took over the government.

Across a driveway from the `Iolani Palace sits the **State Archives** and the main branch of the **state library,** gold mines for researchers. **Washington Place**, the governor's mansion, and historic **Saint Andrew's Cathedral** are two blocks away. This area of Honolulu, with its parks and historic government buildings, is well worth an afternoon's stroll for anyone who lives on the islands or plans to. Fridays at

Carefully stacked rocks and pieces of lava appear mysteriously on lava fields and deserts, to the awe of tourists. Is it the mischievous menehune, Hawai`i's industrious nocturnal elves, up to their age-old tricks? Or just someone practicing balancing skills?

noon the **Royal Hawaiian Band** presents a concert on the `Iolani Palace grounds. (Good luck parking in this area; bring lots of quarters to feed parking meters, or take TheBus.)

As for the other islands, **Kaua`i Museum** in Lihu`e has a permanent display of artifacts as well as changing exhibits highlighting the history and crafts of both Kaua`i and Ni`ihau. **Koke`e Museum** details the history of Koke`e State Park as well as the future of eco-tourism, interpreting the environment for visitors.

In addition, many missionary homes throughout the islands have become small museums. **The Baldwin House** in Lahaina, Maui, and the **Lyman House** in Kona, on the Big Island, are excellent examples of how missionary families lived *after* they had been on the islands for several years. They do not depict the hardship many missionaries endured. Maui's **Alexander and Baldwin Sugar Museum** at Pu'unene is an interesting peek at plantation life; some of the museum attendants lived on the plantation as children and share interesting stories with visitors. Meanwhile, the **Parker Ranch at** Waimea on the Big Island, the largest intact working cattle ranch in the U.S., provides an intimate look at both rich and poor ranch life.

**The Kaua`i Alliance** offers a brochure highlighting all culture, humanities and arts organizations and events on that island. Write P.O. Box 3344, Lihu`e, HI 96766.

"Amateur" Theater

The word "amateur" is less than appropriate in regard to the islands' many theater groups. Former actors and would-be actors, many with professional experience, live in these islands. The quality of musical and dramatic presentations can be very high. If you are a would-be actor and not intimidated by the talent, you'll no doubt revel in the environment.

Plays are presented weekly on most islands. Auditions are usually open to the public and are announced in the entertainment sections of island newspapers. Theater groups are nearly as popular in Hawai`i as they are in England and the following is only a partial list of what is available.

On O`ahu, the **Diamond Head Theater** offers both musical and dramatic productions October through August. **The Hawai`i Performing Arts Company** is situated in the Manoa Valley Theater (performances September to June) and the University of Hawai`i at Manoa has various drama groups at **The Kennedy Theater.** Cultivating budding talent is **The Honolulu Theater for Youth,** ranked the second-best youth theater organization in the United States. **Kumukahua Theater** presents locally written plays as well as productions about the Hawai`i/Pacific region and experience.

The **Maui Community Theater** performs at the historic `Iao Theater in Wailuku and the **Baldwin Theater Guild** presents plays and workshops at Baldwin High School Auditorium. Both adults and children perform with **The Maui Academy of Performing Arts**.

On Kaua`i, the **Kaua`i Community Players** and **Kaua`i Kids at Play** offer musicals, comedies and drama throughout the year. And **Hawai`i Children's Theater** in Kapa`a provides both fun and formal education in the arts.

The Big Island has several groups. The **Hilo Community Players** present Broadway and off-Broadway productions. The **Kahilu Theater Foundation** in Waimea has its own western-style building across from the Parker Ranch Visitor Center.

Radio and Television

In addition to Hawaiian music, classical, popular, jazz, country, rock and "oldies" music are played on various radio stations on most islands. Some stations feature ethnic "hours," with Filipino or Japanese music and news. Cable transmission brings television to most parts of the islands, but Honolulu has the only studios broadcasting network television. Some remote areas of the islands have no cable service, so if you are a TV-aholic, check before you commit to a living space. Most cable stations broadcast on mainland time; shows on national networks — ABC, CBS, NBC and Fox — are usually broadcast an hour earlier than Eastern Standard Time. (For example, prime time starts here at 7 p.m. and winds up at 10 p.m.) All four major islands have community television — non-profit stations that broadcast local information. Cost of cable television is about the same as on the mainland, from $24 per month for basic service plus the usual array of taxes and fees.

High-tech too?

We may be tiny islands swimming in a great big ocean, but we are hardly savages. Most islands are overrun with techies and offer DSL lines, various modes of receiving television such as dishes, digital services, etc., and an array of cell phone service. However, you are well-advised to discuss service availability before you sign a home or business rental or purchase agreement. The amount and quality of service may be limited in some areas.

Movies

Popular movies are presented on all islands, except Moloka`i and Lana`i at about the same time they open at mainland theaters, but if you want to see an art film or anything that diverges from the popular, you'll have to be quick. Chances are it will play only one or two nights, if at all.

Honolulu's **Movie Museum** shows classic, art and foreign films five nights a week, Thursday through Monday. The theater has just 18 seats (naugahyde recliners), and you can bring your own food. Price is $5; $4 for those who belong to the museum's video rental club. **The Honolulu Academy of Arts Theater** also shows *avant garde* films, as do community colleges throughout the islands.

The Annual Hawai`i International Film Festival is one of the cultural advantages of living here. The state-subsidized festival brings two weeks of new and independent films from around the world to all islands, in early autumn. In June, **The Maui Film Festival** takes place and in December, the Maui Film Festival gives residents a Christmas present: Academy Award screenings. Watch for schedules in weekly entertainment guides or pick up free catalogs (limited quantity) at bookstores in late September.

When you are invited to dine at someone's home, at a picnic or *lu`au*, assume that you should bring a dish to share. If asked whether you should bring some thing to the gathering, the polite hostess will say no when she means yes, and you'll arrive to find that everyone but you has contributed. If you want to discuss food with the hostess in advance, ask what she would like you to bring, not if you should

Dining, out or in

The islands serve up an appetizing variety of local foods and ethnic cuisine. Savvy newcomers bypass posh resort restaurants for hole-in-the wall spots, Hawai`i's version of the once-popular American diners. These small mom and pop restaurants offer interesting and authentic versions of tasty local dishes like *manapua* (steamed dumplings filled with pork or vegetables); *musubi* (rice wrapped in seaweed); cone *sushi* (rice in an egg batter cone); plate lunches (any popular meat plus two scoops of rice and/or macaroni or potato salad); *malasadas* (fried hole-less donuts); *saimin* (broth with noodles and fish cakes plus any number of ingredients; so popular that even local

McDonald's restaurants offer a version). All are inexpensive island favorites that can be eaten on the run.

You'll also see lunch wagons on most islands, usually offering one or two specialties. And "all you can" eat smorgasbords are popular on O`ahu.

Here, as on the mainland, families are eating more meals outside the home. The same golden arches and red-roofed pizza places that flourish on the continent dot the roadways of O`ahu, Maui, Kaua`i, and the Big Island. Lana`i and Moloka`i remain franchise-free at this time. Some fast-food franchises offer meals at mainland prices; but most tack the cost of shipping to your bill. You may find, for example, that a $2.99 special advertised on national television costs $3.49 here.

Several national restaurant chains like **International House of Pancakes, Sizzler, Tony Roma** and **Denny's** offer meals in the $15 to $20 range, considered low here. Fancier restaurants cater to tourists and, especially on the neighbor islands, are expensive. Expect to pay a minimum of $40 for a meal in an upscale restaurant. Residents here are more apt to celebrate special events at *lu`au* or potlucks at the islands' numerous parks and beaches.

RESOURCES

Hawai`i is a mecca for the musically and dramatically inclined. These organizations are on O`ahu. Most neighbor islands have similar groups.

- **Honolulu Academy of Arts**
  (808) 532-8700
  www.honoluluacademy.org

- **Hawai`i Academy of Recording Arts**
  (808) 235-9424
  www.nahenahe.net/HARA/

- **Hawai`i Youth Symphony Association**
  (808) 941-9706
  www.hiyouthsymphony.org

- **The Honolulu Boy Choir**
  (808) 596-7464
  www.honoluluboychoir.org

- **Honolulu Youth Opera Chorus**
  (808) 521-2982
  www.hyoc.org

- **Hawai`i Opera Theater**
  (808) 596-7858
  www.hawaiiopera.org

- **Manoa Valley Theater**
  (808) 988-6131
  www.manoavalleytheater.com

- **University of Hawai`i at Manoa Kennedy Theatre**
  (808) 956-7655
  www.hawaii.edu/theatre

Andrea's farewell

It was fourteen months from the time Andrea Heath-Blundell, 46, learned she had lung cancer until the time she died. They were important months. Andrea rejected her husband Brian's offer of a trip to anywhere in the world, telling a friend, as they lay on a beach looking out at the ocean, "Everything that matters is right here."

She had come to the islands as a young woman 18 years before, met Brian and given birth to their daughter Kim, now 14. She was active in her adopted community, the historic town of Lahaina on Maui's west side. Over the years she had taken part in PTA, Girl Scouts, and a community advocacy group.

Andrea's last months were spent absorbing sights and scents, as though she hoped to preserve memories of the beauty she loved, and in quiet times with friends and family. She found comfort planning her own funeral. She died at home, peacefully, and her body was cremated.

About 300 friends gathered at a memorial service at an old prison in the residential section of Lahaina. In bright-colored dresses, mu`umu`us and aloha shirts, mourners carried leis and flowers. Friends and relatives shared memories. Among them was a young woman Andrea had met at a support group for cancer victims. "I'm a new friend," the woman said, "and knowing Andrea has given me strength."

After the ceremony, guests boarded a boat at the Lahaina harbor and traveled silently, watching the sun dip into a glossy sea. A moon rose over the West Maui Mountains and multiplied itself on the ocean. Four flower-laden canoes appeared, a tribute from the people of Lahaina. Kim and Brian scattered Andrea's ashes into the ocean. Flowers, leis and hundreds of petals floated over the water. A friend sang a Scottish song as the flowers drifted out to sea. On the way back to shore, guests shared food and socialized, all as Andrea had planned.

As people here live for the beauty of nature, of sun and sea, so do many people here say their final farewells. Funerals and memorials tend to be intimate and less structured than the funeral parlor wakes common on the mainland. And they are often held at a beach or a garden. In Hawai`i, about 57 percent of those who die are cremated, a larger percentage than any other state. There are two reasons: the high number of Asians who traditionally cremate their dead and the scarcity of land here.

The memorial service of a transplanted resident is apt to be attended by many people from the community, casual acquaintances as well as longtime friends. Explains one *malihini*, "Many of us live far away from our hometowns and relatives so everyone must be your `ohana (family)."

Religion: a litany of faiths

It's Sunday in Hawai`i. More than 100,000 people kneel in prayer, stand to sing, or sit harkening to sermons in 758 churches and temples, or on the beach, worshipping in traditional rituals as well as some unique to these islands.

On the Big Island, the **Honpa Hongwanji Shin Buddhist** temples host a convention.

On O`ahu, **Calvary By The Sea Lutheran Church** members celebrate annual Clown Sunday with Bible stories and personal testimony in mime, song and dance. Participants include the Outrageous Calvary Clown Choir and the Crazy Keiki (Children's) Choir.

In Kihei, Maui, members of **St. Theresa's Roman Catholic Church** sell fresh *lei* in the church vestibule gift shop. A hula dancer will perform during the offertory.

Programs bow to all ages, genders and interests. Later in the month, the **Spiritual Life Center** will lead a three-day pilgrimage to Kalaupapa, Moloka`i's former leper colony. Members of the O`ahu **Jewish Young Adult Group** can attend an End of Summer Beach Party — in November — and children from several churches are invited to "A Youth Lock-In" at O`ahu's **St. John's by the Sea**, billed as an overnight adventure. The

People of various religious beliefs and cultures join hands during a canoe blessing on the Big Island. Tradition calls for blessings, usually led by a kahuna or priest, at a variety of events including the launching of new businesses, buildings, ships and canoes.

G. Brad Lewis

Assemblies of God Church plans a family skating party. **Nu`uanu Congregational Church** will host a program on "Caring for the Caregiver" and **The Central Union Church** seniors group will study "Creative Memories," a program on preserving family history.

O`ahu women may attend a discussion on the "The Feminine Soul" in the **Mystical Rose Chapel** on the **Chaminade University** campus, or the **Kailua Christian Women's Club** luncheon, "Home is Where the Heart Is."

Church Membership

A 2009 Gallup poll found religion was distributed this way:*

Denomination	percent of population of Hawai`i
Christian:	60.6%
Protestant/Other Christian	37.8%
Roman Catholic	22.8%
Mormonism	3.3%
Judaism	0.7%
Agnostic, Atheist	21.0%

excluding those of other non-Christian religions and those who had "no opinion"

And for those re-thinking their religious allegiance, a support group for former Mormons is meeting in a private O`ahu home.

`Aina, the land, has a spiritual meaning for Hawaiians. A gift from the gods, the 'aina supports and nourishes trees for shelter and food to sustain life. It also provides taro from which poi, a most important staple, is made. Above, a taro patch in Hanalei, Kaua`i, where the gods also supply abundant rainfall.

Toni Polancy

There are many paths to worship in these islands. Hawai`i is host to 43 recognized religious groups and at least a dozen new or less-organized faiths. Led by Rev. Hiram Bingham, the first missionaries, Congregationalists, arrived in 1820. They were followed by a variety of priests and missionaries who built schools and churches. Plantation workers, imported from around the world, added other faiths, including Roman Catholic. (See chart.)

The Mormon Church, with 7,000 members and owning 6,000 acres on windward O`ahu, has a long, well-rooted history in the islands. Purchased in 1865 as a place for Mormons from around the world to settle, the "reserve" at La`ie includes **Brigham Young University**; the Hawai`i **Temple of the Church of Jesus Christ of the Latter-day Saints**; and the Polynesian Cultural Center, one of Hawai`i's most popular attractions; plus a hotel, a shopping center and many homes.

And the variety of religions continues to grow. New denominations, such as **Hope Chapel** and the **Assemblies of God,** have ever-growing congregations attracted to lively family-oriented programs. Various New Age services are also available on most islands.

Participating in church activities is a good way to become part of a new community. Most Hawai`i churches are organized to accommodate our transient population and welcome newcomers, winter resdients, military families and tourists.

Most of us are pretty good sports

By Matthew Thayer

With its abundance of clear, sunny days, warm weather, blue ocean and clean air, this island state has lured many outdoor sport enthusiasts to pack belongings in boxes and crates stamped "Hawai`i."

This sports-minded influx continues a long and storied tradition dating back to the first Hawaiians. Hawai`i's initial settlers ruled the seas as master sailors, oarsmen and fishers. They invented surfing and many other games to test their skill, accuracy, strength and courage. One competition involved skimming down the sides of steep cinder cones in wooden sleds that resembled the modern-day luge.

European contact in the early 1800s brought new sports to Hawai`i's shores, as did the influx of plantation workers. Ranchers brought horses to the islands and locals soon embraced events such as rodeo and polo. Baseball, football, basketball, track, bowling and dozens of other sports all found their niche in island life. This athletic base seems to pervade an overall island lifestyle that is healthy, energetic and supportive of most sports, especially those for Hawai`i's youth.

Spectator sports

With no major professional sports teams to claim as their own, Hawai`i fans are big supporters of local college and high school action. The University of Hawai`i is the biggest draw and many of its football, basketball, baseball, softball and volleyball games are televised live throughout the state.

There are opportunities to see the top competitors live when they play in all-star events such as the Pro Bowl and Hula Bowl football games, the Maui Invitational and Rainbow Classic college basketball tournaments. Professional golf tours stop in Hawai`i, including the Champions Skins tournament, the Hawaiian Open and the Mercedes Championships. Islanders also have an opportunity to rub elbows with the pros when they play in various celebrity and charity events during their off-seasons.

Aaah, the drawbacks

The biggest challenges for mainland sports fans who want to keep up with major league baseball or the NFL are not simply things like finding box scores or being able to dig up in-depth information about favorite teams. Not at all. The hardest part is getting accustomed to football games starting at 7 a.m. And convincing mainland friends to stop calling every Monday night and ruining the game by giving away the scores of the tape-delayed contests. The five- or six-hour time difference means games are broadcast hours earlier here. However, there's a good side to the early morning broadcasts — you'll have time to take the family swimming or on a picnic Sunday afternoons.

A few games of our own

Among the big spectator sport heroes here are some *really* big ones: sumo wrestlers. In this intriguing Japanese sport, men who weigh 400 pounds or more wrestle each other in bouts that usually last less than a minute. The sport carries much tradition, from the way wrestlers' long hair is dressed to their humble bows when they've lost a bout. To newcomers, the sport may seem absurd, but to locals and most *kama`aina* it is mesmerizing. Hawaiians are famous sumo wrestlers in Japan and match highlights are broadcast in Hawai`i nightly. Wrestlers are considered national heroes here, as they are in Japan.

Participation sports

Pick a sport that is popular somewhere in the world and there's a good chance it has a league or group of enthusiasts here. Hawai`i's giant waves, strong winds, triathlon circuits and golf courses may be reason enough for some fans to adopt an 808 area code, but for the rest of us, it's just nice to know that after the move it won't be too hard to hook up with a softball league or bowling tournament or bridge club.

Most islands feature a healthy number of public parks and recreation facilities. Through the years locals have petitioned for public pools, athletic fields, skateboard parks, basketball courts, youth centers, tennis courts and even in-line skating rinks. The result has been a gradual upgrading of the sports infrastructure that hustles to meet the needs of a growing population.

Hiking, camping, togetherness

Most of Hawai`i's volcanic mountains are too steep for amateur mountain climbing, but others are perfect for less strenuous hiking to near summits with spectacular views and unusual flora. For safety reasons, you should never hike alone. Group hikes, including weekend or overnight trips, are a favorite with *kama`aina*. A campout under the star-filled sky on a secluded beach like Wai`anapanapa State Park near Hana, Maui, is an unforgettable experience and some families make it a yearly ritual.

Fishing, for a reason

Hawaiians don't kill just for sport. Hunting and fishing are ways to provide food or income, especially on rural outer islands. Most of the fishing is of the deep sea variety and catches include marlin (a`u), yellowfin tuna (ahi) and mahimahi. You'll also see local fishermen casting nets from shore.

Rock lobsters, crabs and shrimp are netted or simply plucked from rocks and underwater caverns. Night-diving for eels and lobsters is popular, too. If you walk the beach at night, you may spot the eerie glow of hunters' search lights under water. Catch is taken home, sold to markets or restaurants, or peddled from homes or out of cars at roadsides.

Fishing tournaments are a western concept, but a few are held on the islands. The most famous is the five-day invitational Hawaiian International Billfish Tournament off Kona (Big Island) shores every August.

Hunting can be a boar

Most islands also have hunks of state land where hunting is permitted with licenses. Among the bounty: feral pigs, goats, pheasant and francolin, a small pheasant-like bird.

Boar hunting is a particularly exciting local sport. Trained dogs scour the mountains for the huge tusked beasts, wild descendents of hogs imported decades ago as food. Boars are vicious when cornered and aren't particularly friendly when they're free. Smart dogs go for the boar's jugular; smart boars go for another very tender part of the dog. It's not unusual for a dog to be severely injured in the encounter. However, the big pig provides a great *lu`au* and is a popular source of food.

(Matthew Thayer, once a Pennsylvania resident, has long been a photojournalist at the Maui News.*)*

Worth considering....

- **Organized camp-outs and hikes** are a smart way to get to know your island and meet new people. Watch the newspapers' entertainment sections for announcements or ask at sports equipment stores.

- **If you like a particular tourist activity** — bike riding, scuba diving, fishing, hunting — and would like to participate often, tell the activity owners or managers that you live here and are available to fill in on tours. Some will let you participate at a low *kama'aina* rate just to cover expenses, rather than have the tour or activity go partly empty.

- **Let your hobby be your occupation.** This is one of the best places on earth to make your avocation your vocation. Like to swim? Snorkel? Fish? Consider a job on one of the excursion boats that traverse the ocean daily. Hankering to hike? Consider a career taking tourists up into those pristine mountains peaks. Or start your own business. Come up with an eco-idea: a new way for visitors to enjoy our out-

... and remembering

- **Fishing and hunting are regulated** and checks by law enforcement officials are frequent. Call the Department of Land and Natural Resources permit office in any county to get more information. Visit hawaii.gov/dlnr or hunting.ehawaii.gov/hunting for more information.

- **If you bring guns or firearms into the state,** you must register them with local police within 24 hours of your arrival. Guns rented or purchased here must also be registered with police. For information, call the Hunting Seasons Hotline at **(808) 587-0171.**

Sooner or later, you'll use *the ocean*

By Blair Thorndike

With the sea surrounding us on all sides, it's little wonder that Hawai'i's most popular athletic endeavors are watersports-related. No matter where you go in the islands, you'll see all manner of watercraft strapped to vehicle rooftops and filling carports — everything from surfboards and kayaks to windsurf rigs and outrigger canoes.

Surfing

Probably the best-known form of Hawaiian ocean sport is surfing. Invented by ancient Polynesians who slid toward shore on huge wooden planks carved from trees, surfing has evolved through the centuries into a multi-million dollar global industry. Aside from the obvious fashion influence spawned by surfers, the sport itself has many levels.

• **Neophytes** can get their feet wet in calmer breaks such as Waikiki or Kihei. Surf schools abound these days, so anyone with the nerve can give it a try.

Matthew Thayer

• **"Weekend warriors"** are another breed of surfrider — career-bound during the work week, these die-hard individuals of any age, gender, shape, and size absolutely live for the weekend, no matter the weather or wave conditions.

• **Obsessed.** Then, taking it to the more extreme end, there are surfers who do little else. Thousands of surfers work night jobs, just to be able to ride waves every day. Ask your waiter or hotel night clerk if he (or she) surfs... the answer will likely be an emphatic "yes."

• **Professionals.** Finally, there are the professionals, who flock to O`ahu's North Shore each winter for a prestigious series of big-wave contests known as the Triple Crown of Surfing. These contests are a must-see for anyone. Some of these professionals earn six- and even seven-figure salaries... not bad for a day at the beach!

Surf's you right

Surfing is best on the North Shores during winter (experts only) and the South Shores during summer (good for novices). Aleutian storms send swell trains southward towards Hawai`i's North Shores from October through March, creating gargantuan waves. Conversely, summer in the Northern Hemisphere means winter below the Equator. Storms off of Antarctica and New Zealand send swells northward that must travel extreme distances and through numerous South Pacific archipelagos before reaching Hawai`i's South Shores, significantly diminishing their size and intensity.

Bodyboarding

The sport of bodyboarding pretty much fits into the categories above, the difference being that bodyboarding (lying down) is easier to learn than stand-up surfing and is less costly (bodyboard: $40; surfboard $400), thereby generally appealing to a broader range of enthusiasts.

Bodysurfing

Bodysurfing is another of the "wave-riding" sports, but is the least cumbersome, as a pair of swim fins is all one needs to propel one's self onto a wave. This sport is popular at the state's sandy shorebreaks, such as Makapu`u on Oah`u, Makena on Maui, and Hapuna on the Big Island.

Windsurfing, kitesurfing

With tradewinds fanning our archipelago nearly year-round, Hawai`i has become a windsurfing mecca. Brought to the islands in the late '60s by nomadic boardsailors who saw lots of windy days and open shoreline, windsurfing has also evolved into a lucrative global industry. Best of all, unlike surfing, windsurfing does not require swells to be enjoyed; just wind.

As with surfing, schools exist for beginners, there are large numbers of daily enthusiasts, and there is a burgeoning professional circuit. Kitesurfing, similar to windsurfing, has also taken off in recent years. Harder to learn, and a bit more of an "extreme sport," kitesurfing is truly best left to the daredevils.

Outrigger canoe paddling

Outrigger canoe paddling is another of the truly "Hawaiian" ocean sports, with roots that can be traced back to the ancient Polynesians. With no method of interisland transportation other than paddling outrigger canoes fashioned from giant trees, the Hawaiians paddled great distances in these watercraft and, in fact, migrated from the South Pacific using canoes fitted with sails. (The name "outrigger" comes from the pontoon-like extension protruding from the hull, called an *ama,* which provides stability).

Today, outrigger canoe paddling is Hawai`i's official state sport. Tens of thousands of paddlers, from pre-teens through silver-haired seniors, enjoy the activity on every island. Canoe clubs abound, with hundreds of members in each. Beehives of activity during the summer months, the clubs serve as the center of the social universe for many, with practice sessions taking place at all hours of the day, from dawn 'til dusk. Participation is open to one and all, and since a club's strength lies in its numbers, newcomers are usually welcomed. Joining an outrigger club is a good way to associate with a broad range of fellow residents.

Each club fields teams of six in many age/gender divisions at huge summertime regattas statewide, with the winners heading to the prestigious State Championships in August. This is followed by a series of long-distance canoe races, culminating in the world-renowned feats of endurance that traverse the treacherous 32-mile-wide Moloka`i Channel. More than 100 men's and women's crews compete in these prestigious events held each fall, with thousands of spectators welcoming the durable paddlers who make it to the Waikiki Beach finish line.

In recent years, and in an effort to remain fit during the "off-season," canoe paddlers have taken to the sea in one-person outrigger canoes.

These high-tech, ultra-light, ultra-expensive watercraft can be seen plying the waters of every island. Races are held throughout the winter months for these specialized boats, with the numbers of participants growing each year.

Kayaking

Another solo paddling sport gaining popularity is kayaking. At the low end of the spectrum are the ubiquitous plastic "scupper-type" craft, often seen in large numbers on trailers headed for beaches where they are rented *en masse* to visitors. At the other end are the high-tech fiberglass "surfski-type" kayaks, used by top athletes for fitness and racing.

Paddleboarding

One type of ocean sport you may see, or even attempt, is paddleboarding. This obscure pre-World War II sport, which can be traced back to the days of Waikiki beachboys and the legendary Duke Kahanamoku, is gaining popularity. When the surf was nonexistent, these bronzed watermen would paddle prone for miles, resulting in stronger arms, shoulders and backs.

Today, paddleboarding is popular with both lifeguards and surfers attempting to stay fit during spells of flat ocean. Today's boards are expensive, ultra-light, hollow craft that are basically a hybrid of surfboard and canoe; flat on top with rounded hulls. Very buoyant and 12- to 17-feet long, paddleboards go much faster than surfboards and races are held every summer, culminating with a World Championship crossing of the Moloka`i Channel in late July.

It's a good bet...

Whether your motivation is exercise, competition or pure recreation, chances are you'll be involved in some form of water sports once you move here. In fact, the islands abound with people who moved here with one goal in mind: to enjoy our ocean.

(When he's not chained to his computer desk, life-long Hawai`i resident Blair Thorndike is an avid surfer and paddleboarder with big waves to his credit and channel crossings under his belt.)

We're healthier

We're outdoors, we're active and usually the weather's fine

A montage of windsurf sails at Ho'okipa Beach, Maui

After-school surfers run for a wave at Wailua, Kaua`i.

Abundant rain keeps the grass green at Hanalei, Kaua`i, and perfect for playing Frisbee.

Swimmers at `Ohe`o Gulch in Hana, Maui, commonly known as Seven Pools.

and more active

A hiker nears the summit of Haleakala on Maui.

Canoe teams take their sport seriously. Near Kona, The Big Island.

A religious experience: walking to Sacred Falls, O'ahu.

A few boys, a basketball and the West Maui Mountains.

Matthew Thayer

A runner ascends from Maui's central valley.

Health: We live longer...

Hawai`i has, for the past 40 years, enjoyed an excellent reputation as the "health state." On the average, Hawai`i residents live four years longer than U.S. mainlanders. Statistics show that men here typically live to age 76, women to age 82.

We are thinner...

Hawai`i has the fewest overweight people in the nation. About 19.7 percent of residents are overweight compared to about 30 percent on the mainland. Our average body mass (fat) index is 24.1; compare to 31.6 for the rest of the country.

We may be thinner and live longer because we are more physically active. The good weather means we aren't as likely to be holed up watching television and nibbling potato chips. Even the oldest among us can be outdoors throughout the year, swimming, walking, hiking and paddling. Hawai`i also has many Asian residents who tend to maintain healthy diets high in fish and vegetables and low in fats.

There are exceptions. Of major concern among health care professionals is the tendency of people of Polynesian ancestry, including Hawaiians, to be overweight and suffer from high blood pressure and diabetes. Whether this tendency is hereditary or dietary is still debated, but in recent years major efforts have been made to educate and change dietary habits, with some success.

We smoke less...

Another healthy statistic: Hawai`i residents are less likely to smoke cigarettes and may be less likely to inhale someone else's smoke. Only about 16.6 percent of Hawai`i's residents smoke cigarettes, according to a recent study by the National Women's Law Center and the Oregon Health & Science University. That compares to about 25 percent for the rest of the nation.

The reason so few of us smoke? The study cited a substantial state cigarette tax, making smoking expensive, and the use of tobacco settlement money to help discourage smoking. But there may be another reason: thanks to the great weather, we are active and less likely to be lying around, filling our time and our lungs with nicotine.

Those low smoking figures, however, do not allow for tourists who make up about 15 percent of the population. Tourists from some parts of the world smoke a great deal, and non-smokers may be exposed to second-hand cigarette smoke in tourist areas. In recent years, most islands have banned smoking in restaurants in an effort to protect employees who could be exposed to long hours of smoke inhalation.

And we gather accolades

In 2003 Honolulu was named the "healthiest city in the nation" by a men's fitness magazine. The city grabbed the highest marks for its climate, geography, air quality and recreational facilities, which contributed to keeping people outside and mobile. Meanwhile, a national children's advocacy group rated Honolulu one of the best cities in the nation to raise a healthy child. And the United Health Foundation ranks us the fourth healthiest state.

However... here are some unhealthy problems

Our nearly perfect climate seems to alleviate such ailments as arthritis and bronchitis, but it doesn't mean you'll never have another cold or totally avoid the flu. Healthcare officials say these minor illnesses are difficult to track since most people simply treat themselves with over-the-counter drugs or "take two aspirins and go to bed," but it is as common for people to complain of flu and colds here as on the mainland. Some say our tropical climate and exposure to visitors from around the world make us more susceptible to infections such as SARS, West Nile virus and dengue fever.

Overall, Hawai`i is healthful, but it is not without health problems.

- **Illegal drugs.** In recent years, crystal meth use among residents has reached frightening heights, endangering everyone's lives in many ways and overburdening the healthcare and social-services systems. See the Crime section of this book in the Trouble chapter.

- **Tooth decay.** Hawai`i does not fluoridate its drinking water, and many of our children have bad teeth. About twice the national average of elementary school-age children here have untreated cavities, and a nationwide study a few years ago showed that Kaua`i children have the worst teeth in the country. The state health department has sought the few thousand dollars it would cost to install fluoride injectors into the state's water system, but efforts to fluoridate the water have failed in the past, partly because people here want their water to be natural and untainted by chemicals.

- **Diabetes.** About 19.7 percent of Native Hawaiians have diabetes. That's 2.5 times the proportion of other residents. A diet high in red meat and a cultural preference for large portion sizes may contribute to the high rate.

Two to watch

- **Typhus outbreaks.** The islands occasionally experience outbreaks of murine typhus, rare in the rest of the nation, but common in third-world countries. Murine typhus outbreaks can follow explosions in the mouse and rat populations. Fleas on rodents carry the bacteria that cause the disease. Infection occurs when flea feces enter a fleabite wound or are inhaled.

- **Asthma.** A Hawai`i Health Survey found asthma nearly twice as common in Hawai`i as in the rest of the nation, with about nine percent of us suffering from asthma. An immunologist told *Honolulu* magazine in 2002 that Hawai`i's air contains many allergens and our warm weather means we are breathing pollen year-round. Other possibilities? Vog, the sulfuric smog from Big Island volcanic eruptions, and dust mites which, like most bugs, thrive in the climate.

- **Suicide.** Hawai`i has the fastest-growing teen suicide rate in the nation, up 126 percent since 1980. The general level of mental health support is considered poor, particularly on neighbor islands and rural O`ahu, says one health care spokesman. Even if you can tap into it, the state mental health system is so heavily burdened it cannot always respond effectively.

A family affair: *ho'oponopono*

Ho'oponopono, an ancient Hawaiian "cure" for illnesses, physical as well as emotional, is still practiced today by some families. In *ho'oponopono*, members of the family gather to resolve a problem or cure a lingering illness. The family chooses a leader, often the oldest family member or a minister or healer. After prayers or a Bible reading, the leader asks each person to admit any grudges he may have or transgressions he may have committed. The ritual can go on for hours or even days, as problems are discussed by family members. Then forgiveness is asked between the individuals involved. The *ho'oponopono* is effective, some doctors surmise, because it uses a very modern psychological "cure": openly discussing problems and getting to their root, instead of letting them fester and multiply.

- **An elderly population.** Hawai`i has one of the highest elderly population rates in the country, and as the Baby Boomer generation grows older, we face a healthcare crisis. For example, on Maui, a social worker calls the long-term care situation "dismal." Recently, 53 people, cured to the point where they did not require acute care and could leave the hospital, waited at Maui Memorial Medical Center for weeks because no nursing care facilities were available. All islands face a similar crisis. Read more in the Retirement chapter of this book.

- **Teen pregnancy.** Teen pregnancy is very high here. Traditionally there is little stigma to being an unwed mother in Hawai`i, where entire families helps raise children, but the teen birth rate is particularly high in economically depressed rural areas.

- **Hospitals.** Healthcare in O`ahu's major hospitals is adequate, judged by the amount of expensive, sophisticated equipment that is the measuring stick throughout the U.S. Queen's Medical Center in Honolulu, for example, has advanced scanning machines used for biomedical research as well as treating patients. But neighbor island residents usually must travel to Honolulu for sophisticated tests such as brain and body scans as well as critical operations, including heart surgery. Neighbor island hospitals vary greatly in quality, say a doctor and nurse interviewed separately.

Health insurance

This state ranks eighth nationally in the number of citizens who have health insurance, down from first place a few years ago. Just 10 percent of our residents are without health insurance compared to a national average of 16 percent. By state law, employers must provide health insurance to employees who work more than 20 hours a week. They can ask the employee to pay one-half of the premiums or 1.5 percent of their wages, whichever is less. (See more on this topic in the Working chapter of this book.)

Two major non-profit health care giants, Kaiser Permanente and Hawai`i Medical Service Association (Blue Cross/Blue Shield), provide most of the health insurance in Hawai`i. In recent years, numerous smaller health insurers have also come on the scene.

The costs

In Hawai`i, as in the rest of the nation, healthcare costs have been climbing in the past few years. Members of healthcare plans are paying more for services, more for prescription drugs, and more for visits than they did a few years ago, and in some cases, getting less. The same problems have plagued health plans throughout the country.

Both HMSA and Kaiser offer a variety of plans. Under HMSA's most popular group plan, clients can choose a participating doctor and HMSA picks up 90 percent of the cost of the office visit. Clients also have access to a wide range of testing services and other healthcare providers.

Kaiser Permanente clients can choose from staff doctors at convenient Kaiser clinics around the state for a low co-pay fee. They have on-site access to routine procedures such as blood tests, mammograms and heart monitoring, as well as pharmacy services. For advanced care, they are flown, usually at Kaiser's expense, to Kaiser hospitals and centers on O`ahu or referred to other facilities as necessary.

Protect your health. Consider this:

- **In a medical emergency, how far is help?** If you have a serious health problem that may require emergency trips to a hospital, consider carefully which island you choose to live on. Hospital care can vary greatly from island to island. You should also consider how long it might take you to get to a hospital in an emergency during busy traffic times. For example, Kaua`i's Wilcox General Hospital is able to handle most emergencies and is generally considered a satisfactory hospital. But if you were to live in Princeville or Kilauea, it could take an hour during rush-hour traffic to reach the hospital.

- **Be prepared to travel elsewhere** for some treatments and procedures. Several healthcare pro-viders recommend bypassing Hawai`i hospitals and traveling to the mainland for serious elective surgery. For example, because of the larger population, hospitals near major cities perform more valve and joint replacements and heart surgery, therefore have more experience. Ask your doctor and hospital to provide statistics comparing hospitals before you have surgery.

- **Avoid cane fields, volcanic residue.** Air quality on these islands is among the best in the world because of the trade winds and our isolated location in the Pacific. But if you have sinus or breathing problems, avoid living near sugar cane fields, still abundant in Maui and Kaua`i. Also be aware of "vog," volcanic residue in the Big Island's air. The cane harvesting process involves burning cane stalks, which creates smoke and black ashy debris that can blow across several miles. Volcanic haze can affect air quality across the Big Island. It's no big deal, unless you already suffer from breathing problems.

RESOURCES

Here's help:

- Any emergency Call **911** or **ASK-2000** from anywhere in Hawai`i 24 hours a day

- O`ahu Suicide and Crisis Center **(808) 521-4555**

- Maui Suicide and Crisis Center **(808) 244-7407**

- United Self-Help All islands toll free **(866) 866-4357** or **(808) 926-0466** (call collect).

- Aloha United Way **(800) 892-2757**

- Alcoholics Anonymous **(808) 946-1438**

- Narcotics Anonymous **(808) 737-6949**

- Catholic Services to Families **(808) 536-1794**

the military

Yeoman 3rd Class Margaret Jean Fusco photographs three friends by King Kamehameha's statue in Honolulu, circa spring 1945. Posing are (left to right): Yeoman 2nd Class Jennie Reinhart; Yeoman 2nd Class Muriel Caldwell and Yeoman 2nd Class June Read.

Photo courtesy of Department of the Navy, National Archives, Naval Historical Center

Look before

you leap into

Assignment: Paradise

The Sciarrottas:
'Bloom where you are planted'

Before becoming a Navy wife two years ago, before moving five times in six months, before being transplanted to O`ahu from Washington state, Kelly Sciarrotta was a pre-school teacher. One of her favorite children's songs included the line, "Bloom where you are planted." Today, that line is Kelly's motto. The wife of Navy chief electrician's mate Santino "Sonny" Sciarrotta, Kelly has been in O`ahu for less than a year when we spoke, yet she had already accomplished a great deal. In addition to settling in at a townhouse and giving birth to baby Katie, Kelly is active both at the military base and in the community. She finds homes for pets at the unofficial base rescue center, counsels other Navy spouses at an organization called Compass, and heads up volunteers training at the nearby city-run dog park.

"You have to bloom where you are planted," she says. "Get involved, do good or at least the best you can, wherever you are."

Kelly has had plenty of opportunity to practice blooming. Sonny went to sea two days after they were married. When he returned four months later, the Sciarrottas spent the next six months in five different locations while he trained as electrician's mate. Sonny requested shore duty in Hawai`i, and got it. After so much traveling, their three-year stint here feels like home.

The Sciarrottas considered putting a down payment on a home in Hawai`i, but decided free Navy housing was a better bargain. They live in a complex of modern townhomes in the middle of busy Salt Lake near central O`ahu. Kelly shops at the Navy exchange a few blocks from their house. It is the largest military mall in the Western Hemisphere and the largest Navy exchange in the world, with most goods discounted about 30 percent. At the mall market, milk costs just over $2 a gallon, compared to as much as $6 a gallon in some local markets.

The family enjoys life in the islands. Sonny, who has been in the military for eight years, says the military "pays a lot better than people give it credit for. The standard of living is getting better because the military needs to keep people in."

Toni Polancy

Kelly, Sonny and baby Katie share living room space — and affection — with a boxer named Vanity and cat called Father Flanagan, adopted from a base shelter operated by volunteers. Katie, born at Tripler Medical Center, was seven months old when this photo was taken.

"It's going to be good, culturally, for the baby," Kelly adds. "You can walk through the swap market and hear 12 different languages clearly being spoken."

"There's tons of stuff to see and do in Hawai`i," Sonny points out. And you get plenty of visitors. The Sciarrottis were expecting 13 relatives to visit and stay at their townhouse, all at the same time.

Next year, Sonny faces a year of sea duty on a fast-attack submarine, probably near the Persian Gulf. That fact hangs over the couple's happy time here.

"When Sonny goes out to sea it is difficult," Kelly says. "Everyone always asks how we military wives do it. We do it because we have to. I focus on supporting Sonny. He needs to know I am strong and that we are okay."

Assignment: Paradise

If you have to be assigned somewhere — if you must pick up your life, pack up your family, leave schools and friends and move because your boss, the military, says so — it might as well be Hawai`i. Why not spend two years or so in a place called Paradise?

As military, you will be here longer than most visitors. You will experience both the best and the worst of the islands, and perhaps take back with you a more realistic picture of life here than anyone else who visits. Most tourists expect idyllic surroundings and posh hotels and special treatment. But you are wiser. You have probably lived in many places and you don't trust picture postcards. You know that the only difference here will be sunshine, a warm ocean, fragrant winds and a wide variety of people, some of whom will treat you and your family with great respect for all that you are doing for our country, and a few who may not.

You've experienced military life already. You expect crazy work shifts, long separations from your spouse and family, crowded housing. You ask little in return: a modest paycheck every month, medical benefits, an occasional visit to the base exchange, and a few days R and R occasionally.

If you are happy with military life, overall, you should enjoy your stay in Hawai`i. Its facilities for the military and families are among the best in the world, in part because the state's mid-Pacific location is vital to United States security. Military cutbacks that slashed funds and closed mainland installations in the late 1990s have done only minor surgery here. And the terrorist attacks of September 11, 2001, added to the importance of the state's military bases. The U.S. Pacific Command, Camp H.M. Smith, is responsible for the defense of over 105 million square miles, or roughly half the earth's surface. Within that area are 43 countries comprised of more than 60 percent of the world's population. That's 1 in every 12 Hawai`i residents.

You, and your family, are very welcome here. The state of Hawai`i needs the military. After tourism, the military is most important to the state's economy. Of the state's nearly 1.3 million residents, 110,500 are "military," either active, dependents, reservists or employees at bases.

Will you like your life here?

Most military members and their families seem to enjoy, or at least be satisfied with, duty here. In 2001 a Navy study polled 3,834 enlisted men and their families and gleaned 22,000 comments about the quality of life in Hawai`i. To the question "Living in Hawai`i has been a positive experience," 78 percent responded that it had been a positive experience; 16 percent indicated they had been dissatisfied and 6 percent had no opinion. A wide array of services is provided for families who accept Assignment Paradise — everything from sponsors to help with settling in to legal advice and a chance to earn a graduate degree, from opportunities for fun to employment and abuse counseling.

Military facilities here are among the best in the world and are getting even better. The government contracts with private industry to renovate and manage military housing on the islands including a $37 million shopping center at O`ahu's Schofield Barracks. The new facility is about half the size of the Navy exchange at Pearl Harbor, already the largest Navy exchange in the world.

MILITARY

Toni Polancy

The Navy mall at Bougainville and Radford Drive in Salt Lake is large.

Hawai`i Military Presence: Land Controlled by the Military

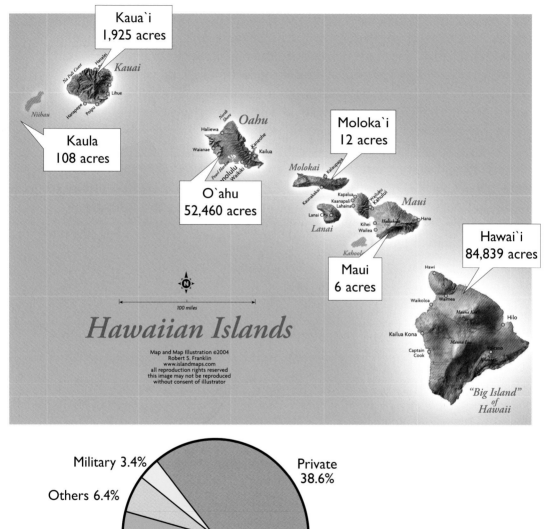

Kaua`i
1,925 acres

Kauai

Kaula
108 acres

Oahu

Moloka`i
12 acres

Molokai

O`ahu
52,460 acres

Maui

Maui
6 acres

Lanai

Hawai`i
84,839 acres

Hawaiian Islands

100 miles

Map and Map Illustration ©2004
Robert S. Franklin
www.islandmaps.com
all reproduction rights reserved
this image may not be reproduced
without consent of illustrator

"Big Island"
of
Hawaii

Military 3.4%

Private
38.6%

Others 6.4%

Six Largest
Private
22%

State
29.6%

Land Control in Hawai`i

Source: Hawai`i State Data Book

- **The Fort DeRussy Armed Forces Recreation Center**. A giant park at Waikiki Beach with lifeguards, tennis courts, picnic areas, and 1,500 feet of beach.

- **The Hale Koa Hotel.** This military-operated first-class luxury resort is exclusively for active duty, retired military, and Department of Defense civilian personnel. Located on 66 acres of prime Waikiki beachfront property, it has 814 posh guest rooms with private balconies; includes live entertainment as well as buffets and Sunday champagne brunches, dinner shows and a sunset *lu`au* on the beach. Room rates are less than half that of comparable civilian hotels. Reservations are made on a first come, first serve basis, a spokesperson says, but rooms are typically reserved up to a year in advance. Interestingly, Hale Koa is self-supporting — no tax dollars are used in its operation.

- **Wai`anae Army Recreation Center.** One of the finest beach facilities on the island of O`ahu, including cabins with full kitchens, a club and water sports. You should note, however, that Hawai`i is experiencing severe drug problems and a rising crime rate. This rural area of the island seems prone to robbery and can be dangerous.

- **Kilauea Military Camp Recreation Center.** On the Big Island, a portion of fascinating Hawai`i Volcanoes National Park is set aside for military personnel of all branches. There are one-, two- and three-bedroom cottages with wood-burning fireplaces and Jacuzzis. If you are bringing your family to Hawai`i and the children are old enough to appreciate and remember walking on a volcano, watching its steam rise from the ground, visit this amazing place. (808) 967-8333 or www.kmc-volcano.com

- **Barking Sands Pacific Missile Range.** On Kaua`i, the military has put every resort offering together in one place: beach cottages, a swimming pool, tennis, racquetball, basketball, a golf driving range, a softball field, beach volleyball, a fitness center, a youth center. There's even a karaoke club and an outdoor movie theater. (808) 471-6752 or cnic.navy.mil/barkingsands.

- **Tripler Army Medical Center.** As you leave O`ahu's main airport and head toward Honolulu, you'll see a large pink building dominating the hills to your left. That's the Tripler Army Medical Center, the largest medical treatment facility in the Pacific, providing healthcare to every branch of the military. Over 850,000 people are eligible for care at Tripler, which is also a teaching hospital in conjunction with the University of Hawai`i.

- **Legal assistance.** Legal assistance is available at all military bases for numerous routine matters: taxes, divorce and child support, auto title transfers, landlord/tenant disputes, wills, powers of attorney. Active duty personnel, as well as their family members and retirees, are eligible.

- **Childcare.** Subsidized childcare centers are available at several of Hawai`i's military bases. For example, working military parents and Defense Department employees can bring children ages six weeks to five years to Hickam Air Force Base's Child Development Center from 6:30 a.m. to 5:30 p.m. daily. Staff to child ratio is low — one caregiver to every four infants or every five toddlers — so the center is often filled and has a waiting list in some age categories. Call Hickam's Child Development Center at (808) 449-9880.

Housing

- **Permanent housing.** After you've received your orders for Hawai`i, begin making arrangements for housing. Submit a DD 1746 (an Advance Application for Housing) to the appropriate personnel on your base or to:
Community Homefinding Referral Relocation Service (CHRRS)
3189 Nimitz Road
Honolulu, HI 96818-3676
(808) 474-1804

CHRRS aides help families find off-base housing, even going as far as providing transportation for the search. They can also supply a list of hotels for temporary housing.

- **Temporary housing.** Several O`ahu hotels specialize in temporary lodging for military families. The Plaza Hotel (Best Western) has a military liaison person and "Welcome to Hawai`i" program. Call **(808) 836-8889** or **(808) 576-6637**. The Harbor Arms Apartment Hotel also welcomes military. Call **(800) 360-5556**.

Toni Polancy

The kindly staff at Hickam family services produces a very thorough informational packet for newly-assigned families. The packet we received in 1999 included a bright yellow flyer imprinted in heavy black type. The information is so succinct and informative that we include it here. **Remember that prices quoted are for 1999. Figure about a 20 percent increase today. All costs quoted are estimates.**

The cost of living in paradise

Living in Hawai`i is enjoyable, but very expensive. Please read this very carefully and make sure you can afford it before accepting the assignment.

The cost of living in paradise is at least 35% higher than it is on the mainland. You should figure out what your expenses and credit debt are per month. Multiply your expenses by 35% and add it to your current budget. Will your pay support that? Do you have enough now in savings to take care of emergencies such as car repair? Do you have an extra $3,000 to rent an apartment here and cover unexpected expenses? If you must take advance pay, add that figure into your monthly expenses. The island is beautiful, but for many, the beaches and fine weather are not worth financial bankruptcy.

…A two-bedroom condo/townhouse rental unit will run $900–$1200 (without utilities) per month; $1100–$1200 for a house rental. It is very hard to find housing at the lower rates. The rents have been flat for the past five years and are not expected to increase in the near future. The current waiting list for junior enlisted members (E-1 to E-9) to receive on-base housing can be 1 to 10 months, maybe longer. For junior officers it's about a 4–12 month wait.

…Landlords require first month's rent and an amount equivalent to the first month's rent for a security deposit. You will need a minimum of $1800–$2400 just to rent your house or apartment.

…Utility costs will generally be paid separately from your rent. Security deposits on utilities can be waived. The appropriate waiver forms are available at your command. Estimated cost of electricity for a family of two living in an apartment without air conditioning is $74 (per month) and for a family of 4 it is $126. Estimated water and sewage is $60 per month for a family of four. Estimated cable TV service is $25 per month for standard cable. Telephone connection services are $46 and estimated $20 per month for basic service. If your rental doesn't have a phone jack, the installation charge is $95. Long distance rates are similar to the mainland.

...Car insurance is higher than on the mainland. Estimate at least $100 per month. Driving record and at-fault accidents can cause the premium to increase dramatically. One speeding violation can increase cost to $135 per month; two speeding violations raises the amount to $208; and a single DUI increases the rate to as much as $600 per month.

...A spouse can easily find employment here, but generally pay is lower than on the mainland and more than half the jobs are downtown. Parking rates can run from $120–$200 a month and gasoline costs $1.63 per gallon on base for the lowest grade. Gas for the second job can run your expenses up an extra $40–$60. A bus pass is $25 per month (student pass is $12.50). Senior citizens (65 and up) pay $20 for a two-year pass.

...Child care costs are very high on O'ahu. It will cost you between $229–$446 per month depending on your household income. Our Child Development Center is considered the best in (the Pacific Air Force) and is currently expanding to accommodate more children. The Hickam Family Day Care Providers Program offers licensed care ranging from $300–$380 per month. The local school system's after-school A+ program is $55 per month. Children on free or reduced lunch program pay substantially less. An employed spouse may find that the net return for working a full-time job is only $100-$300 per month once the costs of child care, parking, gas and lunches are factored in.

The typical family may find that they must adopt a firm budget to remain free from financial worries. There may be no room in the budget for life's unpredictable emergencies. If your spouse worked on the mainland and you have accumulated the debt of a two-income family, you may find yourself in serious trouble trying to pay your creditors, especially if you are only receiving one income in Hawai`i. Please call the Family Support Center's Personal Financial Program Manager to work on your "Aloha" budget upon arrival.

Military housing is being revamped in O'ahu. These newer townhouses are next to the Navy exchange mall.

Tips for settling in

- **Communicate.** Be sure to communicate with family counselors at the base you will be assigned to well in advance of your arrival. Many services are available to help you settle in, such as "aloha kits" including dishes, ironing boards, irons and baby furniture for rent at reasonable rates or for free. Complete packets of information, sent to you in advance of your move, include discount coupons, maps and school data. See the contact list at the end of this chapter.

- **Leave it home.** Bring as little with you as possible. Appliances such as ranges, refrigerators, washers and dryers are provided in base housing and are included in most rental apartments and homes here. Additional furniture can be purchased inexpensively at household sales, thrift and used furniture stores or discount stores. Leave bulky furniture at home. Bring few clothes. See the Moving section of this book.

RESOURCES

Pacific Command's link to all kinds of information for newcomers, families: www.pacom.mil/about/newcomers.shtml

A list of important relocation numbers on military installations: www.pcs-tdy.com/directories/hawaii.html

Your Military in Hawai`i, a helpful magazine-type guide, should be in the information packet you receive from the military or you can download it. You'll need Acrobat 4.0 which you can also download from the site. www.yourmilitaryinhawaii.com

Employment:
www.hawaii.militarycommunities.com

Air Force

Family services/Family support:
(808) 449-0300

Housing:
(808) 449-0317

Hickam:
For Hickam phone numbers and local Military Directory Assistance, call
(808) 449-7110
www2.hickam.af.mil

Hickam community services:
(808) 449-1030 Extension **234**
www.hickamservices.com

Army

Fort Shafter community services and family services:
(808) 438-9285

Fort Shafter housing:
(808) 438-5063
fortshafterhousing.com

Schofield Barracks
Community services and family services:
(808) 655-2400
www.mwrarmyhawaii.com

Coast Guard

General information:
(808) 541-3203
www.uscg.mil

Housing assistance:
(808) 831-2766

Relocation services:
www.uscg.mil/worklife/relocation_assistance.asp

Shipping household goods
(808) 473-4497

Marines Corps

Community services:
www.mccshawaii.com

Personal services:
(808) 257-7787

Relocation services:
(808) 257-7790
www.usmc-mccs.org/rap/index.cfm
www.militarytransitiontimes.com

Navy

www.hawaii.navy.mil/

Family Service Center
Pearl Harbor:
(808) 473-4222

na keiki

the children

We cherish

our toddlers,

but shortchange

our school kids

*Plumeria lei amid blond
curls on the Big Island.*
Photo by G. Brad Lewis

Breanna: "Chop suey" turns one

When Breanna Haulani Aki Gaddis turned one year old, her grandmother's whole Waikapu neighborhood knew it. So did 400 of her family's friends. Breanna's birthday party lasted for six hours, longer than most weddings, and included three bands, tables of catered food, and a room full of presents. It cost more than $4,000.

It was quite a party, well befitting one of Hawai`i's favorite traditions, the baby lu`au. Custom calls for a huge event, often sponsored by the baby's grandparents, to which friends, relatives and co-workers are invit-

Bob Fijal

Breanna and her mom

ed. And for good luck, the party must be held on or after the child's birthday, never before, since it celebrates the fact the infant has survived the dangers of infancy.

Breanna's grandparents, Matthew and JoAnn Aki, had a home and yard large enough to host the affair; but lu`au are usually held in halls or community centers, her mom Brandy says.

"For Breanna's party, we got a little carried away," Brandy adds. "We invited everybody who took the time to ask about my pregnancy or her birth. Usually people come to see you at the hospital and then they never see the baby again, so we wanted everyone to come."

Usually, it's adults who party the hardest at a baby lu`au; in Breanna's case the sunny toddler joined right in, dancing in the arms of guests and laughing at the bands.

No one is quite sure which of Hawai`i's many ethnic groups originated the baby lu`au, but Breanna would qualify no matter which. Her ancestry includes Japanese, Hawaiian, Chinese, Irish, English and French — and that's just on her mother's side.

"Her daddy (Beau Gaddis) is everything else," Brandy laughs. "Breanna is real chop suey."

From cradle to college

Hawai`i appears to be an ideal environment in which to raise children. There's grass to run barefoot in, fruit and flowers to pick, canoes to paddle, mountains to hike, beaches to play on and an ocean to swim in. In addition, children in larger communities here enjoy the same sports and activities as children on the mainland, all provided by liberal government funding and a caring community: Olympic-sized swimming pools, ball parks, skateboarding facilities.

And the islands offer an added boon in today's auto-obsessed society. Our predominantly small towns are, for the most part, convenient and safe for children. Interestingly, Hawai`i children take less Ritalin (for hyperactivity and attention disorders) than children anywhere else in the country.

Traditionally, children are cherished here. Polynesian and Asian cultures honor their elderly, and count their children as blessings. By island tradition, a child belongs not only to his parent, but also to his greater family and to the community. Here, a *lu`au* marks the child's first birthday, celebrating the fact that he or she has survived the first, delicate year of life.

Usually, all children share in this tradition of family and community support. Young *malihini*, or newcomers, may suffer a few taunts from classmates, but overall children under the age of 10 or 11 seem to have little trouble adjusting to life here.

For the offspring of traditional two-parent or extended families, Hawai`i is truly a young child's idyll. Unfortunately, that's not the case for every child today. Here, as on the mainland, times are changing:

'If you want your child in a rarefied environment, well... that's not what Hawai`i is about. It's a multi-cultural society where we learn from one another.'

O`ahu school principal Lea Albert

- About 25 percent of Hawai`i children are born to unwed mothers. Traditionally, that carries little stigma in island cultures, but these children are more apt to live in poverty. Hawai`i has four times more children living in emergency shelters than the national average.

Kid Care

Childcare is big business in Hawai`i, where few employers offer childcare assistance. Most centers these days call themselves pre-schools, with the emphasis on school. Aides at ten centers we called were eager to discuss learning programs. Most pre-schools accept children at age two; only a few accept babies as young as eight weeks of age. Most are open from 6 or 7 a.m. until 5 or 6 p.m. Prices range from $400 to $500 per month, including lunch and snacks. Babies under age two cost extra.

- A good place to start: PATCH (People Attentive To Children), a non-profit childcare resource and referral agency with offices on most islands: Access www.patchhawaii.org or call O`ahu: **(808) 839-1988**; Maui **(808) 242-9232**; Kauai: **(808) 246-0622**; Hilo: **(808) 961-3169**: Kona: **(808) 325-3800**.

- For information on Kama`aina Kids, private childcare throughout the islands, access www.kamaainakids.com or call O`ahu **(808) 599-2807**.

- Even if a child has two parents, they each may be holding down two or more jobs to make ends meet in costly Hawai`i, and have little time left for their child. This can be particularly difficult for newcomers who have no relatives or extended family to help with childcare. If the child encounters problems adjusting at school, there may be no adult available to help overcome the difficulties.

- As a child grows older and enters junior and senior high school, his life becomes more complicated, just as it does on the mainland. Drug problems are more rampant here than in some areas of the mainland.

And here the child has some special problems: an often overcrowded public school system and a mix of cultures that can be stimulating but also frightening. While the gang issue may not be as prevalant or obvious here as in New York or Los Angeles, ethnic groups do tend to stick together, and often clash. It takes a very special teenage *malihini* or newcomer, to adjust with ease.

Asking a less-than-eager teenage child to move to Hawai`i may be asking too much.

Quality of education

When Mary moved to O`ahu with her teenage son a few years ago, it seemed every longtime resident she met had a warning for her. Your son, they said, must attend either a private school or one of two public high schools with good reputations. The schools were in Kahala and Hawai`i Kai, both upper-middle-income enclaves. Since Mary could not afford to live in those neighborhoods, she "borrowed" a friend's address to register her son in Hawai`i Kai. Five years later, she was very satisfied with her son's education.

"At some schools you can get an education," an O`ahu psychologist and father says. "Others are nothing but trouble and drugs. The kid goes to school and comes back beat up. The teacher speaks pidgin. And you wonder why they are not getting an education?"

Put hundreds of young people of various races and ethnic backgrounds together. Factor in youthful tensions. Add a highly transient population and rapid growth that overcrowds school facilities. Figure in a single state-wide school board making decisions for communities miles away. Consider a large turnover of both teachers and students on some islands, and you'll see the tremendous challenges facing the state's public school system, as well as the parents and students.

> 'At some schools you can get an education. Others are nothing but trouble and drugs. The kid goes to school and comes back beat up. The teacher speaks pidgin. And you wonder why they are not getting an education?'
>
> –an O`ahu psychologist/father

About 45 percent of Hawai`i's public school teachers send their own children to private schools, according to a 1990 U.S. census. (No figures were available for 2000.) On the mainland, only 12 percent of school-teachers' children attend private schools. Overall, just under 20 percent of Hawai`i's elementary, intermediate and high school students choose private schools, compared to 12 percent in the rest of the nation.

Teachers sending their children to private schools is not necessarily a condemnation of the schools in which they teach, says Greg Knudsen, director of communications for the board of education.

TerraNova Achievement Test Results

Hawai`i results, by grade, by percentages

Subject and level	National Norm	Grade 3	Grade 4	Grade 5	Grade 6	Grade 7	Grade 8	Grade 10
Reading:								
Low	23	27	23	21	23	30	20	23
Average	54	53	57	58	65	53	62	61
High	23	20	19	21	12	17	18	17
Math:								
Low	23	26	24	22	27	28	24	25
Average	54	56	52	52	51	56	56	48
High	23	19	24	26	22	16	19	27

Source: Hawaii State Department of Education, accessed October 2, 2008.

Scholastic Assessment Test Score Averages

Component	2006		2008	
	Hawai`i seniors	U.S. averages	Hawai`i seniors	U.S. averages
Mathematical	509	518	502	515
Reading	482	503	481	502
Writing	472	497	470	494

Source: Hawaii State Department of Education, accessed September 22, 2008.

A lifeline for parents

Your toddler Tim has been having temper tantrums. What should you do?

Call Parent Line and get professional advice. Dial **526-1222** from O`ahu or **(800) 816-1222** from any neighbor island and child and adolescent development professionals will answer questions about kids from birth through 17 years. Topics include, but are not limited to, single parenting, sibling relations, discipline, homework, eating concerns, breast feeding, divorce and death. The line also welcomes calls from students. The confidential line is staffed by the state Department of Health from 8 a.m. to 6 p.m. Monday through Friday and 9 a.m. to 1 p.m. Saturdays.

Hawai`i spends about $11,000 annually per pupil, according to the National Assessment of Educational Progress. That figure drops somewhat when the higher cost of educating special needs children is deducted. A private school may spend twice that amount.

What tests say

On Scholastic Assessment Tests, which compare high school students throughout the nation, Hawai`i students score several points below the norm on all subjects. The National Assessment of Educational Progress, a measurement known as "the nation's report card," also scores Hawai`i public school students below norm in all subjects. These tests determine knowledge of science and the ability to use what is learned to solve problems. Only students in notoriously poor school districts such as Washington, D.C.; Guam; Louisiana and Mississippi score lower than Hawai`i.

At the same time, in 2007, only 35 percent of the schools in the state have met Annual Yearly Progress, according to No Child Left Behind (NCLB) standards. The No Child Left Behind Act requires continual improvement of reading and math test scores, and schools across the nation are also having trouble meeting the controversial standards.

Furlough Fridays?

Few moves by the state have angered its citizen like Furlough Fridays. At a time when President Barack Obama was pushing for more time in the classroom, his home state created the nation's shortest school year, closing schools for 17 days in 2009 and 2010 for budget-cutting reasons. Hawai`i's 171,000 public schools students receive only 163 instructional days, compared with 180 in most districts in the U.S.

At this writing, Furlough Fridays faces several lawsuits; school days are expected to be restored. But Furlough Fridays indicate the power government holds in a one-school-district state...and how little Hawai`i's leaders care about its kids.

Hawai`i's many private and religious schools fare much better on the tests, but even the scores for religious schools declined dramatically from 2002 to 2003. Private school scores also fell, although they are still much above national averages.

A high turnover of both students and teachers in some areas adds to problems. At O`ahu schools near military bases as many as 70 percent of students come and go within a year, Knudsen says. That means a teacher must constantly be working to bring new students up to speed — and the rest of the class suffers.

Pay your child support, or else

Don't come to Hawai`i hoping to escape child support payments. Hawai`i is one of the toughest states in the nation when it comes to protecting children's support rights. The Child Support Enforcement Agency, a federal-state entity, can garnish wages, intercept tax refunds, report to credit bureaus, file liens against property or file a criminal complaint in court.

The statute also gives the state the authority to revoke or suspend drivers' licenses and recreation licenses of a person in arrears for at least three months.

David Scull / Honolulu Advertiser

Children skip up the steps to Maunaloa Elementary School on Moloka`i. An intensive reading and writing program helps students at the old plantation town overcome language and literacy problems. Students have several reading periods throughout the day and at least two chances to write; then each child takes a book home every night to read with parents.

One very big school district

The structure of Hawai`i's school district is sometimes blamed for its problems. Instead of each community having its own school board and financial responsibility for its school, there is one centralized school board on O`ahu with jurisdiction for the entire state. This is the only state in the nation with such an autonomous one-district system. The state government (and the concerned public) occasionally debates breaking jurisdiction into individual boards for each county or maintaining the present statewide system.

Public school or private school?

About 18 percent of Hawai`i students attend private schools which have very good reputations but are costly — from about $4,000 to $17,000 annually. Is it necessary for your child to attend a private school to get a good education in Hawai`i? Not absolutely. The quality of public school education varies greatly from school to school. And school assignments can be bolstered by additional attention from parents with homework and assignments, teachers advise.

O`ahu journalist Patrick Williams, 26, reflected on his experiences in both Hawai`i public and private schools. He attended Punahou School, considered one of Hawai`i's finest private high schools, on scholarship.

"I went to public school until seventh grade and then to Punahou. In public school, I was always the brightest kid in the class. School was a cruise, easy," Williams remembers. "But when I went to Punahou, I just bombed. I had to start all over. I had to learn to study, how to take notes, and I did. But that was the difference. A big difference."

Of the 135 private schools in Hawai`i, 44 percent are parochial. Here is a sampling of some of Hawai`i private schools and their costs.

School	District	Grade	Pupils	Tuition
Punahou School	Honolulu	K-12	3,771	$17,300
Iolani School	Honolulu	K-12	1,840	$15,600
Waldorf School	Honolulu	pre-12	325	$4,500–12,600
Holy Trinity School	Honolulu	K-8	105	$6,950
St. Andrews Priory	Honolulu	K-12	435	$12,910–13,610
Seabury Hall	Maui	6-12	370	$16,100
St. Anthony Jr./Sr. High	Maui	7-12	360	$9,200
Hawai`i Preparatory Academy	Big Island	9-12	570	$14,900–19,200
St. Joseph High	Big Island	7-12	350	$5,075–7,525
Island School	Kaua`i	K-9	333	$7,235–10,975
Kahili Adventist	Kaua`i	K-12	40	$5,270–6,260

Source: Honolulu Magazine, Private Schol Guide 2010, http://www.honolulumagazine.com/ Honolulu-Magazine/September-2009/Private-School-Guide-2010/

Ideally, the current centralized concept equalizes the schools. Teachers and funding are allotted per student, and are the same whether a student lives in highly populated Honolulu or rural Hana. Kindergarten through second grade is allotted one teacher for every 20 students; grades three and up have one teacher for every 27 students. (Actual classes in some areas are much smaller and some are larger with an aide helping out.)

Critics have pointed out that the state also centralizes much of its school decision-making and authority, adding layers of bureaucracy. They argue that financial decisions should be made closer to home, within the school community. Some studies indicate that school districts perform best when principals control their own budgets and are accountable for student achievement. The less centralized a school district is, the better student performance becomes. Or so the theory goes.

Despite its critics, Education Week magazine credits Hawai'i with having the most equitable system in the nation. The state school board consists of members elected from every county. They hold business meetings twice a year in every corner of the state, hearing concerns from parents and school administrators.

"When you have real economic downs, like Hamakua (a major sugar plantation on the Big Island) closing, the community is depressed, but the schools are not affected. The basic funding continues," the board of education's Knudsen points out.

A few charter schools

In recent years, many community-based charter schools have sprung up in the islands. Authorized by the Legislature in 1999, charter schools use public money and are part of the Department of Education, but operate largely independently of the state school administration.

Some charter schools have special goals. Hakipu'u Learning Center in Windward O'ahu, where more than 85 percent of the students are part Hawaiian, stresses self-sufficiency and trains students to "become stewards of the land." Students go to a taro farm, an ancient fishpond and the beach every week for lessons in ecology, culture and physical education. Students also take part in weekly interest groups such as surfing to learn about ocean swells, snorkeling to learn about fish and *limu* (seaweed) identification, and photography to learn about art. They must write about each project.

A very special school

You will hear a great deal about The Kamehameha Schools. The highly regarded schools came about through the will of, and continue to function through the estate of, royal family member Bernice Pauahi Bishop. The Kamehameha Schools gives preference to students with Hawaiian blood, and tuition is low or free. With one campus on O'ahu and one each on Maui and the Big Island, the schools serve approximately 4,800 students.

Attending Kamehameha Schools is considered a privilege, and controversy has arisen over its Hawaiians-only policy. But students at the Maui campus made a very positive impression on a Caucasian substitute teacher there.

Matthew Thayer

"I thought I'd died and gone to heaven!" she says. "The students were polite, responsive and wanted to learn. This is the way teaching was meant to be, but I had never encountered this before in my teaching career."

She had spent 12 years as a full-time public school teacher in Hawai'i.

Too many students; too few schools

Hawai'i schools are the largest in the nation in individual enrollment. Until 1998, when enrollment began to level off, the school system had increased by an average of 3,000 more students each year for several years. Currently, the number of students is holding steady. Still, a Department of Education school performance review found one-third of the state's 243 schools overcrowded. Forty percent lack library and office space. Many others are in need of repairs and some still are not air-conditioned.

Kamali`i Elementary, a school built in 1998 to relieve overcrowding in fast-growing Kihei, Maui, was packed by its second year. Enrollment surpassed planning estimates by over 130 children. Principal Sandra Shawhan was dealing with an overload of students who she said were "coming from everywhere" — from a nearby public school, the island's expensive private schools, the mainland and places as far away as Austria. She had to move two teachers, originally scheduled to teach special subjects like computers and music, to regular classroom duty. Two classes that boost children's interest in learning thus were eliminated.

Kamali`i was one of the state's first multi-track schools, functioning year-round with students on various nine-month schedules; other Hawai`i schools are following suit to alleviate crowding. About 60 percent of the state's schools are now on varying schedules, which seems to work well.

Non-English speaking students

Educators sometimes blame low verbal scores on students' wide variety of ethnic backgrounds.

"We still have a long way to go to improve student achievement," says Knudsen. "We have a large share of people who do not speak English as their first language, and pidgin English is a factor here."

A Department of Education report says the percentage of students needing special education of some sort, including instruction in speaking English, has doubled in the past two decades to about 8.7 percent of the school population. More than 30,000 of the state's 183,000 public-school children either are learning English or have recently graduated from English as a Second Language classes.

The percentage of students needing special education of some sort,including instruction in speaking English, has doubled in the past two decades to about 8.7 percent of the school population.

Hawai`i's immigrant and migrant students come mostly from Asia and the Pacific Islands, and speak a range of languages for which it is difficult to find qualified teachers. Most children come from the Philippines, Samoa and the Marshall Islands.

Adam's story: keep trying

Adam, a Caucasian newcomer, faced special problems when he entered public middle school on Maui a few years ago. He was blond, overweight and exceptionally intelligent, all perceived as negatives by some classmates at his new school. Adam was repeatedly teased and taunted by classmates. He was pushed, punched in the arms and his books were knocked away.

His parents, who had been teachers on the mainland, addressed the problem several times with school authorities.

"For the most part," says his mom, "they were polite, but did nothing to solve the problem."

Adam's father remembers a "local" teacher who asked, "What's the matter, *haole* boy? You can't take it?"

Eventually Adam got along better with his classmates, but his grades began to fall. One day Adam explained to his mother that he had learned to cope by not bringing attention to himself, by not being too smart.

Worrying that their son was wasting his intelligence, his parents helped him obtain a scholarship at a high-priced private school. His grades improved, but Adam said he felt out of place with such wealthy students.

Still concerned, his parents enrolled him at St Anthony's, a Catholic school in the very "local" town of Wailuku. There he thrived.

"The mix of students, part local, part *haole*, neither rich nor poor, and stressing good grades and ethics was just right," his mother says.

Adam eventually graduated with honors and won a scholarship at a military academy. Ironically, despite the problems he encountered, attending a school in Hawai`i became a plus for Adam, his father says.

"If he had gone to school in, say, New Jersey, with its high population and competition, Adam would probably not have the appointment (to the military academy). But in Hawai`i there was little competition."

Adam and his parents kept trying, until they solved the problem, and the ending was happy.

Teacher shortages

For generations, the state has needed qualified teachers. Many are imported from the mainland. In the first half of the 1900s, teachers were even given housing as incentive to move. However, the lure of the islands can fade quickly and many teachers return to the mainland, some within months of arriving here. (See Scott's story in the Moloka`i section of this book.)

Today, as Baby Boomer Generation teachers retire, the shortage worsens. The Department of Education hired 1,552 teachers for the 2001–2002 school year, a 71 percent increase in vacancies since 1996–1997. About 57 percent of new hires come from out of state. For the 2004–2005 school year, there were 357 teacher vacancies.

Teachers' wages are about average for the nation, enough to support a family in most mainland communities. But adjust that by 30 to 40 percent for the higher cost of living and the state's high taxes, and pay is the lowest in the country.

The average salary for a public school teacher here during the 2001 to 2002 school year was $44,306, up from $40,536 the year before. That ranks as the 17th highest in the nation. But when the cost of living is factored in, the figure shrinks by almost $13,000, to just over $30,000.

> **Teachers' wages are about average for the nation...But adjust that by 30 to 40 percent for the higher cost of living and the state's high taxes, and pay is the lowest in the country.**

Many teachers hold second jobs, reducing after-school time they could spend with students. In the past, disgruntled teachers have protested low wages by refusing to perform after-school extras such as advising clubs and supervising extra-curricular activities. In research for this book, we encountered several former teachers who had gone into more lucrative professions, such as real estate, the travel industry or insurance sales.

Teachers cite another factor for high turnover among new or recruited teachers: because all teachers in the state fall under one school system, teachers with seniority can "bump" new teachers to take jobs in the most desirable locations. Teaching jobs in busy O`ahu or less rural parts of Maui are deemed more desirable than those, for example, on very rural Moloka`i or Lana`i.

Too few books, supplies

Teachers who do remain on the job sometimes spend their own money to buy extras for students. Teachers are allotted a fixed amount of money each year for supplies and receive that money all at once. When it's depleted, some teachers go to weekend garage sales to find supplies like paint and craft items.

"I spent $2,000 of my own money one year," a teacher says. "I didn't realize it until I did my taxes."

At Roosevelt High School in O`ahu, science department chairwoman Jennifer Williams has 24 textbooks for 60 students in her sophomore biology classes, a *Honolulu Advertiser* story reported. Williams spends her own money to buy used biology texts that students can take home to study. And her shortage was not unique. An *Advertiser* survey showed that six out of 10 teachers, contacted at various schools, did not have enough textbooks to assign each student his own.

At Moanalua and La`ie elementary schools on O`ahu, parents conduct fundraisers to finance books for their children's education. A letter to the editor of a Honolulu newspaper points out that such efforts are laudable, but supplying books for students is the responsibility of the state. "The basic foundation for our education system is to provide the proper facilities, current textbooks and well-trained and motivated teachers... I am embarrassed that our state will not provide these services while our children, who are our future, suffer."

Racial and ethnic incidents

Racial or ethnic incidents occur at many Hawai`i schools, interviews for this book determined. They are not limited to public schools, nor are they limited to Caucasian students, although light-skinned pupils seemed to bear the brunt of harassment. The incidents range from young students being teased to teenagers in tougher neighborhoods being intimidated and threatened. (See Adam's story, this chapter.)

Most incidents go unrecorded, but a few make headlines. The State Department of Education agreed to pay $25,000 to a Maui intermediate school student. A suit, filed by the child's mother in 1995, claimed her son had been attacked by classmates numerous times, and charged that the school breached its duty to provide a reasonably safe and secure environment for the boy. As a direct result of the assaults, the child allegedly suffered injuries to his face, back, ribs and other parts of his body. The mother charged that the attacks were racially motivated in part because her son is Caucasian.

The school's principal disagreed on the cause of the attacks. "I don't dispute the attacks. But I don't believe it was racially motivated," she told the *Maui News.* Many Caucasian students attend this school and encounter no problems with ethnic groups.

'Saving face'

Another mother, one with two teenage children in public high schools, says ethnic differences make it difficult to solve youthful problems.

"Many of the parents who come from Pacific Islands have different rules for dealing with crisis, for dealing with problems, and it is not to talk it out or go to court. It's by yelling or threatening or fighting it out," she says.

"My son knows that saving face is very important in some of these cultures and he has learned to slide around it. He related one episode where he just said, 'Hey man, it's okay. I didn't mean to push you. It's just a game.' So by him backing down, the other kid was able to save face, which was very important for his cultural standing."

Hawai`i's rich ethnic mix can mean problems at some schools, school communications director Knudsen commented in 1998.

An editor comments...

An editor of this book, a college graduate student who grew up in Hawai`i, offered an unsolicited comment on ethnic problems.

"This section... is written as if *haole* (Caucasians) were the only folks moving to Hawai`i. It is my experience that Asian kids moving to Hawai`i blend right in. Indeed, the (Asian students) from North America often say that they feel more comfortable in Hawai`i than they did (in North America)," he writes.

"It is also my very own experience that many *haole*, including locally-born ones like me, can suffer more than just a few taunts. This is also not limited to public school. I went to `Iolani (a private elementary and high school on O`ahu) and was harassed daily and mercilessly for my first two years there."

Consider home schooling your child?

"Alternative" lifestyles are generally accepted in Hawai`i and, especially in rural areas, some parents choose to take responsibility for their children's education. Approximately two percent of Hawai`i families home school their children.

"The [home schooling] laws in Hawai`i are some of the best, and the Department of Education is very supportive of families" who choose to educate their children at home, Gail Nagasaki, formerly of the Home School Support Group, writes in her newsletter "Home School Adventures: Programs for Parents and Youngsters."

No special training or governmental approval is necessary, but parents must notify their local school principal and follow state procedures. The parent is responsible for the child's total educational program including athletics, and must keep a record of the planned curriculum. After grades 3, 6, 8 and 10, children are required to take standardized tests to assure they are progressing.

How does a parent go about teaching a child?

"It depends on your philosophy of learning," writes Nagasaki. "On one end of the spectrum are families who believe in a school-like approach, with a teacher or tutors, assignments, regular hours and such. On the other end of the spectrum are those who believe children can't help but learn and that life and play are their best teachers. Most of us start with some sort of formal curriculum and eventually evolve into our own programs."

Support groups on all major islands offer opportunities for children and parents to meet, network, share ideas and offer each other support and encouragement.

- **Contact your local school administration** office and ask for Form OIS-4140 or call the state school superintendent's Hotline on O`ahu at (808) 586-3587.
- **For more information on the Internet:**
  www.doe.k12.hi.us/myschool/homeschool.htm
  www.hawaiihomeschoolassociation.org

"I have one Caucasian family right now saying they want to transfer to another school because their child doesn't want to be the only *haole* in class. But we cannot transfer the student based on that. It's a race argument," Knudsen said.

"Some people come here with very low tolerance for anything different than where they came from. Others thrive on the diversity," he points out.

The discipline code

The state's 39-page discipline code spells out appropriate disciplinary action for major offenses; individual schools can have their own discipline code for dealing with minor infractions. The centralized school system actually allows more freedom for principals to handle individual problems, Knudsen maintains.

Some public school defenders point out that Hawai`i students are getting a lesson here they would not get on the mainland: studies in human relations. Students here benefit from playing and working with people from a variety of cultures. The world is becoming homogeneous as more countries are opened to international business, and island young people may be better equipped for life in the global community.

> 'Some people come here with very low tolerance for anything different than where they came from. Others thrive on the diversity.'
>
> – Greg Knudsen,
> school district spokesman

And an editor for this book asks a relevant question: What makes Hawai`i different from mainland schools, where gang activity is commonplace? Perhaps the problems here are, in the long run, no worse. Perhaps the problems here, in most schools, are fewer than at mainland schools.

What students say

Melissa McOmber, 17 when we interviewed her, grew up on the tiny island of Lana`i. She says she encountered some teasing as a Caucasian, some prejudice in school, but not much, probably because as such a longtime resident she was considered a part of the island society.

However, Melissa sees a change in student attitude today.

"Going to school and growing up is different here now then when we were younger. Everyone knew everyone; we were very close; until third grade we were all brother and sister. Then it started to get different.

"I baby-sit for a few *haole* blonde kids who get it worse than me because they were not born here. I think kids are much more vicious (about ethnic teasing) now. There's probably more resentment now (as more new people move into the islands)."

Another teenager, who prefers not to use his name for this story, came to the islands six years ago. He spent his first year at an intermediate school and his second year at high school. He says he saw no racial problems; just what he calls "ethnic differences."

"It's not like you're just walking down a hall and someone yells, 'White boy!' like that. People don't just yell, 'White boy' if they don't know you. It's more like if they know you. They don't have anything against the person… they are just joking around, trying to intimidate you."

Some schools celebrate their students' ethnic differences, which seems to diffuse problems. At Kahuku High School in windward O`ahu, where about 25 percent of the students are Caucasian, principal Lea Albert says most of her students benefit from the rich mix of cultures. Each year 3,000 to 5,000 people attend Kahuku's May Day celebration at the nearby Polynesian Cultural Center. Photos of Samoan, Tahitian, Tongan, American and Ukrainian students in full costume dance across a bulletin board in Albert's office.

Albert suggests parents instill an attitude in their children that "you're coming to learn and to benefit" from the array of cultures.

"There are many fine people in the world and in this school many parents want the multi-cultural experience for their children," she says. "That's the real world. If you want your child in a rarefied environment, well… that's not what Hawai`i is about. It's a multi-cultural society where we learn from one another."

Drugs and alcohol

In recent years, a great challenge has arisen for police, social workers, teachers — and anyone who cares about children. Highly addictive crystal methamphetamine (ice) has affected many families. Hawai`i leads the nation in the percentage of arrested men who test positive for ice. In 2002, ice overtook alcohol as the primary substance abused by adults admitted to island treatment centers. Parents addicted to the drug force their families to live a nightmare and may abuse their children financially, physically and emotionally.

Although the incidence of school children using ice is relatively low, the easy availability of pot and other drugs here is a special threat. Researchers say the switch from smoking pot to smoking ice is natural, because both have the same physical effects. But ice has a more powerful high.

One teacher compares drug availability in Hawai`i schools today to when she attended a California school in the 1960s. "The availability is the same," she says, "but drug use is starting much younger. Eighth graders are doing what we did in high school. But it's not just Hawai`i, it's a change of the times. From what I hear from new parents coming into the school district, the risk of gangs and drugs is higher there (on the mainland) than here."

The A-plus after-school program

Through a special program called "A-Plus," Hawaiian public schools baby-sit about 21,000 children of working parents after regular school hours. The children are kindergarten age through sixth grade.

Hawai`i was the first school district in the nation to have such a program, started in 1990 when the state had a revenue surplus. A-Plus costs $20 million a year to operate. Only $5 million comes from the $55-a-month fee paid by parents. Fees are reduced for children from low-income families. But one parent criticizes the need for such a program.

"They have the A-Plus program for latchkey kids and it's 'Wow! Look what we are doing for you.' But if we weren't so heavily taxed by the government, if we didn't need two-income families to survive, we wouldn't have latchkey kids," he says. "It's like they stabbed you in the artery and gave you a bandage. And we're suppose to say 'Thank you very much for the A-Plus program!'"

His comments do not take into account that two-income families have become the norm on the mainland and in many parts of the world. A single mother defends the program: "For single parent families, which there is a growing number of these days, the A-Plus program is a godsend. How can one parent come home at three in the afternoon to care for a child after school? Even if you are lucky enough to work one job you still probably work until five. What are you going to do?"

Tips for adjusting to your new school

For Parents:

- **Choose your school or community before you choose your home.** Some schools have few problems; others have many. "You hear, 'I just chose the house with the Monier tile roof, the sunken living room'," an O'ahu psychologist says, "when you should be hearing 'I chose (a home near) a good school for my kid'."

- **Visit several schools.** Ask for a copy of the state discipline code and the individual school's discipline code. Ask how that code is enforced. Talk to teachers and principals. How do school authorities handle drugs, fights, swearing and insubordination?

- **Ask for a list of incidents reported in the past year.** How often were police called and for what reasons? If you are not satisfied with the answers, consider searching for a home in an area with fewer problems.

- **Ask for help.** Ask the school counselor or registrar for any additional information or suggestions that may make your child's transition to a new school easier. Their responses will be helpful and may also be a measure of their concern and expertise.

- **Attend parent organization meetings**, if possible, both before your child enrolls and after. Is there a parent advisory system set up to help operate the school?

- **Suggest your child take part in sports and community youth programs.** Most communities offer football, basketball, softball, volleyball, track, tennis, wrestling, surfing, soccer and canoeing. Some sports do not require much skill or equipment. If you move in summer, don't wait until school starts. Visit your neighborhood youth center soon so your child can get acquainted with some fellow students.

- **Prepare your child for cultural encounters.** Explain that Hawai'i includes many cultures and your child may now be a minority. Tell your child he may be harassed or bullied. If he is, ask him to let you know and also to tell a teacher or counselor at school.

from parents, students and teachers

- **Be at home when your child returns from school**, at least during his first few days at a new school. Relax and talk about the child's experiences. If you cannot be there, try to have an older sibling, friend or relative at home to greet your child.

- **If your child has persistent problems**, see a school counselor immediately. Schools can't fix problems they don't know about, a teacher points out.

For Students:

- **Changing school is both a challenge and an opportunity** to start fresh. Consider what went right for you at your past school and repeat this. What went wrong? Avoid those actions.

- **Keep quiet and observe during the first few days or weeks** at your new school. Most of Hawai`i's kids and many cultures present in Hawai`i don't like show-offs. Kids who act up are especially looked down upon.

- **Stay cool. Don't overreact.** Remember phrases like "white boy" or "haole" are not necessarily name-calling, but communication from a culture that is different from your own.

- **Avoid asking silly or obvious questions or comments.** Questions like "Wow, do you people eat raw fish?" may sound friendly to you, but may seem intrusive to other students.

- **Avoid fights. Period.** The cultural differences here make fighting dangerous. In some cultures, parents will back up their children and encourage them to fight. The truly strong person is sure of himself and does not have to prove his power. He walks away from conflict.

For more details on Hawai`i schools, tests and services, including how individual schools rank, visit www.doe.k12.hi.us/standards on the Internet.

Higher education

Often, Hawai`i families who can afford it send their children to the mainland for a college or advanced education — and for good reason: the islands can be provincial. The fortunate student who attends mainland colleges and returns to Hawai`i brings a valuable perspective which will serve her or him well.

Although Hawai`i's economy has been improving in the past few years and there are some statistics indicating the trend is changing, about 18 percent of Hawai`i's higher education students attend college on the mainland, and an estimated 75 percent of them do not return to the state. In addition, many students who attend college here move away, lured by the greater availability of jobs, better paying professional positions, and lower living costs. Neither colleges nor high schools track students closely after they leave, so no one knows exactly how many students forsake their island homes forever.

That's not to say the 82 percent of Hawai`i college students who go to college here do not receive a very decent education. Most attend the University of Hawai`i, which serves every populated island through local or on-site programs and satellite hookups. Programs are designed to match island needs: oceanography, linguistics, food services, astronomy, Pacific and Asian studies and travel industry management, as well as more traditional courses.

The University of Hawaii and its ten community campuses serve over 50,000 students. Its $470 million budget (20 percent above the national average and about 10 percent of the total state budget) faced about $155 million in budget cuts in 2010 and 2011 due to the down economy.

In past years, UH has rated low on some college surveys, but seems to be moving up. U.S. News and World Report in 2004 ranked the UH schools of education, business administration, law and social work as 73rd in the top 100 programs in the country. And research grants have increased from about $16 million in 2000 to $25 million in 2004.

Hawai`i students also have a choice of three private O`ahu colleges and universities: Chaminade, Brigham Young and Hawai`i Pacific, as well as several specialized institutes and colleges.

The University of Hawai`i

The University of Hawai`i, with nearly 60,000 students at its 10 campuses, has many points in its favor:

- **Tuition and fees.** Tuition for Hawai'i residents goes to $4200 in 2011. Non-residents will pay $11,606.

- **Programs varied.** The main campus at Manoa on O`ahu has strong master's and doctorate programs, in addition to a very broad under-graduate program.

- **Prestigious research.** Hawai`i's unique geography — Mauna Kea mountain on the Big Island, the Pacific Ocean, the tropical climate — makes UH a natural for research. Its research program is among the top 70 university programs in the nation, according to the Carnegie Foundation for the Advancement of Teaching. And the university's mid-Pacific location makes it perfect for a strong Asian-Pacific business program at a time when that part of the world is emerging economically.

- **'Acceptable plus.'** The graduate school received an "acceptable plus" rating from the Gourman Report, which cites UH's programs in agricultural economics, anthropology and botany.

Still, UH has a relatively poor reputation. A 2003 survey found students dissatisfied with everything from the lack of parking to a new computer enrollment system, to old dorms and a lack of quiet, late-night study areas. Test scores are low compared to national university averages, and many faculty members choose to send their own children to the mainland for a higher education.

The Fiske Guide to Colleges says of UH, "Overall, the academic atmosphere is very laid back" and quotes an education major: "Everyone more or less does his or her own thing and tries to just get by with decent grades."

In *The Price of Paradise*, published in 1992, UH professor of economics Sumner J. LaCroix offers several reasons for the university's poor image. He pointed out that 90 percent of UH students hold jobs, compared to about 63 percent at mainland universities. That means UH students have little time for study and for the campus activities that add dimension to the college experience.

Fewer than 20 percent of students live in campus housing and so must waste valuable study and social time traveling to and from the university. The few campus housing facilities that exist often go to students from the mainland or other countries.

In an interview for this book, LaCroix said Hawai`i students differ from mainland students in that they don't want to graduate from college with a debt.

"So they work in addition to school and many work not 20 hours, as you would expect, but 30 to 35 hours per week. Almost full-time," he says. "I think they are afraid that after-college debt will force them to the mainland [to live]. And there is also a cultural aversion to debt here."

"I wish," LaCroix says, "they would borrow and enjoy their college years. They'd get more from their college years ultimately."

LaCroix argues, fairly, that students who apply themselves and do research before choosing classes can, and do, get a solid education at the University of Hawai`i.

Use the phone or Internet to find out more about:

- **The Department of Education, O`ahu**
  www.doe.k12.hi.us

- **Hawai`i Department of Education**
  (808) 586-3230
  Superintendent's hotline
  (808) 586-3587

- **View test score reports for individual school:**
  www.doe.k12.hi.us/myschool/
  sat-hcps-terranova.htm

- **The A-Plus after-school program**
  www.doe.k12.hi.us

- **Hawai`i State Teachers Association**
  www.hsta.org
  (808) 833-2711

- **Non-teacher employment**
  (808) 586-3422

- **Hawai`i State Parent Teacher Association**
  www.hsta.org
  (808) 834-7872

- **Teacher employment information**
  (808) 586-3420

- **Hawai`i Public Charter Schools**
  www.hcsao.org/hicharters/profiles
  (808) 586-3570

- **Kahuku School on O`ahu:**
  www.k12.hi.us/~kahukuhs

retirement

"It is important for us

to utilize our *kupuna mana`o*

(the wisdom of our elders)

because after they're gone,

who will teach us?"[1]

—Richard Kalolo`okalani Keaulana

Courtesy of Josephine Falk

Josephine Falk, O`ahu, at age 70

"On the mainland, in many places, I think the elderly are made to feel like a nuisance. Here, it is a custom, because of the Oriental and Hawaiian cultures, to appreciate and respect old people. And it carries over to how everyone treats you. You feel it."

—Josephine Falk, 86, O`ahu

A change of life

Josephine Falk was 66 when she came to O`ahu to visit her daughter. It was Josephine's first visit to the islands. She disembarked at the Honolulu airport, savored the warm fragrant breezes, smiled up at the sunshine and promptly called other relatives in snowy Pennsylvania.

"Rent out my apartment," she said. "I'm never coming back."

Many tourists fall in love with the islands and decide to stay, but Josephine faced a stiffer challenge than most. She had been a cleaning lady and babysitter all her life, so she had no pension with which to support herself — only her Social Security check of a few hundred dollars a month.

For a few weeks, she lived with her daughter's family in Kailua, a half-hour drive from Honolulu. She learned all she could about life in the islands by reading and talking with residents, and she found that Hawai`i is one of the kindest states in the nation to retirees. People who retire here collect all standard federal benefits, such as Medicaid and Social Security, and the state offers other incentives for seniors. All employer and government pensions and Social Security income is tax-exempt. (Hawai`i is one of only three states that exempt such monies. But a state statistician warns that those exemptions do not include private pension plans such as 401K and deferred compensation plans.)

Honolulu, the state's largest city, is ideal for healthy retirees — convenient, clean and, in most areas, relatively crime-free. And there's plenty of activity for those who enjoy beaches, free entertainment at hotels and shopping centers, and pleasant places to just sit and watch the crowds go by.

> **Josephine was 66, alone, and had only her Social Security for support when she "retired" to Honolulu.**

In Hawai`i, statistics show, people on an average live four years longer than on the mainland, and the warm weather eased Josephine's arthritic pain, enabling her to enjoy a more active life.

Another boon to seniors is TheBus, Honolulu's efficient public transportation system, which makes it easy for elderly residents to relinquish their drivers' licenses and still stay mobile, traveling all over the island to social events and free meals at senior citizen centers. Seniors enjoy drastically reduced bus fares.

More important, though less tangible, says Josephine, is the gentle aloha spirit and respect for the elderly so evident in Hawai`i.

"On the mainland, in many places, I think the elderly are made to feel like a nuisance. Here, it is a custom, because of the Asian and Hawaiian cultures, to appreciate and respect old people. And it carries over to how everyone treats you. You feel it," she says.

Another difference: "You are younger in Hawai`i," Josephine says. In her hometown, she was considered elderly. "In Hawai`i, 66 is just middle-aged. Many people work until they are in their mid-seventies or older."

Josephine hoped for a job in one of Waikiki's many gift shops, where today employees earn as much as $20 an hour plus commissions. But shop owners prefer employees who can speak at least a little Japanese. Josephine had extensive child care experience, so she answered a newspaper ad for a nanny and was quickly hired to care for the two sons of a Chinese couple in a fashionable section of Honolulu. At the same time, she took lessons in Japanese language.

"In Hawai`i, 66 is just middle age. Many people work until they are in their middle seventies or older."

Next, she went apartment hunting, answering more than twenty ads before finding a first floor apartment within her budget near Waikiki's Ala Wai Canal. The mainland owner wanted a tenant who would keep the apartment clean and safe, so the rent was a bargain. At $400 a month (in 1978), it covered only her landlord's maintenance fees and utility costs. (Comparable apartments in Waikiki cost about $1200 to $1400 today.) In effect, she was "house-sitting," a common way for responsible people to reduce housing costs. Wealthy people from all over the world buy homes and condominiums in Hawai`i as part-time residences or as investments. Thefts and break-ins are common, so absentee owners occasionally offer reduced or free accommodations to trustworthy people who guard and maintain their residences. Such situations are very difficult to find, however, and more often go to people already established in the islands.

Meanwhile, Josephine put her name on a three-year waiting list for a federally-subsidized apartment in one of several O`ahu senior citizen complexes.

Her daughter soon moved back to the mainland, but Josephine remained in Honolulu. Though alone, she was happy. She made friends. She walked a few blocks to the beach each day after work. On her days off, she took long bus rides, exploring the island.

"Oh, I missed my family," she says. "But I could call them. Or take out the albums with the family pictures and reminisce. And they visited often."

In addition to studying Japanese, she took lessons in Hawaiian culture and hula, offered free to senior citizens. By the time the children she was caring for outgrew her, Josephine has learned enough Japanese to secure a job in a Waikiki gift shop. She began dating the uncle of the gift shop's owner. She was over 70 and still working full-time, but she is quick to say, "Enjoying it too. I like meeting people from all over the world."

Eventually an apartment became available in a new, federally subsidized complex for the elderly. Airy, with a large living room/ kitchen combination, bedroom and ample storage, it was close to markets and malls.

In her mid-70s, Josephine stopped working at the gift shop, and for several years, took part in a federally-funded "grandparent" program at a school for handicapped children. She continued in that role until she was 81.

Toni Polancy

A resident peers down from the eighth floor of a building at the Makua Ali`i Senior Center, a subsidized housing complex in Honolulu. Near the Ala Moana Shopping Center, the convention center and grocery stores, Makua Ali`i is in an area of Honolulu with a high elderly population.

Today Josephine Falk spends her days in a wheel chair at Hale Makua, Maui's community nursing home. A sign behind indicates birthdays for the month, a rainbow of cultures.

At 86, she lamented not having a job. She continued to ride TheBus daily, striking up conversations with travelers from all over the world. She swam often at Kuhio or Ala Moana beaches.

"I know if I lived elsewhere, especially where it's cold, I would be bedridden or confined indoors during the winter," she said at the time. "Here, each morning I wake up to sunshine and I can't wait to get out and enjoy the day."

She had, she felt, adequate medical care in Hawai`i, at least as good as she would have had in Pennsylvania, and when she retired she began taking advantage of subsidized house-cleaning help and van services. Like most elderly people, Josephine wanted to be self-sufficient, living in her own apartment as long as she could. Apartment complex managers assessed her physical and mental capabilities each year, and Josephine always worried that they would someday decree that she must leave her apartment. That did not happen.

One morning, when Josephine was 89 years old, a friend found her lying on the bathroom floor of her apartment, unable to get up and calling weakly for help. She was taken to Queens Medical Center in Honolulu, as efficient a hospital as might be found anywhere in the United States. After several weeks at Queens and at a Honolulu nursing home, Josephine was transferred at her request, to Maui, where a daughter had moved a few years earlier.

Josephine has been at Hale Makua, Maui's community nursing home, for two years, and her condition continues to worsen. She is often confused, and asks about members of her family back in Pennsylvania, sisters and brothers long dead, children and grandchildren whose faces she cannot remember. Like Hawai`i, the nursing home is a mix of cultures and languages which easily confuse elderly residents, but aides are gentle and patient.

Would Josephine be better off in her hometown? Her family asks that occasionally, as they email each other from across the world. The answer, they decide, is no. In Pennsylvania she would be confined indoors. Some of the nursing homes there smell of urine. And who is left anyway? All 12 of her siblings are dead.

These days Josephine uses her good leg to push her wheelchair out to the nursing home's garden and tries both to remember and to forget. To forget that she is old; to remember the things that brought joy to her life. She studies the mist lifting off the West Maui Mountains, watches a plumeria blossom drift from its branch. She smiles as volunteers conduct a *bon* dance, as a visiting preacher strums his ukulele.

She will tell you, if you ask her, that she is lucky to live Hawai`i.

Caring for our kupuna

Hawai`i has a long and proud history of caring for its *kupuna*, its elderly. The word *kupuna* means ancestor, but also carries a gentle essence of wise, beloved.

As on the mainland, the trend here is to help seniors live on their own for as long as possible. On most islands, seniors who need it have access to free or very low-cost assistance with housekeeping; daily meals delivered to their door by programs such as Meals on Wheels; community meals served daily in at least one senior center on each island, and at several sites on O`ahu; van service to doctor appointments, grocery stores, and to the many senior centers for recreation and socializing.

Living in Honolulu is convenient for seniors, and they may be able to live there independently longer than on neighbor islands where there is little or no mass transportation and health care is limited. But the state faces a tremendous challenge now and in the next ten years. Hawai`i has a larger percentage of elderly residents than any other state, and by 2020 one in four residents will be 60 or older, the state Executive Office on Aging projects. One resident in six is that old now.

Traditionally, Hawaiian and Asian `ohana (family) care for their *kupuna*, usually in the family home. In 1997, only about two percent of Hawai`i's 65-plus population lived in long-term care facilities.

But economics and customs are changing. Today, nearly 70 percent of Hawai`i's women, the customary caregivers, work outside the home. And some of Hawai`i's elderly are the hippies, surfers and other newcomers who flocked to the islands in the 1960s, 70s, and 80s. They may have no one here to help care for them. Society and the government are providing more of the services once supplied by relatives.

> By 2020, one in four Hawai`i residents, some of them the hippies and surfers who flocked to the islands in the 1960s and 1970s, will be age 60 or older. 'We have a tsunami about ready to hit and we're not ready for it.'
>
> –John McDermott, ombudsman
> Executive Office on Aging

Plenty of *assisted* living

Within the past few years, the numbers of "assisted living" facilities, for elderly people who need only minimal help with day-to-day tasks have multiplied. Like other housing in the islands, they tend to range from very basic to very posh.

But the real challenge comes in caring for elderly who require more assistance, who need regular nursing or extensive help with day-to-day life. In some respects, the very poor elderly, like Josephine Falk in this story, are more fortunate than middle-income seniors, who can quickly lose their homes and savings to pay for nursing costs, no matter where they live.

Most of the assisted-living projects are in highly-populated O`ahu: an $88 million high-rise in Waikiki, a $183 million continuing life-care project in pricey Kahala, a $22 million senior retirement community near Punchbowl, a low-rise assisted living project in Kapolei and the 162-unit assisted-living complex, Kulana Hale II, near Beretania and Kalakaua streets, where several other elderly complexes are located. With its $28 million cost guaranteed by the U.S. Department of Housing and Urban Development, 40 percent of Kulana Hale's units will be reserved for low-income residents whose annual income doesn't exceed about $22,000.

The cost; the conflict

Nursing home costs in Hawaii are 44 percent higher than the national average. At this writing private room at a nursing home costs $306 a day in Hawai`i, compared to the national average of $212 a day.

Alaska had the highest daily average at $577. Louisiana had the lowest at $127 a day, a 2008 MetLife survey of nursing home and assisted living costs found. The cost of aging is among the highest in the nation in Hawai`i.

A private room in a nursing home here costs an average $271 a day. The cost of assisted-living services averages $3,753 a month, according to a 2007 survey by MetLife.

Concerned legislators have attempted to alleviate the problem, considering bills that would create a state-sponsored long-term care benefits program and provide a tax credit to those who buy private long-term care insurance.

But in some cases the payout amounts from these plans would hardly make a dent in the rising cost of long-term healthcare for an extended illness. And some insurance plans are confusing and full of loopholes.

> "Our nursing homes are basically full. Some people think, 'I have a cushion; I have money.' But there are no beds available."
>
> –John McDermott, ombudsman
> Executive Office on Aging

Josephine Falk, in the preceding story, is also fortunate that she has grown old ahead of the pack, before the hundreds of thousands of "baby boomers." Already the lack of nursing homes is affecting the rich and poor alike. Throughout the islands, people wait in hospitals for nursing home vacancies.

"Our nursing homes are basically full," says John McDermott, ombudsman for the Executive Office on Aging. " Some people think, 'I have a cushion; I have money.' But there are no beds available."

Kupuna Care, a state program, was designed to help elderly people stay at home as long as possible by supplying in-home care and assistance. But its programs are full and there is a waiting list.

The number of elderly is increasing across the nation, but Hawai`i has an additional problem, McDermott says. Many of our young people, potential healthcare professionals, move to the mainland where they can get better-paying jobs. That means fewer physical therapists, nurses' aides and social service workers to care for the growing number of elderly here.

"We have a tsunami about ready to hit and we're not ready for it," McDermott says.

Boarding homes

When the elderly become infirm and can no longer care for themselves, they are at the mercy of health insurance and the services it will provide, says a physical therapist who works with the elderly. In the islands, where large nursing homes are scarce, a person needing extensive care may have to live in a household run by an ethnic family other than his own. For

---

Retiring to Hawai`i?

Do this first:

Ask yourself a few questions before you finalize your plans to retire to Hawai`i. Or, if you have a spouse, talk about these topics before you make your decision.

- If you are part of a couple, do you both really want to come?

- Do you expect to live here forever, or just for a few years?

- If you plan to stay, what provisions can you make here for later years, when you are no longer able to care for yourself?

- Would it be wiser to live here a few months of the year and closer to your family or friends for the rest of the time?

- Visit a senior citizen center and/or an assisted living center near the area where you hope to live. Can you picture yourself living in this environment?

➤ **TIP:** Services vary greatly from island to island.
   For more information:

   Big Island: **(808) 961-8600** or www.hcoahawaii.org

   Kaua'i: (808) 241-4470 or www.kauai.gov

   Maui, Moloka'i and Lana'i: (808) 270-7774 or
   www.co.maui.hi.us/departments/housing/aging.htm

example, many Filipino and some Asian families accept boarders. However, the cultural and dietary differences can be a shock for seniors, the physical therapist said, making them feel even more alone and isolated.

Residing in a private home can be a loving, pleasant experience for some. Or it can be a nightmare. Adult Protective Services investigated 381 cases of abuse in one recent year and 157 were confirmed. Hawai`i has no law requiring criminal background checks for people who work in care homes. It is one of 14 states that doesn't.

Despite years of opposition from care home operators, state laws approved in 2003 began permitting unannounced inspections of licensed care homes. The first year of inspections found few serious problems, according to the Office of Health Care Assurance, which oversees Hawai`i's 545 adult residential care homes.

Go home?

Many transplanted elderly opt to return to their hometowns before advanced age sets in.

"Once you get to the point where you hardly leave your apartment, you might as well be in inexpensive Duluth (Minnesota) or Sun City (Arizona) or someplace in Florida," says one caregiver. "And (if your family lives on the mainland) it sure will be a lot easier for your family to visit and help out."

OBTAIN MORE INFORMATION:

- **The Senior Information and Assistance Handbook**
PuSend for a copy of the Senior Information and Assistance Handbook published by the City and County of Honolulu's elderly affairs division. This booklet includes a very complete list of services and resources.

For a copy, write:

Elderly Affairs Division
715 S. King Street #500
Honolulu, HI 96813

or go to

www.elderlyaffairs.com

The website will also lead you to a variety of helpful information.

Death with dignity?

Some very ill elderly say they would like to have the choice to end their lives. Hawai`i, typically a liberal state, has long been debating the pros and cons of physician-assisted suicide, or "death with dignity."

"We've gathered reams of research on all its legal, medical and moral ramifications," says Yasmin Anwar, an editorial writer for the *Honolulu Advertiser*. "But with both sides as polarized as abortion foes and supporters, we don't expect this issue to be resolved any time soon, let alone become a law."

Another twist: moving parents here

Another scenario comes into play in Hawai`i. Since 1970, the state has experienced a 60 percent increase in population. Many of those who moved here are middle-aged now, heading for retirement themselves, and back on the mainland, their parents are becoming old and need the care and security of adult children nearby.

"We get many, many calls from family members thinking of moving mom out here," says Mildred Ramsey, former director of gerontology, Child and Family Services for Hawai`i. "It is very traumatic to bring them out here and expect them to make such adjustments. They have been living, maybe most of their lives, in familiar territory, maybe with old friends. Their activity level is set."

And, of course, many people dream of retiring someday to Hawai`i. They make that a lifelong goal. If you've dreamed of living in Hawai`i, hoped for it for much of your life, don't you owe it to yourself to come?

A real estate broker, herself elderly, comments: "I see it often. People retiring and trying to live a dream. And that's all right if they come here when they are young enough to be active and enjoy life here. But so often, a couple gives up everything to come, and then one of them gets sick and they are far away from family and friends."

"It can be very sad," Child and Family Services' Ramsey comments. "Some seniors retire here. Sell their home on the mainland. Ship all their furniture, put all their money into a new home or high rent. Then they want to return (to their hometown) and it's so expensive, their retirement savings are used up."

CALL AARP

There's a branch of the American Association of Retired Persons on each major island.

Area code (808)

Big Island	334-1212
Kaua`i	246-4500
O`ahu	843-1906
Maui	661-0159

Hawai`i State Archives

Once, Hawai`i residents lived shorter lives than residents on the mainland U.S., possibly because so many here worked at tough jobs, in hot weather, on plantations. By 1950, existence grew somewhat easier for everyone and life spans were about equal. Today, Hawai`i residents can expect to live several years longer than their mainland counterparts. That may be because the warm weather lets us stay active longer.

Life Expectancy
[Average expectation of life in years]

Year	United States Both sexes	Male	Female	Hawai`i Both sexes	Male	Female
1910	50.0	48.4	51.8	43.96	44.04	43.83
1950	68.2	65.6	71.1	69.53	67.77	71.67
1970	70.8	67.1	74.7	74.20	72.12	76.44
2000	76.9	74.1	79.5	(NA)	(NA)	(NA)
2004	77.8	75.2	80.4	80.8*	78.2*	83.3*
2007	77.9	75.3	80.4	(NA)	(NA)	(NA)

NA Not available.
Source: U.S. Department of Health and Human Services, National Center for Health Statistics.
*Source: Hawaii State Department of Business, Economic Development & Tourism, Population and Economic Projections for the State of Hawaii to 2035 - DBEDT 2035 Series

8 good reasons to retire to Hawai`i

1. **Longer life span.** On the average, statistics say you may have four more years of life here than on the mainland. And you may be thinner and more active. Hawai`i has the fewest overweight people in the nation.

2. **Tax exemptions.** Hawai`i is one of only two states that exempts all pension and Social Security income from state income taxes.

3. **Low property taxes.** Hawai`i senior homeowners also enjoy exemptions on the state's already low property taxes.

4. **Stimulating friends and activities.** Hawai`i retirees include some of the world's brightest and most successful people. Talented retirees and visitors often share their gifts through classes in writing, painting, dance, languages.

5. **Warm weather, better health.** Hawai`i's warm weather is kind to some ailments associated with aging, such as arthritis. Temperatures hover in the mid-70s to mid-80s on most parts of the islands during the day. They rarely fall below 65 on the shorelines, even at night.

6. **High respect for elderly.** Respect for elderly tends to be high in Hawai`i, thanks to the strong influence of Hawaiian and Asian cultures.

7. **Mobility.** People age 65 and older can ride TheBus all over O`ahu at a discounted cost. That could mean you'll stay mobile and active longer.

8. **Plenty to do.** Bountiful beaches, golf courses, parks, senior centers —and senior citizen discounts on many activities.

8 good reasons NOT to retire to Hawai`i

1. **Loneliness.** Once the thrill of living in paradise wears off, it's possible you'll miss your family and old friends more than you imagined.

2. **Helplessness.** You may become ill far from family, perhaps before you've had time to make reliable friends.

3. **Housing.** Inexpensive elderly housing and assisted living is difficult to find. Assisted-living arrangements exist in Honolulu, but they are very costly at this time. It can take two years or more to secure government subsidized housing on some islands.

4. **Distance.** Ideally, your annual budget should include a few thousand dollars each year for travel, to reinforce ties with family and friends and to help children and grandchildren visit you.

5. **Costs.** Food and medical costs are high and include a four percent state excise tax.

6. **Poor public transportation.** On the neighbor islands, public transportation is almost nonexistent. Seniors who relinquish their driver's licenses must depend on cabs, van service, or friends and relatives to transport them.

7. **Lack of care homes.** On some islands, boarding homes for the elderly tend to be operated according to ethnic backgrounds. If it became necessary, could you adjust to living in a household with customs and diets different from your own?

8. **Limited medical care.** Seriously ill patients must be airlifted to Honolulu for some sophisticated procedures.

Assisted living and/or continuing care

Most retirement complexes offer services such as two or three meals a day, transportation, housekeeping, dining rooms, lounges, activities and events, paid utilities (except phone) and basic cable, resident managers and emergency alarms. Some also have extended-care facilities so residents can remain "at home" if they become ill. Costs, rules and ambiance vary greatly. A major difference: in some complexes, buy-in fees are returned if the resident leaves; in others they may not be.

An advocate for the elderly warns that complexes that offer "continuing care" may not really be equipped to handle a person who needs a nursing home. She suggests you visit all areas of the complex, interview people who already live there, and ask an attorney to review any contract carefully.

A resident and the complex's mascot enjoy the scenery at Pohai Nani Good Samaritan Kauhale, a retirement village in Kane`ohe, O`ahu.

chapter 11

pili

ho oipoipo

romance

Adam and Eve
started it all
in a place
called paradise

About 20,000 people marry in Hawai`i every year; that's 55 a day. Just about one half of them are visitors who come to the islands for its beautiful backdrops — an ocean sunset or Kaua`i's famous Fern Grotto. The rest are kama`aina, often celebrating their new life in ways unique to these islands.

Mabuhay! Emily and Rufino are wed

One by one four men rose from long tables that filled the Lahaina Community Center, raised glasses of champagne and saluted newlyweds Emily Maniago and Rufino Villanueva:

"Mabuhay!" "Okole maluna!" "Banzai!" "Cheers!"

The 800 guests at the Villanueva wedding toasted the second generation Filipino couple according to modern Hawai`i tradition — in Filipino, Hawaiian, Japanese and English — representing the islands' ethnic diversity.

According to Filipino custom, several "sponsors" helped plan and finance the huge event. Chosen by the couple's parents, sponsors are longtime family friends whose role includes premarital counseling and advice to the young couple.

Emily's religious heritage is Jehovah Witness; Rufino's Roman Catholic. At their wedding in the garden of an ocean-front resort, Rev. Piula Alailima of Polynesian heritage performed a non-denominational ceremony. Alailima is minister at Lahaina United Methodist Church.

Photo courtesy of family and Beach's House of Photography

Loreto, one of Rufino's six siblings, prepared food for the reception that lasted five hours. It included traditional Hawaiian *lu`au* food like *kalua* pig and *haupia*, a coconut pudding.

Family and friends contributed hours of entertainment to the wedding reception. Emily's brother Jerry performed a traditional Tongan slap dance, his friend a Polynesian fire dance. Emily's nephew Frederick Maniago, from Moloka`i, sang a solemn Hawaiian chant. Emily's three sisters Anna and Lorna Maniago and Brenda MacPhetridge performed a *hula*.

According to Hawaiian tradition, the new husband sits in a chair as the new wife dances a wedding *hula* in front of him. The Villanueva reception put a new twist on that: Leilani, a family friend, performed the wedding *hula* in front of guests.

Altogether Emily and Rufino's wedding and reception blended at least six cultures. And formed a culture of its own: Hawai`i *hou*. New Hawaiian.

Dating, mating, wedding, wanting

In the early 1900s, when male workers by the hundreds were imported to labor in Hawai`i's burgeoning sugar industry, there were 223.3 men on the islands for every 100 women. Women were so scarce that "picture brides," chosen by their husbands from photographs or through matchmaking relatives, were imported from the Philippines, Japan and other countries.

Today, the ratio has closed, and the number of men and women in the islands is about equal.

Today, it's apt to be the romance of paradise, not work or the necessity of mating that draws people here. For many young, single people Hawai`i is an adventure, a time to wait tables, surf and soak up sun before moving back to Minnesota, marriage and a desk job. For others, perhaps recently divorced, it is a place for fresh starts and new relationships.

> "You're white and you want that brown-skinned man. Or a man wants an Asian wife."
>
> —Jennifer Terrance, Compudate

Couples also come for romantic reasons: newlyweds starting a new life together, older-weds hoping to rekindle romantic sparks under the tropical sun or simply fulfilling a longtime dream in paradise.

Will those coming here for romantic reasons find what they are looking for?

Dating tourists

For anyone seeking short-term relationship, Hawai`i is a dream come true. The high number of tourists (about 150,000 are in the islands at any one time) means a constant influx of new people from around the world. Longtime bachelor Tom Guthrie, happily married now, remembers a roommate who was "popular with the ladies."

"I never knew whose slippers were on the doorstep," he says. "It depends on how guys want to play it here. If they just want to get laid there are planeloads of *wahine* (women) arriving every day. Some guys would hang out at the airport to catch them as they got off the planes. They'd have their surfboards on the car and just ask, 'Hey, you want to go to Hana?'"

Marital Status, by Sex

Marital status	1990		2000	
	Male	Female	Male	Female
Total, 15 years and over	441,420	428,783	481,768	484,107
Never married	152,188	106,715	166,715	125,609
Now married, except separated	241,961	237,260	258,532	254,359
Separated	6,425	7,539	6,837	8,468
Widowed	9,053	38,530	10,728	47,439
Divorced	31,793	38,739	38,956	48,232

Source: U.S. Bureau of the Census.

Marital status data for 1990 were from the 100-percent data while the marital status data for 2000 were from the sample data.

The State of Hawai`i Data Book 2004 http://www2.hawaii.gov/dbedt

Guthrie grows pensive. "What freaks me out," he says, "is that I know a lot of people in my age group who are alone. There must be something freaking them out that they don't settle in with one person."

Several single professional women, eager to find permanent relationships, said they rarely or never date tourists, primarily because the relationship would be brief.

"It's very easy to get dates with tourists. They are at hotel bars literally waiting to be picked up," a *kama`aina* in her 30s commented. "But, at my age, I am looking to get married. I don't want to leave Hawai`i and I would not marry a tourist. So why would I date someone who doesn't live here?"

Dating kama`aina

Both sexes complained that the islands have small *kama`aina* or resident populations, limiting choices. "Everybody knows your business," complained a neighbor-island bachelor. "It's like living in a small town, except that on the mainland you could get in your car and drive away, meet new people. Here, you can't do that."

The small neighbor island population makes "cheating" risky. A bachelor in his 50s was emotionally involved with three women at the same time. They found out, called each other, and all three dropped him.

The choice of companion may be limited, but Hawai`i is a wonderful place to date, an O`ahu radio announcer in her 20s points out. There's so much to do here and most of it is free: romantic places to hike and swim and just talk.

A 48-year-old medical secretary wouldn't agree. She was leaving Hawai`i after five years. Never married, she did not exactly come looking for a man, she says. Still, she admits, it would have been nice to find one.

"Men and women come here for different reasons," the secretary insists. "Women come here usually to change spiritually, to get closer to nature. A lot of single men, on other hand, come here to bum out, live on the beach, chase women, live on the edge.

"On the mainland I used to say, 'What kind of job does he have? What kind of a car does he drive?'

"Here it's 'Does he *have* a job? Does he *have* a car?'"

Meanwhile, a Honolulu twice-divorced father of two complains that Hawai`i's *haole* (Caucasian) women are too independent.

"Well, it takes a certain amount of chutzpah to get here," he says. "Some of these women came alone, left friends and relatives. I met one woman who sailed over on a container ship, for god's sake! Another one had hitchhiked all over the world. These are very tough women. They don't need a guy. Some guys maybe think that's good. Not me."

Tropical fantasies

The relatively small population of the islands does make it difficult for some people to find a perfect match, commented one former dating service executive.

In Hawai`i, people use the dating services not because they are desperate, but because they are particular, she insists. They want to fulfill romantic tropical fantasies.

From O`ahu singles: great (free) dates

"The absolute worst possible thing to do on a first date," says a bachelor in his 50s, is to go a movie. "You sit there for two hours, not talking, staring at the screen and wondering what your date thinks of you."

Hawai`i's idyllic ambiance is free — and dating provides some of the island's best bargains. Here are suggestions from O`ahu singles for romantic, free or inexpensive dates. Some ideas are applicable to any island.

- **Walk.** Take a moonlight walk, scheduled regularly at the Honolulu Zoo (971-7195). Under a full moon, parks assume a wondrous appearance. Call the Nature Conservancy (537-4508) and ask for hiking and nature walk schedules.

- **Be romantic.** Stroll on any beach. Pick up a pretty shell or a piece of coral and offer it to your date as a souvenir. Tell your date you are taking the shell home as a reminder of the beginning of your relationship.

- **Check the *Honolulu Weekly*** or the entertainment and community sections of newspapers for free concerts or lectures. Choose any subject that will interest both of you. A lecture on relationships can be especially appropriate and provide topics of conversation.

- **Park.** The tops of Tantalus or Pacific Heights are great for enjoying the view. Or, drive out to the windward side of the island. Have a sunset dinner at the Crouching Lion Inn, then park at La`ie Point. Watch the waves, talk and get to know each other.

- **Hike.** Get up early and drive to Makapu`u lighthouse with backpacks full of water, fruit, and food. Hike up to the lighthouse and watch the sun come up. Then hike over the cliff to the inlet and dive off the rock or bask in the sun.

- **Picnic.** Ka`ena Point Nature Preserve has sand dunes, endemic coastal plants, albatross nests, whale watching. Or rent kayaks, take along a lunch, and paddle to Mokulua islets off Lanikai/Kailua. Or trek up to Kapena Falls off the Pali Highway. Or try the easy hike up Makiki; it has plenty of romantic spots for picnics.

- **Enjoy free or inexpensive shows and entertainment.** Hawai`i's many performers appear at book stores, on shopping center stages, and in free or inexpensive resort shows. Perfect for a casual date.

- **Be spontaneous.** Call at 4 p.m. and suggest the two of you go down to the beach to watch the sunset at 6. Bring a bottle of champagne or wine and two glasses. For an extra romantic touch, tie long thin ribbons on the glasses or wrap the bottle in a flower lei.

"You're white and you want that brown-skinned man. Or a man wants an Asian wife," she says. Or, conversely, a woman may dream about men like the ones she left behind, and buttoned-down east coast professionals can be difficult to meet here.

Tropical realities

Mixed-race relationships are common here, where cultures blend so smoothly. Many lead to interesting and fulfilling lives, but fusing cultures can put added stress on a relationship, warned two social workers.

"Mainland young people come over here and are fascinated by locals. Maybe it's the dark skin," says one. "But about a year or so after they are together, things start to fall apart. I see this happening over and over. There is not a strong bond between men and women in some cultures. The guys like to be with their buddies and want to hang out with them and (some of them) don't treat women very well."

Men dominate in some Pacific Island cultures, where communal living is common, "so the wife is left to care for the children and just be with the women, and mainland women just aren't brought up that way," she says.

Social workers see much spousal abuse, she warns, and it is not limited to any particular race.

"On the mainland I used to say, 'What kind of job does he have? What kind of a car does he drive?' Here it's 'Does he have a job? Does he have a car?'"

Cultures aside, commented the second social worker, the stress of everyday life rears its ugly head in any relationship. "With the added problems here of very high food and housing costs and low-paying jobs, that puts a strain on any relationship," she says.

High expectations

Maybe, romantically, we expect too much of the islands. Some couples come hoping fragrant breezes, moonlight walks and the flutter of cool sheets will repair a rent relationship. A man now in his late 50s sold his family farm in the midwestern U.S. and moved his family to the islands several years ago because, he says, his wife was dissatisfied and dreamed

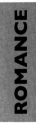

Escaping to Paradise

Not every woman is seeking a relationship; some women are trying to escape one. Hawai`i, an ocean away from their troubles, seems a safe haven for women who fear for their lives.

"We get calls every week from women on the mainland who want to start their lives over again [here in Hawai`i], to get away from abusive relationships," says Carol C. Lee, executive director of the Hawai`i State Coalition Against Domestic Violence.

But, Lee says, "We need to let these women know how difficult life in Hawai`i is. How difficult it is to get jobs, how scarce affordable housing is, how expensive child care is here, that only O`ahu has inexpensive mass transportation."

Most shelters give preference to women in immediate danger, Lee says, and that means women who already live here, whose antagonist is on the island. A woman who moves here from the mainland would be away from immediate danger and might not be accepted if the shelter is crowded.

On the other hand, the coalition often helps Hawai`i women escape abusive situations in Hawai`i, Lee says. They are sheltered on the islands until they can escape to the mainland.

Domestic violence is a leading cause of homicides both on the islands and on the mainland. Of the 58 murders in Hawai`i in a recent year, 40 percent occurred in homes, according to the Hawai`i State Health Department.

of living here, and he wanted to save his marriage. The family found financial success in a business, but marital happiness nonetheless eluded the couple and they eventually divorced.

"Maybe it's the Adam and Eve thing," he muses. "After all, this is supposed to be paradise. You come looking for perfection. The expectations are too high. Or maybe it is people who are not happy who come here, looking for more in their lives. This is a wonderful place. I'm glad I came. But maybe if whatever you are looking for is not there, where you are, maybe it does not exist."

The trauma of divorce can be doubly difficult here, far from supportive family and friends. In some cases, there's an urgency to finding a partner, any partner who can help pay the bills, who can stave off loneliness and help you survive in paradise. A 42-year-old divorced attorney is only half joking when he says, "It's so expensive here. I need to find a wife."

Homosexual relationships fare no better in paradise. A spokesperson for gay rights blamed Hawai`i's "play environment" for the break-up of many gay relationships shortly after the couple arrives in the islands. "One of them may be serious and working hard; the other is off playing and maybe meets someone else," he says. "I've seen it happen over and over again."

A wealthy spouse?

The islands are famous for being costly — and they are also well-known for attracting the wealthy. Among the singles here are those seeking rich spouses. There's a clichè: "You can fall in love with a rich man as easily as a poor one. You just have to find one first." And you'll find one faster in a neighborhood where rich men swing their golf clubs just a few feet from your *lanai.*

"Oh sure, such men exist," says an attractive 42-year-old woman. Hoping to find a wealthy husband, she lives in an upscale O`ahu resort where she admits she cannot afford the $2,600 monthly rent.

Watching a male foursome tee off across sweeping greens, she adds, "But most of them have wives. And even if you do find a rich, available man, there are hundreds of beautiful woman here, many hoping to marry money. And even the poor men are dating women 20 years younger than they are."

> "After all, this is supposed to be paradise. You come looking for perfection. The expectations are too high."

Former lovers

Former lovers have a way of showing up in Hawai`i. Four single women related similar experiences. They had lived on the islands for several years when an ex-boyfriend or ex-husband sought them out and visited, hoping to rekindle youthful sparks on a romantic tropical isle.

"He was just a friend I had once worked with, and we had had a very short affair years ago. We kept in touch and when he was available he called and it all sounded very romantic — him coming to visit. But it had been eight years and we really didn't have anything in common any more. I enjoyed showing him around the island, but that was it," says one woman.

Another woman: "I knew as soon as I picked him up at the airport that it wasn't going to work and I said, 'Uh, oh, what am I in for?' So I had to be honest about it and just tell him, 'No. Sorry. We're just friends.' "

"Actually," says a third woman, "I think we're better preserved in Hawai`i. Seeing a paunchy old mainland flame can be a bit of a shock."

The fourth woman enjoyed a happier encounter. She and a recently-divorced man she dated in college over 20 years ago are planning a long-term relationship.

Have you checked your lover's background?

It has been three-quarters of a century since "picture brides" were common in Hawai`i. But way back in 2003 the state took measures to protect the modern equivalent, mail-order brides. A century ago, picture brides, chosen by their spouses from blurry photographs, came from Asian countries to marry plantation workers. Today's version is apt to be a woman from anywhere in the world who responded, for example, to email or an Internet ad. The law allows anyone living abroad and using a for-profit matchmaking service to check up on the intended spouse's past. Hawai`i is only the second state to pass a law allowing foreigners to get the criminal conviction and marital history information about prospective spouses living in the United States.

▶ **TIP: Don't search for a potential mate;** just look for good friends of either sex, Maui resident Beth Baughman advises. "You find people when you are giving — when you make bonds with people."

▶ **TIP: Become involved in activities** that will put you in contact with people whose interests are similar to yours. Join an investment group, a Toastmasters (speakers) club, or go on a Sierra Club or Nature Center hike, join a paddling team, visit the local Internet coffee shop.

It's the law

Marriage

If you are living with your spouse without the benefit of a legal ceremony, think twice about coming to Hawai`i. Common law marriage is not officially recognized here.

In common-law marriage, a couple lives together as husband and wife and displays to the community that they are bound together as such, but are not married according to the laws of their jurisdiction. In other words, they have not applied for a marriage license or gone through a legal ceremony performed by an authorized person.

Whether your marriage will be recognized in Hawai`i depends on where you are coming from. If you are from a country (other than the United States) where common-law marriages are recognized, Hawai`i will also recognize the marriage. But if you are from a state which recognizes common-law marriages, Hawai`i may not consider you legally wed.

Those whose marriages are not valid by Hawai`i law do not have rights which the law gives to legally recognized spouses. They may not have a claim to their spouse's social security or other benefits. However, children born to unwed couples enjoy full rights.

Send for:
• *Getting Married*, a pamphlet from the Hawai`i State Health Department, 1250 Punchbowl Street, Honolulu, Hawai`i 96813.

• *Marry Me on Maui*, a pamphlet from the Maui Chamber of Commerce, 250 Alamaha Street, N16A, Kahului, Hawai`i, 96732

Ironically, although Hawai`i does not recognize common-law marriage, it was the first state in the nation to institute a "Reciprocal Beneficiary Relationship" law allowing unmarried couples many of the same benefits as those in official marriages. These include the right to shared medical insurance, joint property ownership and inheritances. The law, in a test stage at this time, is generally considered full of loopholes. Legislators and political groups are seeking ways to clarify the issue.

ROMANCE

Divorce

Hawai`i is no place to bring a shaky marriage. Hawai`i has a "no fault" divorce law, but you must live in Hawai`i for a year before you can file for divorce and three months before you can file for legal separation. Simple uncontested divorces can be granted a few weeks after filing. Complex or contested cases can take much longer, but about 95 percent of divorces in Hawai`i are uncontested cases, handled amicably, according to Attorney Peter J. Herman in *A Practical Guide to Divorce in Hawai`i.*

Each year, about 5,500 people divorced in this state. It is not necessary to find fault with a spouse or to prove adultery, cruelty or desertion. The person seeking the divorce must simply show the court either that:

1) the marriage was irretrievably broken, or

2) the couple has had a legal separation in Hawai`i for two years and have not reconciled, or

3) the couple has a legal separation from another state and the time has expired or

4) the couple has lived apart without a formal separation for two years and there is no chance they will live together again.

Do-it-yourself divorces are legal in Hawai`i, although author Judith R. Gething, in her book *Sex Discrimination and the Law in Hawai`i*, strongly recommends that attorneys be consulted by both sides if children are involved.

Hawai`i's version of same-sex marriage

In 1997 Hawai`i was the first state to pass a law extending many different-gender marital rights to gay couples. Additional laws granting further rights and benefits under the Reciprocal Beneficiary Act were approved in 1999, and more may be added as time goes on.

Same-sex couples, or any two people wanting to be treated as a couple, can obtain a reciprocal beneficiary certificate, similar to a marriage certificate, from the state health department. They must:

• Be at least 18 years old;

• Have not married nor be part of another reciprocal beneficiary relationship;

- Be legally prohibited from marrying the other person under the Hawai`i marriage law;
- Have not consented to the reciprocal beneficiary relationship because of force, duress, or fraud;
- Sign and file with the Department of Health a notarized declaration of the relationship; and
- Pay an $8 registration fee. (Another $8 to terminate the status.)

Under reciprocal beneficiary, the rights include many of the same personal and financial rights given traditional couples. Among them:

- **Equal rights to visit a spouse in a hospital**, to make medical decisions during a spouse's illness (if the spouse is unable to) and to make decisions such as disposition of the body if a spouse dies.
- **The responsibility of one spouse to support the other.** The law affects, with some reservations, health insurance benefits offered traditional married couples and affects government and private retirement benefits such as pension plans, insurance and workers compensation benefits.
- **Rights of inheritance and real estate.** When one spouse dies, the other has the senior rights to the deceased spouse's estate much as in a tradtional marriage. A same-sex couple can also own real estate in much the same way as traditional couples.

For more information and opinion, scroll "reciprocal beneficiary Hawai`i" on the Internet or go to the health department's website: www.hawaii.gov/doh/records/rbrfaq.html

Despite its wide-reaching effects, the Reciprocal Beneficiaries law has been criticized by some gay organizations as being an attempt to circumvent the issue of same-sex marriage. Some of the benefits, it is claimed, have eroded over the years. Any couple planning to register should study to see which benefits the law affects and whether the law will apply to them. It would also be wise to seek the advice of a knowledgeable attorney.

Menage a trois — Maui style

A Maui bachelor tells this delightful story.

He and a female acquaintance went snorkeling together near Molokini crater. As usual on first dates, conversation had been friendly, but stilted.

Bikini-clad, his companion lay on a float in the water, her eyes closed, a dreamy smile on her face. He gazed at her longingly, wishing he could muster the courage to tell her just how lovely she looked.

Suddenly, she began to giggle. "Hey!" she squealed. "Cut it out. You're tickling me!" Chuckling again, she swatted at the water.

Photo courtesy of stock.xchng

It appeared something was nudging her from under the raft and, of course, she assumed it was her male companion. She thought he had dived into the water and was engaged in amorous, rather bold, frolic.

A few seconds later, a dolphin poked his face up out of the water and peered at her — his large mouth curved in what seemed like a smile.

"That dolphin did what I didn't have the nerve to do," the bachelor laughingly recalls. "He made the first move and it really broke the ice. I knew just how far I could go without getting her mad — and it was a lot further than I thought!"

Some *kama`aina* who heard this story cast it in a mystical light. Dolphins, they say, are so tuned in to humans that they can read our minds. The cetacean Cupid, they contend, had sensed the man's yearning and was lending a helpful hand — or nose, in this case.

Success stories

So where in Paradise does one find a potentially perfect mate? Here, as elsewhere, a potential spouse is likely to appear when you aren't looking, when you are satisfied with yourself and your situation. In exotic Hawai`i, many people meet their mates in very ordinary ways: at churches, at civic and business organizations, at work.

Beth and Doug — and "their tree."

• At work

Beth Holiday and Doug Baughman, both in their mid-40s, met at the Maui County Fair. She was staffing a booth inside a hot, sticky tent. Doug was stationed at a booth outside, near a shady tree. Beth bought a soda and took a break under that tree. They struck up a conversation, continued talking for the four days of the fair, and communicated often by phone for three weeks before a first date.

Rene and Garth: those hands.

One year later, they married.

"There's a lot more to it than running into each other," Beth says. "We both worked on ourselves and were ready to be in a relationship. We were both happy and enjoying our lives. The only reason to take on a partner was to augment our lives, make them even better."

• At home

Rene Scardino and Garth Panzer were roommates in a shared house with several other people, a common living arrangement in the islands.

Rene was New Age; Garth was very conservative, and their relationship was "hate at first sight" for nearly a month. Then they began taking long walks in the Upcountry Maui moonlight. One day Garth offered to rub Rene's sore shoulder with his healing hands. She looked up at him and thought, "What took you so long?" They married a few months later and have remained so for 15 years.

• At church

Sometimes looking — and praying — helps. Photographer Steve Strand prayed for a beautiful Christian wife for several years before meeting Valeria Franco, a Brazilian immigrant at his church, Hope Chapel. Their faith stresses pre-marital abstinence and a fulfilling family life. Steve and Valeria married within a year and now have two young children.

Steve and Valeria have Hope.

• On the phone

Modern technology is especially helpful for people living on isolated islands. Rob Manning called from the mainland hoping to sell private label wine to Holly Lang, a Hawai`i magazine publisher. She didn't buy, but something clicked and they communicated for three weeks via phone and email. Then he invited her to a wine festival in the wine region of Northern California, where his family has a ranch.

Holly and Rob "clicked."

Each was divorced five years and relatively happy with their lives. At that first meeting, "Neither of us had great expectations," she says. But, that first date was, Rob says, "As though we had known each other forever." Ten days later, he flew to Maui. After a two-week visit, she proposed. He moved to Maui and they were married ten months later.

trouble

From the

unpleasant

to the illegal

Photo by Matthew Thayer

Residents flee a tsunami that washed over part of Hilo in 1946, destroying much of the waterfront and causing 159 deaths.

Nature's fury

The seven Hawaiian Islands, floating like a tiny lifeline in the center of the vast Pacific Ocean, look vulnerable… and they are. Those yellow sirens on tall poles in and around beaches are designed to alert residents of approaching disasters, like hurricanes and, worse, tsunamis.

Tsunami

What is a tsunami? Imagine an ocean giant taking an enormous breath and inhaling miles of water, then spewing it back in a gargantuan wave traveling 500 miles an hour, hitting the shore and crashing over people, homes, even towns. Tsunamis, the stuff of legends, occur only rarely, usually decades apart; but they can cause many deaths and much damage.

Hawai`i telephone books include a section devoted to tsunami evacuation routes. If those yellow sirens sound, or if the ocean recedes get away from the ocean as quickly as possible, and head for the mountains.

Major tsunamis slammed Hawai`i in 1946 and 1960. The 1946 tsunami caused 159 deaths and over $26 million in damage, much of it in Hilo on the Big Island. Survivors describe residents flocking to the ocean in awe to watch the water recede, then running for their lives as a tremendous wave sucked at the shore, swallowing people and structures.

Considering the dangers lurking out there, some locals find it puzzling that newcomers pay millions of dollars for oceanfront homes.

> **"Hawaiians know it's no good you live right on the ocean. More safe live back in town."**
>
> – elderly woman, Big Island

"Hawaiians know it's no good you live right on the water," says one elderly Big Island resident. "What for you do that when water all around us? You can look at it everyday anyway. More safe live back in town."

Hurricanes

As dangerous weather goes, hurricanes seem almost tame. Unlike tornadoes, which pop up in unexpected places with little warning and can take hundreds of lives, hurricanes usually announce themselves well in advance of their arrival. Whirlwinds form out in the vast Pacific and head toward the islands, spin offshore from one island to another, a dervish dancing this way and that, finally hurtling off to dissipate somewhere in the ocean. Meteorologists track these strange ballets for weeks. And long-time residents have seen the scenario played out so many times they tend to grow nonchalant.

In September, 1992, Kaua`i watched Hurricane Iniki perform an eerie pirouette offshore of the Hawaiian islands, threatening first the Big Island, then Maui. Just as it was poised to strike O`ahu, Iniki turned and roared straight into Kaua`i, its eye passing directly over the island. Winds of up to 165 miles per hour pummeled the island for five hours, causing $2 billion in damage.

While Iniki's arrival was devastating, advance warnings helped save lives. On Kaua`i, four people died as a result of Iniki: one from a heart attack, one by flying debris, and two fishermen at sea. Residents had plenty of time to evacuate oceanfront homes and condos and head for shelters. Those who remained cowered under mattresses in bathtubs or crowded together in windowless stairwells, listening to debris torpedo their homes. The democratic hurricane ravaged homes all over the island, chewing up mansions as well as cottages.

Those who did not witness the devastation have had a difficult time relating to it. In 1993, a year after Iniki hit Kaua`i, Maui residents were ignoring a hurricane hovering off their shores. A Ha`iku resident summed up the attitude: "Relax, if it's going to hit here, the tsunami sirens will sound. We'll have plenty of time to go to a shelter."

Flash floods

In some parts of the islands, when it rains, it pours. Rains can pound down steep mountain creeks, congregate in quiet ravines and turn dry ditches and "runoffs" into cascading rivers. Every few years, lives are lost in flash floods, mostly passengers in cars swept away or overturned by the raging waters.

An impending torrential rain can be difficult to detect and come suddenly. Campers and hikers are occcasionally stranded or lose their lives in sudden pounding downpours.

A real estate agent may tell you that the house you want to rent or purchase is in a flood zone; a landlord may not. Use common sense. Talk to neighbors, civil defense officials and stop at police stations in the area in which you are considering a home. Ask about weather conditions and whether flash floods are ever an issue.

Know your way around dangerous island weather

- **Prepare.** Each summer assemble a hurricane kit including flashlights, batteries, medical supplies, canned food and water. Extensive instructions and evacuation routes are printed in the front of Hawai`i telephone books. Be familiar with your route.

- **Protect** important papers, memorabilia. Rent an inland bank safety deposit box for family photos, small heirlooms and all important papers or keep them in sealed waterproof (plastic) boxes that can be easily carried and taken with you to a shelter.

- **Live a few blocks inland.** While modern technology makes it easier to track tsunami and issue warnings, some people feel more comfortable living at least a few blocks from the ocean — and home insurance costs less.

- **Mortgage and homeowner's insurance,** costly here, is a must. Be aware of which natural disasters your policy covers. Your mortgagor may insist you purchase flood insurance if your home is in a flood zone and state law also mandates flood insurance in some areas. If you rent and your important belongings cannot be quickly packed and taken to a shelter, purchase renters insurance.

- **Drive wisely.** Sudden downpours can turn island roads into rivers. Do not attempt to drive your car through water that is deeper than one-fourth of your auto's wheel. Seek higher ground or park your car in a safe area well away from flood waters and wait out the storm.

- **Play it smart.** Hiking? Take a cell phone along. If you are trapped by floodwaters, attempt to reach a high, safe ground; stay there; call for help and wait for rescuers. Don't attempt to cross raging creeks. Swimming or boating? Read and heed wave and weather warnings.

- **Boating?** Be sure there's an EPIRB, an emergency position indicating radio beacon, on board.

Read more about volcanoes and vog in the Big Island section, Chapter 14: Which Island?

This article, by Kaua`i writer and media producer Mary Earle Chase, first appeared in Kaua`i's *The Garden Island News*.

Don't fool around with Mother Ocean

by MARY EARLE CHASE

The headline read: "Fisherman drowns off Kilauea." The article went on to tell, in a few paragraphs, of the death of Eric Myers, age 28, off Waikalua Beach.

We see these stories all too often here on Kaua`i. Someone swallowed up by our waters. Usually, it is the unforgiving ocean, but recently lives have been lost in the mysterious "blue room" in the West Cave and in the pool beneath Wailua Falls. Water has its way with us; its power too strong even for our willful ways.

The difference in this drowning was that I knew Eric Myers. He was not a fisherman. He was a computer graphics designer and programmer, one of an elite few on the Mainland hired by cutting edge technology companies to blaze new trails in the cyberbush.

He came to Kaua`i whenever he could to escape the world of glowing computer screens and embrace nature, raw and unprogrammed. He fell in love with a piece of land on the ocean at the end of Waikalua Road and managed to buy it. He put up a teepee.

A local fellow showed him how to place nets to catch lobsters on the reef by his secluded beach. He took two of his friends there one Saturday to help him. The ocean was rough but he seemed to know where to go and where not to. His friends followed.

Something went awry, and Eric and his friend Glenn found themselves struggling against a ferocious current. His other friend, John, tried to help, but before he could reach the two of them, Eric slipped away. He was found later with an obvious blow to the head. Waves, rocks, currents, they will have their way — even with experienced fishermen.

Many of us on the island know people who have been taken by the sea. Perhaps we have waged our own brief battles.

Eleven years ago, when my husband and I were visitors here, we unwittingly snorkeled into a swift current at Makua (Tunnels) Bay. My brand new snorkel filled with water and I could not purge it. Choking, I grabbed at coral, but the current ripped me away. I panicked.

Fortunately, my husband Bill grabbed me and said, "Swim!" If I hadn't he would have knocked me out. When we made it back to the beach, a couple of local folks were standing at water's edge with surfboards, telling us they had been ready to go after us.

I thanked God they didn't have to.

Since then, I have maintained the utmost respect for the waters of Kaua`i. Perhaps I am overly cautious, doing most of my ocean swimming in summer when Hanalei Bay is like a lake. I hover around my children as they snorkel on boogie boards and watch nervously as my older son tries out his surfboard. When I hear sirens or see the fire-rescue truck speeding toward Ha`ena, my stomach churns and I pray.

Mother Nature's love is not unconditional. She demands that we stay awake, respectful, and in awe of her power.

Matthew Thayer

Honolulu resident John Cook holds a warning sign along a Waikiki street in July of 2004. Cook said he has been unable to work since he was beaten and nearly killed in an unprovoked attack several years ago. Cook said he was exiting an elevator when a drug dealer who was being evicted mistook him for the condo's manager. He said he was beaten, robbed and left for dead. After a long recovery, he said he was especially frustrated when his assailant did not go to jail. "Nobody goes to jail," Cook said. "The police do all the work and they document it, but the judges let them go." Cook said Waikiki can be a nice place, but people need to be careful.

Crime

Lloyd Yonemura, registrar at Moloka`i High and Intermediate Schools, is greeting 75 public school registrars from around the state. They have come to the quiet island of Moloka`i for a weekend conference that includes an optional mule ride to Kalapaupa, the Hansen's Disease colony and a hike through a rainforest.

"If you leave your car anywhere, don't lock it," he advises attendees. "Take everything out, okay? Take your purses and cameras with you. Leave your car unlocked and the windows down."

That way, he explains, thieves will know there is nothing to steal. They can rifle through your car conveniently, without having to jimmy open the glove compartment or the trunk. Or, they may bypass the car completely, assuming it contains nothing of value.

Hawai`i doesn't have much violent crime. But robberies and non-violent crimes, spurred in recent years by an epidemic of crystal meth use, continue. Hawai`i's sliding doors, easy-open jalousie windows, and trusting lifestyle make burglary a breeze for even amateur bad guys. Many burglaries occur during the day, while people are at work.

For details on crime in Hawai`i, visit the website of the state attorney general: hawaii.gov/ag

"You are far more likely to come home to a ransacked apartment than get shot waiting for a bus," Honolulu magazine reported a few years ago.

That's comforting — unless you happen to be in the apartment when it's targeted, like Sharon, 28, was. She and a friend, sleeping in the loft of a condominium, left the sliding doors to their second floor balcony open. The loft looked directly down on the doors. And, after all, they were on the second floor. How could anyone break in?

"Easy," said a policeman who came to investigate the theft of Sharon's purse from a kitchen counter. He placed one foot against the exterior wall and hoisted himself effortlessly to the balcony. Then he showed Sharon and her neighbors a large footprint that indicated the thief had done just that.

Sharon's purse contained her credit cards, driver's license and car keys. Her car was gone from the parking lot.

"You don't have to get physically beaten to be mugged," Sharon mourned. "I feel violated."

Carefree tourists make especially easy marks. Much of the stolen property never turns up again. Only about 10 percent of the crimes on O'ahu are solved. The rate is higher in the less populated outer islands.

Ice: the worst

Police usually blame crime increases on the curse of the islands: the use of crystal methamphetamine or "ice," a highly addictive stimulant that can cause erratic behavior, depression and hallucination. Keith Kamita, chief of the state's Narcotics Enforcement Division, has said up to 45 percent of the cases handled by his office involve ice.

Ice is an extremely violent drug that has everyone from lawmakers to housewives in Hawai`i on alert and has caused law enforcement to change the way it responds to crime on the street, says an Associated Press story in the *Maui News*. Social workers have predicted that at current rates of methamphetamine use, every person in Hawai`i will eventually be affected by the drug, through an auto accident or a theft, if not by direct involvement with a family member.

Pakalolo (pot)

A car stops for a light in a relatively busy Maui roadway. A disheveled man, about 40, comes up to the car window. "*Pakalolo*. You want?"

It's the only time in the 14 years I've lived here that anyone has offered to sell me pot, but visiting friends say they are approached often to buy marijuana and other drugs. Drug dealing is so common it becomes part of the tourist scene, an anecdote to scribble on a postcard and send home to friends. On most islands, community attitude toward pot is relaxed and in some quarters a strong sentiment exists for legalizing marijuana.

However, locals warn visiting friends — and each other — not to hike too deep into Hawai`i's mountains, to obey *kapu* (no trespassing) signs. Occasionally lone hikers do not return and residents look at each other with raised eyebrows. Did the hiker get lost, fall from a cliff, tangle with a wild boar… or wander upon someone's *pakalolo* patch? Police make occasional raids on private gardens and stashes.

DUI laws: guilty until proven innocent

When you accept your driver's license you are agreeing to Hawai`i laws governing driving and liquor ingestion. If officers suspect you have been drinking, they do not have to read you the Miranda rights. Under the implied consent law, you have already consented to submit to breath or blood testing. You do not have the right to remain silent, nor the right to counsel prior to taking the breath or blood test. A first offense conviction can result in mandatory counseling, suspension or restriction of your driver's license, community service, time in jail, and/or a fine that ranges from $150 to $1,000. In Hawai`i you are legally intoxicated with a blood alcohol level of .08 percent. If you are in an accident, you can be charged with drunk driving if your alcohol level is .05 percent — for some people that is as little as two drinks.

For more info...
go to
hawaii.gov/dot/highways

Speed, the kind that kills

A legal drug kills many island residents each year and because our neighbor islands have small populations, serious and fatal accidents hit home. Many longtime Maui, Kaua`i or Big Island residents know someone who has been killed or injured in an accident involving liquor.

In recent years, nearly half of the state's fatalities involve alcohol. Fortunately, the number of fatalities have been dropping.

In recent years speeding and roadway racing, especially on O`ahu's busy H-1 highway, has contributed to numerous deaths and residents are forcing police and lawmakers to pay attention. It's not that Hawai`i's laws are lax; in fact, they are among the toughest in the nation. But traffic monitoring is relaxed on all islands. Driving 15 to 20 miles over the speed limit is an accepted way to travel on neighbor islands. Law enforcement sets up periodic road checks to weed out drunken drivers during holidays, but usually ignores speeders, drunk or sober, at other times. The islands' easygoing lifestyle, an attitude of "no bother, let be" may be at play. Island lifestyle also encourages partying… and to many that means drinking. And driving. And speeding.

Trauma, shock... and aloha

If you are a tourist who suffers a crime, you'll feel terrible trauma and shock, for sure. But, you'll also experience a generous dose of something else: *aloha* spirit.

Each island has a visitor-assistance program. Police or hotel staff refer victims to the programs where they get help canceling credit cards, changing airline reservations and extending hotel stays if family members are hospitalized. The programs are financed in part by the Hawai`i Tourism Authority, which spends about $200,000 on visitor assistance every year. In addition, many businesses, including hotels, car-rental agencies and airlines, donate products or services. Volunteers help by driving victims or offering advice and support.

"To a certain extent, it's a way of saying, 'We're sorry that you had this bad experience' and we are trying to help in any way we can, and hopefully to change some people's perceptions of Hawai`i after they've been victimized," Murray Towell, president of the Hawai`i Hotel and Lodging Association told *The Honolulu Advertiser*. "You don't want them to be going and telling their friends that they had this bad experience."

Efforts seem successful. Visiting crime victims occasionally write letters of thanks, printed in newspapers, for the kind treatment, the *aloha*.

Murder

When murder occurs, in Hawai`i as on the mainland, police look first to family and friends. Family violence is also on the rise here, in part because of drug and alcohol abuse.

Family Court in O`ahu allegedly has a zero tolerance policy toward domestic violence. Offenders who violate the terms of their parole can be sentenced to serve time in Hawai`i's cramped prisons, including tents at O`ahu's Halawa prison.

Bars and brothels

Hostess bars are legal on O`ahu; prostitution is not. "Korean" bars or hostess bars, all with the word "club" in them, are common in O`ahu and generally understood to be strip bars. They are legal and well-attended by both locals and tourists. In O`ahu, they are so numerous that Honolulu has no red-light district to which prostitution is contained; bars are scattered throughout the island. Such facilities are less available and less visible on the other, less-populated, islands.

Nothing illegal here... just another form of diversion on O`ahu

The state legislature has at times considered how to deal with the problem of prostitution; crackdowns are common and efforts to clean up Waikiki seem fruitful. A few years ago, prostitutes calling out to customers were part of the Waikiki ambiance. Today they are seen, but rarely heard.

Prostitution, a petty misdemeanor, carries a fine of $500 and up to three days in jail for a first conviction. Like drugs, prostitution is considered by some visitors as just another tourist attraction; to others it is offensive. Whatever your attitude toward prostitution, it is not so rampant that it should in any way affect your decision to live here, unless you are planning to run a bar or other nighttime entertainment.

Gangs in paradise

Hawai`i has about 1,000 documented gang members, Honolulu gang prevention police Officer Dean Shear has said. The word "gang" evokes images of crime and brutality, but gangs can vary from a bunch of kids spray-painting walls to armed villains extorting money and dealing drugs. A gang, by police definition, is a group of three or more who

1.) associate on a regular basis;

2.) have a name;

3.) claims territory or "turf";

4.) engages in criminal behavior.

Shear has seen Polynesian gangs from the mainland whose sole purpose is to deal drugs.

"We're positive they have family here, and it's only a matter of time before there's trouble," he told a gathering of Windward O`ahu parents and educators. He sees illegal drugs, particularly "ice" (crystal methamphetamine) as the major gang problem.

Sidney Rosen, author of *Toward a Gang Solution*, counts about 50 gangs on O`ahu. Rosen says there is gang activity on all islands and it's no different on the mainland. Gangs vary from graffiti groups whose primary activity is defacing property, to gangs that deal in drugs, steal, extort and instigate inter-gang violence that can, and does, end in injury or death. In recent years, murders and shoot-outs have been blamed on adult gang activity, its members involved in drugs or gambling.

Youth gangs tend to be drawn along ethnic lines. On O`ahu, Kahuku School Principal Lea Albert has identified several groups, including Tongan Krip Gangsters, Hau`ula Boyz, La`ie Boys Incorporated and the North Shore Boyz.

Meanwhile, some neighbor island students and educators insist the only teenage gang activity comes from "wanna-bes" who take on gang colors and dress: a bandana around the forehead or thigh, a tattoo or burn that signifies membership. Several schools forbid wearing headgear, a way to prevent gangs from displaying their colors.

A neighbor island high school freshman puts it this way: "There's wanna-be gangs, no real gangs. Sure, every place has gangs. I guess they think they're in gangs but anyone who lives on the mainland, like in Chicago or if you live in California, areas like that, you'll know what a real gang is."

Disorganized crime?

It is generally acknowledged that organized crime exists in Hawai`i. At times over the years it has seemed to be more disorganized crime, in part because Hawai`i is divided into so many ethnic factions. Beginning in the early 1960s, syndicated crime in the islands is believed to have been headed by Koreans, local-Asians, Samoan and Hawaiian bosses or sub-bosses. At least two murders — one in the victim's bed, another in a cane field — are believed linked to organized crime. But violence and murder also occur over gambling and drug turf.

'A disaster from the civil rights standpoint'

In Hawai`i, police can hold suspects for up to 48 hours without charging them or allowing them to post bail. That is longer than any state in the union, according to Honolulu attorney Eric Seitz, who called the State Supreme Court ruling allowing the holding "a disaster from the civil rights standpoint." Civil rights attorneys argue that holding suspects without bail violates their constitutional rights.

"The local syndicate was like a guerrilla force of unknown strength," write Gavan Daws and George Cooper in *Land and Power in Hawai`i*. "It was known to be out there, a factor to be reckoned with in the equation of modern Hawai`i. But how big it really was, what territories it controlled, what high ground it might be seeking to occupy — these were things that few or none outside of organized crime knew."

Organized crime got a slow start here in part because until the mid-1940s prostitution and gambling were either legal or tolerated. Ironically, lotteries and other forms of legalized gambling have been voted down in recent years for fear of tarnishing Hawai`i's clean, wholesome image, yet prostitution has been a large part of island history.

Weeding out crime

On O`ahu and some of the sister islands, civilians and police working together have had success in cutting down on crime. The Honolulu police sponsor numerous programs such as Seniors Against Crime and The Community Policing Team which has volunteers walking "beats" to report crimes. The Waikiki By Night program takes concerned citizens on walks spotting potential crime. Volunteer parking lot patrols have also contributed to a drop in auto break-ins on some islands, especially at beaches, where such crimes are frequent.

The Ho`ike Information line on O`ahu provides the public a contact point to obtain answers or referrals for police-related questions. Call

(800) 529-3352

weekdays during business hours. If you are phoning from the mainland, consider that the time is five to six hours earlier here.

The good news? Murder still shocks

When fugitive Shane Mark drew a gun and killed undercover policeman Glen Gaspar in a few years ago, everyone was shocked. Imagine. In the middle of a Kapolei ice cream parlor! Right in a shopping center full of people!

It was front page news for several days. And that's the good news — that violent crime is still rare enough in Hawai`i to shock our populace.

Crime has decreased some in recent years.

State statistics show violent crimes are down a bit and property crime is down a great deal in very recent years. However, the violent Index Crime rate increased 15.7% over the course of the last decade. However, as the islands grow in population, violent crimes such as rape, robbery and aggravated assaults, have increased.

The most common types of crimes against tourists are car break-ins, stolen cars, purse snatchings, and occasionally condominium or hotel-room break-ins. Tourists have also been physically assaulted, but such violence is rare.

All those numbers don't yet mean that Hawai`i is a dangerous place to live or to visit. Percentages seem  high because the islands have for years had such low crime rates. Even with the increases, Hawai`i has a violent crime rate far below California and lower than the national average.

Other statistics show:
- Juvenile crime rates continue to drop, but Hawai`i has a very high rate of juvenile alcoholics, in part because drinking alcohol is accepted and considered normal in some cultures. Road racing — a popular "sport" among the young — combined with drinking, kills a disproportionate number of Hawai`i's young people, especially on the island of O`ahu.

- Firearm registrations also are increasing: up 16.2 percent since 2000; 45 percent of those were handguns.

- Statistics say 90 percent of the crimes on O`ahu go unsolved, although the rate is much better on the less-populated neighbor islands. Here's how neighbor islands fared in 2002, the last year for which figures were available

Big Island: The Index Crime rate fell 2.4 percent. The violent crime rate decreased 21.6 percent and the property crime rate dropped 1.6 percent. Hawai`i County's total, violent, and property Index Crime rates in 2002 were the lowest in the state.

Maui: The Index Crime rate in Maui County decreased 4 percent, with the violent crime rate falling 11.9 and the property crime rate down 3.7.

**Kaua`i:** Major increases were reported by Kaua`i County, with the total Index Crime rate increasing 28.2 percent, the violent crime rate rising 84.2 percent, and the property crime rate up 25.8 percent. Kaua`i County's violent crime rate in 2002 was the highest in the state.

In matters of manners, safety...and the law:

- **All front-seat drivers and passengers must wear seat belts** whenever the car is moving. Failing to use a seat belt carries a $77 fine. In addition, children ages 4 to 17 must be belted when they are riding in the backseat and children under three must use a child safety seat. Failure means a $100 fine. By the way, this state has the highest seat belt compliance rate in the nation, over 90%. Police occasionally conduct "Click it or ticket" campaigns throughout the islands, checking for seat belt use.

- **Stop for pedestrians at designated crosswalks** and intersections. It's the safe and polite thing to do, but failing to yield to a pedestrian also carries a steep fine. And remember that it is illegal to pass a vehicle which is stopped at a crosswalk or to drive your car into a bicycle lane to pass a car.

- **Don't jaywalk...**and don't assume you are safe in a crosswalk, either. Many pedestrians are killed or injured each year, especially on busy O`ahu. More than half of persons injured or killed are elderly.

- **You aren't likely to see "No Littering" signs** in Hawai`i — but throwing any debris from a car, moving or not, is illegal.

- **It's the law. You must turn off your car's engine** if you leave the car. You must also lock the ignition, remove the key and set the parking brake.

Do tourists cause accidents?

It's the weekend and there's less traffic than usual along Kahekili Highway on windward O`ahu. Although he's driven the road hundreds of times, Ted Sakai, administrative assistant to the state director of public safety, is enjoying the scenery, the deeply-ridged Ko`olau Mountains.

Suddenly the car in front of him stops. Sakai slams on his brakes.

"At first I was mad," he says. "I couldn't understand why on earth someone would come to a complete stop on the highway. Then I realized it was a car with tourists.

"Then this guy sticks his head out the window and climbs up on top of the roof of the car and takes a picture. And I'm behind, stopped, watching."

Most longtime Hawai`i drivers have encountered similar situations: tourists jumping out of cars on busy roads to take a photo in front of a sugarcane field. Tourists watching for whales and almost driving over the *pali* (ocean cliffs). Tourists U-turning on a narrow road to go back to a waterfall.

So, do tourists cause accidents?

Bob Siarot, district engineer for state highways on Maui, says he often gets calls from local folks with complaints about visitors' driving habits. Some of the complainants must travel the notoriously wriggly road to remote Hana. Its speed limit is a grueling 10 to 20 miles an hour for much of the 50-mile trip and can take as long as three tortuous hours. There's even a souvenir tee-shirt: "I survived the road to Hana." Residents boast of making the trip in half that time.

"Hana people call and say tourists drive too slow and they get angry and call me. But usually tourists are going at the speed limit. It's actually the locals who are making the road unsafe for everybody by passing," he says.

Okay, so do tourists *contribute* to the accident rate?

"That's very difficult to surmise," Siarot insists. "Accidents are caused by both drivers. If a resident becomes impatient because a driver is slow, then the resident causes the accident. It's caused by bad judgment. People like to blame others for accidents, but really you've got to blame yourself."

So, relax, he says. This is Hawai`i. Hang loose. Slow down.

More homeless, more helpless

You see them everywhere and sometimes where you least expect them. You see people huddling under highway overpasses, under picnic benches, under bleachers, under portable school buildings and under banyan trees, their possessions stacked beside them or overflowing shopping carts. The number of homeless people living in Hawai`i's public parks, beaches and streets has increased by 61 percent since 2000 to at least 6,000 people, the highest ever, according to state report on the homeless issued in 2003.

Hawai`i's increase in poverty is among the highest in the nation, U.S. Census figures say. They show 11.4 percent of the state's population, or about 142,000 people, living in poverty annually.

Several charities, from churches to government programs and institutions, offer food and/or shelter to homeless individuals and families, but social workers say hundreds of people are turned away each night.

At Honolulu's Institute for Human Services women's shelter, space is so tight that homeless women throw numbers into a hat, hoping to win a safe place to sleep for the night. Those who lose the lottery are turned away, to be exposed to elements which, even in gentle Hawai`i, can include robbery and rape.

Homelessness here, as on the mainland, is blamed on a variety of factors, including the federal Welfare Reform Act of 1996, which limited families to five years of welfare benefits, and a national trend to turn the mentally ill away from hospitals.

While it might seem that being homeless in balmy Hawai`i is less unpleasant than suffering in frosty New York City, Hawai`i adds its own face to the figures: decades of failing to build affordable homes in one of the highest-priced housing markets in the nation; enormous drug problems that tear families apart; insufficient mental health programs and facilities.

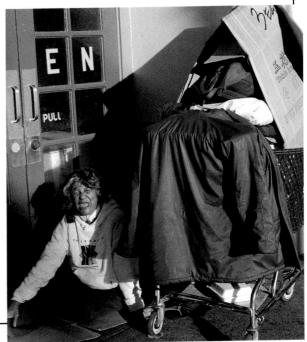

Lee S tack photo

Chinatown, Honolulu, has its share of homelessness.

Creatures

Late one night, Maui resident Margaret Norrie awoke to a nightmare. As she lay in her waterbed, she experienced a crawling sensation. Leaping up, she felt a fire-like pain singe her thighs. Norrie flipped on a light to see scores of tiny red fire ants attacking her flesh. Screaming, shivering in pain and horror, she ran to the shower to wash off the maroonish mess.

Fire ants didn't get their name because they're red, but because their sting is like a second-degree burn. According to entomologist G. Nishida in his book, *What Bit Me?*, they "… grab the victim's skin with their mandibles while driving stingers into the victim. They tend to sting several times without letting go… blistering… and may eventually scar."

The pain may be accompanied by a rash, faintness, blurring of vision, chest pains and abdominal cramps. If stung extensively, there may be nausea, vomiting, dizziness, perspiration and even shock. While Norrie did not experience those severe reactions, the red welts covering her thighs lasted for several days.

For some reason, many years ago, a rumor passed across the world that Hawai`i had no pesky insects. That's only partially true; poisonous insects are relatively few here. There is only one kind of snake established here — a harmless, tiny, blind snake — and rabies is unknown in the Hawaiian islands, says Nishida, natural science collections manager at O`ahu's Bishop Museum. Nevertheless, an abundance of creeping, crawling, biting and otherwise scary critters makes for interesting island conversation.

Like plants and people, insect transplants grow and thrive in Hawai`i's ideal climate. If you choose to live in a house or cottage, instead of a regularly-sprayed condominium, you will come to have a grudging respect for huge cockroaches that look you in the eye, spiders that swath your yard in webs, swarming termites and tiny midges that find their way into the house despite your every attempt to block them.

> 'To live here is to learn to live with bugs.'
>
> – Carlo Carbajal

Old-time Hawaiians often built their houses on stilts to discourage moisture and flooding, as well as to escape ground-dwelling bugs. It didn't always work.

Mosquitoes

Mosquitoes were once unknown on the islands. A legend says that whalers, angry because missionaries were discouraging island women from being friendly, loosed the first mosquitoes near a missionary house at Lahaina, Maui. Whatever their introduction, mosquitoes are *kama`aina* now, setting up nurseries in any stagnant water they can find, from rainforest mud puddles to *lanai* flowerpots.

One of the problems with mosquitoes, Nishida said in an interview for this book, is that they transmit heartworm to pets, especially those left outdoors overnight.

"If left untreated, your pet can die from heartworm,"a painful way to go. Be sure to give your pet monthly heartworm pills, available from your veterinarian. And, of course, protect yourself. Mosquitoes can carry malaria, dengue fever and other diseases, deadly to humans.

Centipedes

Hawai`i residents like to trade centipede horror stories. We'll swear we've encountered centipedes a foot long and measure off two feet with our hands as we talk about it. We are, of course, exaggerating. Centipedes are so ugly and move so quickly that they tend to appear larger than they actually are. Nine inches is about the largest Grant K. Uchida, an entomologist with the state department of agriculture, has seen. The ones hiding under leaves and wood in my backyard — and occasionally landing in my pool — are five to six inches. For the record, centipedes can't swim.

Maui resident Marty-Jean Bender, a biology teacher, remembers waking on two nights to find a centipede hovering near her sleeping child's open mouth. Bender's first reaction was that of anyone seeing a centipede: swat it away. But that can be foolhardy — the centipede bites with two pincers, injecting a venom to which some people are extremely allergic. The Chinese consider the centipede one of the five evils of the natural world, and anyone who's slipped his foot into a shoe and been bitten would agree.

Some of the nasty things said about centipedes are true, Uchida says. They tend to head for cozy beds, occasionally biting unknowing sleepers who scare them. But centipedes aren't out for blood, they are just trying to stay warm.

There's a commonly held belief that if you find one centipede, its mate is lurking nearby. That's not usually true, Nishida says. Centipedes don't travel with mates; if you see two or more at the same time it may be because their usual nesting places have been disturbed or because the humidity is not right for these "narrow comfort-range animals." Or they may just be out hunting for food — which does not include you.

One last thing. Superstition says it's bad luck to talk about centipede encounters, and if you talk about centipedes, you're sure to see one. So forget we mentioned the subject, okay?

Only in Hawai`i

Here's a fundraiser you aren't likely to see in, say, Buffalo or Boise. When the Big Island's East Hawai`i Cultural Center and Hilo Community Players learned their gallery and theater was infested with termites, they found a unique way to raise funds for the fumigation tenting. They invited residents to bring pieces of termite-ridden furniture to be placed inside and fumigated along with the building. The cost? A $20 tax-deductible donation.

Ants, ants, ants

There are over 40 species of ants in Hawai`i, Nishida says. Some prefer sugar; others prefer protein or fats. Answer the phone while you're making a meat sandwich and your food can be covered with the tiny creatures when you get back. In waving ribbon formation, they march en masse up walls, across bathroom tiles. Kill a few and replacement troops appear, undaunted.

Ants can tunnel through concrete floors, into the grout between ceramic tiles, erect nests in tape recorders and telephones, and have been known to ruin computers. Kill a centipede or roach and leave it in your shower — ants will carry its body away to their nests within a few hours.

"To live here," says artist Carlo Carbajal, who awoke in his cottage one night to find a centipede walking across his face, "is to learn to live with bugs. They are simply a part of your life here. You cannot escape them. But the worst is the ants. They or their scouts are everywhere!"

Spiders, all kinds

Like most Hawai`i spiders, cane spiders (also called banana spiders) are shy and relatively harmless. They don't bite unless cornered — they'll just scare you to death. Cane spiders commonly have three-inch leg spans, but islanders report spotting some as big as a man's hand. Brown and hairy, they are sometimes mistaken for deadly tarantulas, which do not live in these islands. Cane spiders are actually beneficial, eating other household insects, but their sinister appearance makes it hard to appreciate their timid nature.

Numerous other kinds of spiders live in the islands. The infamous Southern black widow shows up occasionally and the brown widow is common, often found hanging around outside homes. Brown and black widow spider bites are dangerous and require a doctor's attention.

Brown widow? Yes. Brown widows are common around both the exterior and interior of Hawai`i homes. Dr. G.B. Edwards, an arachnologist with the Florida State Collection of Arthropods in Gainesville, says the brown widow's venom is twice as potent as black widow venom. However, brown widow spiders do not inject as much venom as a black widows, are very timid, and do not defend their web. The brown widow is also slightly smaller than the black widow.

Nearly every spider will bite if cornered but most cannot penetrate your skin. Crab spiders spin enormous webs that drape backyard shrubs, hang from telephone wires or send shivers down the spines of unwary hikers. The bite of these spiders, a gardener says, causes aching welts. The violin spider is another one to watch out for; the bite is serious.

Daring jumping spider

Be on the lookout for this little fellow, common inside most homes. He is so small and playful looking — usually a half inch or less — that when a "daring jumping spider" hops onto your desk or your countertop you'll be more startled than frightened. You may be tempted to either squash it

Geckos, the good guys

They frighten and fascinate tourists, who watch transfixed as geckos converge on a porch light or slither across a hotel wall. The little lizard with the round digits is Hawai`i's mascot and you'll learn to love, or at least tolerate, him.

Having a gecko take up residence in your home is considered lucky and the chances are you'll have at least two or three of various sizes "laughing" loudly and darting about at night. Fascinating as they are, geckos can grow to several inches in length, deposit egg sacs, and leave little ice-cream-cone droppings that are a nuisance, especially when they land in your toaster or computer. You'll want to keep tight screens on your windows.

with your finger or just watch it, fascinated. However, this spider's bite is "sharp and painful and produces pale, raised bumps surrounded by redness, accompanied by blistering and swelling," according to What Bit Me? "The swelling can be severe, extending beyond the immediate bitten area… A dull throbbing pain and itchiness may last several days."

Best to squash this cute little spider as soon as you see it. Numerous other insects — hornets, fleas, mites — make our paradise less than perfect. The state department of agriculture makes valiant efforts to keep snakes, bugs and other pesky creatures away.

Fleas, ticks and their hosts

Fleas and ticks have been a problem on the islands for years. So have cats. Feral cats breed in colonies throughout the islands and many of the cats are flea and/or tick-infested. It is common, for example, to find litters of kittens at beaches and parks, begging for food yet frightened of people.

Island humane societies work hard to combat feral dog and cat problems. Some societies loan cages for volunteers to capture cats and a few veterinarians offer free or reduced-cost spaying and neutering for such animals. Some programs try a life-sustaining approach: cats are caught, vaccinated and neutered, then released back into the wild in monitored colonies. Some homeowners and restaurant owners appreciate cats because they help to alleviate another island problem: rats.

Rat tales

Who came first? The rat or the mongoose? Actually, whalers and traders were the first to arrive here. Rats hitchhiked to the islands on their ships, went forth and multiplied. At some point, mongoose were imported in an ill-planned attempt to control the rats, but they are daytime creatures and rats are nocturnal, so their paths rarely crossed. Now the mongoose has become just another interesting island creature. You'll occasionally see them — blond flashes streaking across rural roads.

Today, most islands have rodent control pro-grams. Those metal bands wrapped around palm tree trunks, glinting in the sun, prevent rats from running up the trees, a favorite nesting place.

Outbreaks of murine typhus, carried by bacteria on the fleas of rodents, occur regularly throughout the islands and especially on Maui, which suffers annual spurts in mouse populations. Typhus is a very serious disease that can cause brain damage or death.

In a true-life Pied Piper tale, the city of Honolulu once made a major assault on a rat-infested Waikiki banyan tree after a rat ran up the mayor's leg, ironi-cally, during a press conference to discuss the rat problem. Defense, and offensives, against rodents include traps and heavy spray guns to scare the long-tailed creatures out of sewers.

On the personal level, it's important to keep yards clear of trash. An aggressive cat or dog also helps the effort by discouraging pests from moving in. However, you must keep your pets from eating rats or mice, full of bacteria and loaded with lice.

Ukus (head lice)

Don't be upset if your school-age child comes home with head lice, known here as `ukus. Lice epidemics are common even in mainland schools; in Hawai`i's tropical weather, they are almost unavoidable. Teachers conduct regular checks for the sticky whitish-gray nits (eggs) or tiny lice that are almost invisible in hair. Children who have lice are sent home to parents for treatment. Over-the-counter shampoos are available, or you may ask your doctor to prescribe a stronger treatment.

Roaches

You'll also become accustomed to looking a two-inch-long cockroach in the eye. Call it a water bug, if that lessens your aversion. You'll even learn to prefer large roaches, which visit in ones and twos, to the smaller mainland varieties that invade by the hundreds.

Hawai`i hosts many kinds of roaches, but most can be kept under control by cleanliness and chemicals. A small light-colored version, the German roach, is especially plentiful here.

Tented and taken

When upscale Honolulu houses are "tented" for termites, there's an added cost. It's not for chemicals or clean up; it's for protection.

About every five or six years, wise residents have their houses tented for termites. During the process, owners leave the home for at least 24 hours, spending the night with friends or in a hotel. While they are gone, exterminating company workers pull a huge cover over the house. A machine pumps in a gas that seeps into cracks and crevices, and kills all insects inside.

The tent stays on overnight. After it is removed, workers open windows to let the gas escape. Windows remain open for several hours before it is safe for the family to return to the house.

But some families return to a house that has been cleaned out of more than insects. They find valuable possessions gone, taken by burglars who take advantage of the easy access. A wise homeowner protects his house. That can be hiring a guard, asking neighbors to be on the alert, or setting up impromptu security from a car parked nearby. In affluent neighborhoods, homeowners sometimes hire round-the-clock security guards to protect the temporarily vacant house from burglars.

Frogs and toads

Hawai`i's amphibians come in two sizes—tiny and tremendous. The little coqui frog, only about five centimeters long, is causing an uproar in the Hawaiian islands. The coqui hitched rides on plants from the Caribbean in the mid-1980s and noted that Hawai`i has plenty of mosquitoes and other insects to eat and no snakes or natural predators. Like so many of Hawai`i's *malihini,* they stayed and multiplied. Male coqui have a loud, incessant night-time mating call that has been the object of many complaints and newspaper articles. State agriculture specialists tackle the problem with everything from nets to a caffeine spray, with minimal results.

Bufo marinus

Meanwhile, that fat leathery blob thudding across your yard at night — or landing in your pet's water dish — is a *bufo marinus*, a really big, bad toad. You'll chuckle when you see one and your pet will want to play with it, but you both should stay away. The frog emits a toxin from glands behind its ears that can be deadly to pets. The toxin remains dangerous even if the toad lies squashed in your driveway or road, a state agriculture specialist says. If you can't control your pets, you can get rid of bufos by catching (while wearing thick gloves) and carrying them (in a lidded bucket) off to some mountain forest. But do keep them away from the dogs and cats and kids. Children and teenagers, by the way, have been known to use the toxin as a stimulant.

No doubt you'll learn to live with and respect all these island creatures eventually and you will certainly overcome any fear you may have. If they become too great a nuisance, you can always spray. And spray. And spray again. Some residents report success with electronic devices to ward off rodents.

"I vowed I wouldn't use chemical sprays," says one newcomer. "But dealing with bugs here is like giving birth. You're in labor and all your good intentions are forgotten. It's like, 'Bring on the drugs.' "

Protect your home, your pets, yourself

- **Pill or gel your pet.** New advances in flea and tick control make it easy to keep domestic pets flea free. Monthly pills seem to work well, as do gels applied between the animal's shoulder blades.

- **Clean up your yard.** Eliminate any stagnant water, virtual "nurseries" for mosquitoes. Trim palm trees often, keep yards free of litter, store grain and any food in rat-proof containers, and keep tight lids on trash cans. Most cats are too smart to attack a rat, but a rambunctious dog can discourage rats. Be careful. Rat bites are dangerous. If bitten, rush to an emergency room.

- **Spray?** Chemical sprays, applied around the exterior of homes and judiciously inside, help to avoid insect problems. Many residents, however, simply put up with the creatures or find ecologically-sound ways of dealing with them. Ground cinnamon is said to discourage ants. And a solution of 3 cups water, 1 cup sugar and 1 teaspoon boric acid sprinkled near nests kills the colony. Bay leaves keep bugs (weevils) out of staples like flour and rice.

- **Consider these ecologically-safe tricks.** Plantation camp residents had some interesting ways to deal with insects. They put water-filled jars under each leg of the kitchen table, discouraging ants from crawling up. And the same system worked to keep crawling creatures off beds. It's also wise to avoid bed covers and dust ruffles that extend to the floor, ladders for crawling bugs.

- **Maintain a humorous outlook.** Have faith that eventually you will become accustomed to sharing paradise with a few of God's less-welcome creatures.

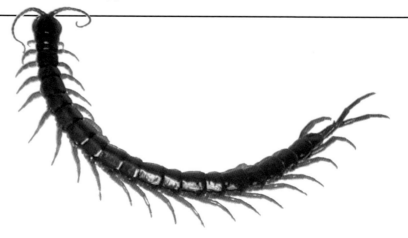

Matthew Thayer

ka\`ne\`e

\`ana

moving

Lighten

your

load

Cargo containers are unloaded from ships at the Honolulu harbor. About 95 percent of Hawai\`i's consumer goods are imported. In addition, some newcomers bring whole households of furniture and belongings.

From New York to Maui...cautiously

It takes a lot of nerve to move to Hawai'i. And a double dose if you've never visited the islands. But that's what New Yorkers Coe Huston and Danielle Dewey Huston did a few years ago.

Coe is a videographer; Danielle is a veterinarian. Danielle's education took the couple to the Caribbean for three years. When they returned to Manhattan, the Hustons got back into their hectic city lifestyle. But they missed the island tropical life--warm sunny days, an aqua ocean to swim and an easier pace.

"We'd work and work and save to take a vacation, to get back to the tropics, " Coe says.

"We wanted to start our family," Danielle adds, "and we wanted to raise our kids elsewhere than Manhattan."

Hawai'i seemed a smart place to settle. The couple had first-class qualifications...but would their work be needed on the islands?

And which island would be best for them?

Danielle stayed in New York while Coe went to Kaua'i and landed a job with a sailing company, taking tourists on ocean trips and teaching them to sail. He enjoyed the work, but it was rough and dangerous. He remembers rescuing tourists regularly.

Coe tried Maui next, got a video job...and the island felt right.

"More opportunity than Kaua'i and less busy than O'ahu," Danielle says.

Danielle secured a position in a Kihei, Maui, veterinary clinic even before she left New York. She came simply, with just two suitcases and the couple began visiting thrift stores, buying some furniture and items they needed.

After a year on the island, Danielle and Coe felt sure Hawai'i was the right choice for them. They sold their apartment in New York and bought an apartment in a medium-priced condominium complex in south Kihei. Then they shipped a container with their furniture, rugs, and other items from New York to the islands. They had been storing the furniture, without cost, with relatives.

"I would do it the same way again," Danielle says. "It's wise to take a move to the islands step by step like we did."

Toni Polancy

Two-year-old Max, Coe and Danielle Huston enjoy a breezy day in paradise.

The Hustons had moved from Manhattan to have a better life for their future children and, according to plan, Danielle soon became pregnant. The birth of tow-headed Max brought new questions: How would mom and dad work and still care for the tot?

The Hustons considered opening their own veterinary clinic...then Danielle got an idea. In busy New York, it's not unusual for veterinarians to visit patients in their homes.

"The service is really good for old animals or pets who would be scared traveling to a clinic," Danielle says. And it's a major convenience for elderly people who might have trouble bringing a pet to a clinic or people working long hours with little time to spare.

A mobile service would eliminate the cost of an office and employees and allow Danielle to work on her own schedule, making time to be with baby Max and keeping weekends free for family life.

Danielle was a little apprehensive. Would Maui pet owners warm to what was, for many of them, a new concept?

The concerns were short-lived. Before long, both *malihini* and *kama`aina* pet owners were responding to newspaper advertising and word-of-mouth endorsements. Within months, the couple had a full schedule of appointments.

Coe assists Danielle, driving to clients' homes or apartments all across the island. He helps with tough assignments like gently holding a huge, frightened dog while his wife administers a shot.

"There's a part of moving to Hawai`i that's selfish in some ways."

— Coe Huston

Especially appreciated, Coe points out, is the euthanasia service that allows a beloved dog or cat to die at home, in its owner's arms.

Two years ago, their business well established and their family started, Danielle and Coe bought a house in Kula, part way up Maui's Haleakala mountain.

Danielle advises Hawai'i newcomers to relax, be open-minded, willing to try new businesses and new ideas.

Another consideration: "I had no idea how isolated I would be from my family, especially now having a baby. Lucky we have things like Skype," Danielle says. Her mother is moving to Maui to be near her only grandchild.

Having a child has made Coe introspective. "There's a part of moving to Hawai'i that's selfish in some ways," he maintains. "You are moving away just at the time when parents are getting older and needing you most. You shed some of your responsibility when you move so far away. When you have your own child, you realize that."

Their work takes the Hustons to all parts of Maui, lets them interact with all cultures.

"The warm weather, the beautiful sunsets, postcard images get boring after awhile. It's not enough to sustain a life. You have to become more connected with the cultural aspects, with people," Coe says.

"(On the islands) we are all from someplace else and we have to make each other our family…It breeds a sense of community here. Here, people help each other in intimate ways like families do."

Moving

How much "baggage" will you bring?

Almost everyone moves to these islands with more than they need. Until you've lived here for a few months, it's difficult to envision how simple your needs will be. Several island newcomers offered this good advice:

- **Don't bring anything you can buy here** — and with the advent of Kmart, WalMart, Sam's Club and Costco, almost anything can be bought here.

- **Do bring cherished items** that can't be replaced — mementos, family photos, keepsakes.

- **Be judicious** about bringing family antiques or favorite pieces of large furniture. You should consider that Hawai`i's climate (very damp in some places; very dry in others) and insects (termites) can damage some furniture.

More Good Advice

- Visit several islands, if possible, before you choose one on which to settle. The islands vary greatly in ambiance, opportunities, cost, and safety.

- Once you've moved, don't look back for six months to a year. It takes that long to get even a little accustomed to life here, advised several newcomers.

- Temporary housing — a place to reside for a few days or a few weeks while you search for permanent housing — is difficult to come by on all islands. Most people arrange with a travel agent to stay in a vacation condominium for a month or so while they search for a more permanent home. A rental agent can be useful, or check the newspaper classified ads or Craigslist.com.

Your move

may be less stressful if you plan it for months when fewer tourists are on the islands. That's usually May, September and October. More available flights, rental cars and short term apartment rentals are available.

Bringing a little

On the plane

Most rental apartments are geared to tourists and include all appliances, utensils, pots and pans, even coffee pots. So a few large suitcases will probably hold all you really need to begin life here: casual clothes, sandals, sneakers or loafers; a few toiletries, perhaps a small radio, cell phone and laptop computer. And even most of those items can be purchased here relatively inexpensively.

Consider paying the extra fee to bring several suitcases with you on the plane instead of shipping items. Airlines continue to increase costs, but so do shippers and the post office...so paying for extra luggage may be less expensive than shipping or mailing.

Via the post office

If you decide to bring more than a few suitcases of belongings, a friend or contact on the island to which you are moving is

My story: a new life and a new business in 2 suitcases

At age 50, I bought the franchise for a new business on Maui (Homes and Land real estate magazines) and left a job as managing editor of a daily newspaper in Pennsylvania. I brought with me to the island, to start my new life and my new business, only two large suitcases and two carry-on bags.

One suitcase included minimal clothing: shorts, jeans, swimsuits, a few casual tops...and two "outfits" (simple skirts and blouses) for business. A "carry-on" held important personal papers and information for starting the magazine.

Another suitcase sheltered three pairs of sandals and memories with which I could not part: photo albums and mementos of my daughters' childhoods. I included a couple of favorite videos to play when I became lonely in my new environment.

Once here, I bought a TV/VCR immediately (for "companionship") and would eventually purchase the office equipment I needed from garage sales and stores on the island. Those things were less expensive to obtain here than to ship, even back in 1991 when shipping was much less expensive than it is now.

I return to Pennsylvania about ever two years and occasionally bring back other items long stored in my sister's Pennsylvania attic... Christmas ornaments, a collection of dolls, more photo albums, favorite books. All the special objects that make up a life here on the islands or elsewhere. —*Toni Polancy*

a valuable resource — someone to whom to send boxes so they'll be on island when you arrive. You should check all resources available in your area and compare prices. However, one of the least expensive ways to ship is via parcel post from your U.S. post office. Pack your valuables in strong cardboard boxes and make sure none weighs more than 70 pounds. Seal well with a strong plastic tape, wrapped both vertically and horizontally.

Save $$$ with "media rate"
Books, videos and DVDs may be shipped via the U.S. Postal Service at "media rate" which is considerably less costly. Your packages may take a month or more to appear at your doorstep, but when you first move here you'll be too busy to read, watch or listen anyway. Mark your box "media rate" and be sure the postal rep gives you the lowest rate.

- **Your best bet:** Pack up your boxes, mail via slowest and cheapest rate, and use the intervening time, while you wait for your belongings, to find an apartment. Or you may pack the boxes and decide to have a friend send them later, after you have an address. Once you've lived here for a few months, you'll also have a better idea of which items you really want.

- **Packing your boxes to store for shipment later?** Mark the boxes 1, 2, 3, etc. and make a corresponding list of what is in each box. Take the list with you to Hawai`i. Have the cartons shipped as you need them, referring to the list and asking for the boxes by number. Why not just mark the contents of the box on the outside? Because "Grandma's antique silver" might prove a little too tempting for thieves.

More good advice:

- **Keep a list of boxes and contents** so you can track which have arrived. If you are sending many boxes, it can be extremely confusing if sent at different times.

Time of the year
Your container of furniture may take longer during the busy pre-Christmas season when commercial goods are being shipped in.

- **Compare costs.** Visit a mailing center such as Mail Boxes, Etc. and ask for the lowest rates. Get estimates from national shippers on the Web. Try UPS.com, FedEx.com, DHL.com. For lowest post office rates, go to the window. Their website (USPS.com) does not automatically calculate lowest rates.

- **Use several smaller boxes** instead of large ones. Shipping may be less expensive and will certainly be more convenient. For example, United Parcel Service (UPS) calculates cost by size as well as weight of boxes. A large box can throw you into a higher price range even though it does not weigh as much as it might. At this writing, the cost of sending a 70-pound box (the maximum allowed) from mainland U.S. to Hawai'i is $107. Check with post office for details, maximum size.

Bringing a lot

Using a mover

If you cannot bear to part with your furniture, do like the Hustons did — store it to ship later, after you've chosen a residence. A legitimate moving company will pack your items in special 'vanpacks" and ship them to Honolulu with many other people's possession in an ocean shipping container. If you live on a neighbor island, your items will be forwarded from O'ahu to your island on a separate barge. The process takes several weeks.

Across the ocean

Folks who want to move massive amount of good ship them via "container," basically a very big box that protects the items from most of the damage that could occur on a cross-ocean voyage.

A Matson Navigation Co. representative says it costs (in 2010) from $4,200 to $7,300 to move household goods from a mainland port (Los Angeles, Oakland, Seattle or Portland) in a 20-foot or 40-foot container. Be sure to get a full quote and follow directions carefully. It's important.

A container goes by space, not by weight. In other words, you can put a certain amount in the container no matter how heavy it is (grandma's baby grand!).

How much furniture can you get in an ocean container?

A Horizon Lines representative suggests this: in your home or yard, measure off an area 19 feet, 4 inches in length; 7 feet, 8 inches in width; and 7 feet, 10 inches in height. Try stacking all your items in that space…at least imagine them in that space. Is it enough? Is it worth the cost?

Less than a full load?

If you don't have enough goods to fill a container, you should contact a freight forwarder who consolidates shipments. Forwarders collect various clients' items until there is enough to fill a container.

DHX is one of the largest, operating from many areas of the country. Depending on how busy the forwarder (also called consolidator) is, you may have to wait days or weeks for the container to fill up and begin its journey.

You can check the Internet for forwarders from your area at www.forwarders.com.

IMPORTANT: Packing according to shippers' regulations may require a professional packer or mover. You should be aware that a container is four feet off the ground and "packing" may require a forklift. Also know that you must hire a moving company or truck to get your furniture from the docks to your house after you arrive on island. Moving to a neighbor island is more complicated, but only slightly more. Get full details and reservations well in advance. Timing can be a problem.

Shipping a car

Matson Navigation and Horizon Lines also move cars from the west coast of the United States to the Hawaiian Islands. At this writing, the cost for a standard-sized vehicle hovers around $1,000 to O`ahu or a neighbor island. Horizon ships leave Oakland once a week, and the journey takes a week and a half. But your car is not guaranteed to be on a particular shipment, so it's difficult to count on the exact time it will arrive.

Phone numbers under Resources, at the end of this chapter, will give you current costs. The car must be empty during shipping and the gas tank must be less than one-half full.

Should you bring your car? The cost of shipping your auto versus buying here is a calculation only you can make. If your car is relatively new, if you are tied to a lease, if you are still making payments on a car you have purchased and owe more than you would net selling it, you may want to ship it. New cars are expensive here; used ones are quite reasonable. (See Autos in the Necessities chapter of this book.)

A scam?

Imagine turning your cherished possessions over to several men in a big truck. The truck drives away…and you never see the possessions again. It happens. Read North American Van Lines' website for ways to avoid a scam.

www.northamericanvanlines.com

Keep important documents at your side

One of the most important reminders we can give you is this: have all personal papers, medical records, prescriptions and important documents within easy reach during your transition to Hawai`i. These papers should travel with you at all times, in your carry-on luggage. The best way to transport them is in an expanding file with compartments, available at office supply stores. **Before you travel, duplicate the papers and leave a copy with a friend, as backup in case any are lost.**

Healthy advice

- If you take prescription drugs, be sure to ask your current doctor to provide enough medication for at least three or four months while you settle in and find a new doctor. Be sure to bring all information relating to the prescription, as well as your current doctors' phone numbers and addresses.
- Bring all your family's health records and inoculation records, including copies of X-rays and mammograms, so future tests can be compared.

PERSONAL RECORDS
- Birth certificates of all family members
- Citizenship papers
- Children's report cards
- Passports
- Inoculation records
- Marriage license
- Child custody documents
- Medical records
- Adoption papers
- Death certificates
- Wills
- Annulments of any previous marriages
- Divorce papers

FINANCIAL RECORDS
- Motor vehicle title
- Property deeds
- Insurance cards and documents
- Savings account books
- Stock certificates and other investments
- Household goods shipping information
- Checkbooks
- Credit cards
- Names and addresses of companies where you recently opened or closed accounts
- Bills due during the time you move as well as records of any you have paid in past three months (in case questions or problems arise)
- Military: Armed Forces identification cards and copy of application for allotment (if any)

Trans-ocean shipping companies

- **Matson Navigation Co.**
  (800) 462-8766
  www.matson.com

- **Horizon Lines**
  (808) 842-1515
  www.shipmyvehicle.com

- **Aloha Cargo Transport**
  (800) 327-7739
  Pacific Northwest freight
  forwarder to Hawai`i

Trans-Pacific and Inter-island

- **U.S. Postal Service**
  (800) 275-8777
  Toll-free information on mailing
  and shipping boxes weighing up
  to 70 pounds
  www.usps.com

Inter-island shippers

- **Young Brothers Limited**
  (808) 543-9447
  www.HTBYB.com

Moving companies
  (Among many listed in the
  Honolulu phone book)

- **Island Movers, Inc.**
  (United Van Lines)
  (808) 832-4000
  www.islandmovers.com

- **American Movers**
  (808) 216 1005

- **Bekins Hawaiian Movers, Inc.**
  (808) 862-6055
  www.bekins.com/moving/
  Bekins-Hawaiian-Movers-Inc

- **Pacific Transfer**
  (Atlas Van Lines)
  (808) 676-9120
  www.pacifictransfer.com

Get the children involved

Long-distance moves are especially traumatic for young children. Here's a way to make the move easier. Let your child choose four or five favorite toys, dolls or stuffed animals and help pack the toys in a separate box. Let your child decorate the outside of the box with colorful magic markers and help address the box. Take the child with you to the post office when you mail it and let him wave goodbye to his "friends." Tell him they are traveling to Hawai`i first and will be waiting for him to come, too. Once your child arrives on the islands, opening his special box and seeing familiar faces — Bert or Ernie, Barbie or Sponge Bob — will soothe the transition.

Should your pet come along?

You've probably heard stories about Hawai`i's stringent quarantine law for pets. You may have heard a variety of comments, everything from "You have to quarantine your pet for four whole months!" to "The new rules mean you don't have to quarantine at all."

Both comments are correct. After more than 80 years of quarantining incoming pets, the state of Hawai`i in 2003 eased restrictions to the point where you can choose whether your pet will be quarantined for 120 days, 30 days, less than five days or — if you follow guidelines exactly — your pet can be released to you at the Honolulu airport.

You must get complete instructions at least 4 months prior to moving.

Call or write
Animal Quarantine Station
99-951 Halawa Valley Street
Aiea, HI 96701-3246
(808) 483-7151 or fax (808) 483-7161
Or visit the Internet:
www. hawaiiag.org/hdoa/

Your decision depends on how much time you have to prepare the animal prior to the move and your ability to exactly follow stringent requirements from the state's animal quarantine station. Today, about 75 percent of incoming animals avoid incarceration and are released to their owners at the Honolulu airport.

If you follow all procedures carefully, your pet's current veterinarian can administer the mandated vaccinations and microchip prior to your pet coming to Hawai`i. The vet will also prepare documents for you to present to authorities when you arrive here.

IMPORTANT: Whichever quarantine method you choose, you must begin by getting complete instructions from the Department of Agriculture's Animal Quarantine Station at least four months prior to your move. Contact information is listed here. We do not list the criteria because more changes in qualifications and procedures are possible and it is important that you get correct, up-to-date information.

The vaccination and testing time is crucial, there's a lot of paperwork, and the regulations are complicated. Counting veterinarian visits, travel containers and quarantine fees, the process of bringing your pet may cost close to $1,000. And if you or your hometown veterinarian makes a mistake, your pet may be sentenced to several days, a month or as long as four months incarceration.

Methods of traveling

Once a pet is pre-qualified for quarantine, it can be shipped to Hawai`i. The pet must arrive at the Honolulu airport for inspection; it cannot arrive at any other island. You should get specific instructions from your airline for shipping your pet; however, be aware that the airline may not have the latest information or be savvy about Hawai`i quarantine requirements.

Your pet must be in a waterproof pet carrier with plenty of air circulation, such as the standard plastic kennels available at most pet stores. You will pay less for your pet's air transportation if it travels on the same flight as you. Be warned: your pet is considered freight and may be shipped on a "space available" basis on some airlines. Also, some airlines will not ship animals during hot summer months.

You should also know

If you decide to bring your pet and you do not have the advance time to avoid quarantine, you should know that your pet would probably survive the ordeal with a minimum of trauma if you can reduce incarceration time to 30 days. We have interviewed more than 70 pet owners whose pets endured 30 or 120 days of quarantine. By far, most dogs and cats survived 30 days with little trouble, but 120 days seemed very difficult, and some owners attributed personality changes in their pets to the long confinement.

Continued

Here's a book that may save your pet's life

Leptospirosis, flash floods, deadly toads, dangerous plants. There's a lot to know about caring for you pet in the islands. *The Hawai`i Pet Book* includes a variety of resources and information useful to island pet owners, from ways to save money on flea controls to finding a place to live. To purchase a copy, go to www.amazon.com, visit your local bookstore or send $20 to us at Barefoot Publishing, Inc., 815 Kupulau Drive, Kihei, HI 96753. We'll pay postage.

Pet-friendly housing help:

The Hawaiian Humane Society shares a list of pet-friendly apartment buildings on O`ahu. Write to them at 2700 Wai`alae Avenue, Honolulu, HI 96826 or visit their website at www.hawaiianhumane.org. *The Hawaii Pet Book* includes pet-friendly apartment complexes on neighbor islands. Remember that most apartments in Hawai`i are individually owned and the landlord may not allow animals, even if the complex does.

The O'ahu quarantine facility is clean and well managed, but its purpose is to isolate animals. Quarantined pets are held in large indoor/outdoor cages with plenty of room, but have little interaction with humans and no socialization with other animals. Cats seem to handle this better than dogs. Dogs are eager for attention from visitors. Owners, friends or volunteers can visit pets at the quarantine center daily.

But the real question is...

Quarantine aside, the real question is, should you bring your pet to Hawai'i? Only you know how much you love and will miss your pet, but please consider this:

- You may have difficulty in finding a place to live that allows pets. Temporary housing that accepts pets is particularly scarce on all islands.
- You will probably be extremely busy securing a job, setting up a new life, making friends. Will you have time to give your pet the attention it needs?

A faithful friend awaits his master's return at Kapa'a, Kaua'i.

Your moving budget

Here's a list for calculating your moving costs to Hawai`i, including some items you may have forgotten.

Cost

1. Flight from home to Hawai`i for yourself . . . . ._____

    for each member family . . . . ._____

2. Shipping car

    travel to coastal city (L.A. or San Francisco) ._____

    over-night stays enroute . . . . ._____

    stays in coastal city as you wait to ship the auto . . . . ._____

    food during trip and stay . . . . ._____

    auto rental while you wait for your car to arrive in Honolulu

    or outer island (cost per day times number of days) . . . . ._____

    additional shipping to outer islands . . . . ._____

3. Purchase or lease car (if you have not sent yours)

    lease deposit . . . . ._____

    to buy new . . . . ._____

    to buy used late model . . . . ._____

    to buy used "cruiser" . . . . ._____

4. Shipping furniture

    cost to move furniture to coastal city for shipping . . . . ._____

    cost to pack and ship to Hawai`i . . . . ._____

    additional costs to outer island . . . . ._____

    storage while you house hunt . . . . ._____

5. Housing

    hotel or short term apartment . . . . ._____

    permanent housing . . . . ._____

    rental deposit - usually one month's rent . . . . ._____

    first month's rent . . . . ._____

    utility deposits and turn-on cost: phone . . . . ._____

                                 electricity . . . . ._____

6. Living cost while you search for job (three-to-six months)

    food costs . . . . ._____

    estimate $80 per person per week for adults . . . . ._____

    estimate $50 per person per week for child . . . . ._____

                              total living Costs _____

Total living costs _____ **+** Total moving costs _____ **=** Total cost of your move _____

Sending plants

Plants must go through a cumbersome quarantine and inspection before being allowed into Hawai`i, so household plants are best left behind. Those that go through inspection must be free from insects, disease and sand, soil, earth or deteriorated peat. Contact the address below for details.

U.S. Department of Agriculture
Animal and Plant Health Inspection Service
Terminal Box 57
Honolulu International Airport
Honolulu, HI 96819

moku 'aina
'aina hea?

which island ?

An important decision

that will affect

your success or

failure here

For detailed information
on any island, go to:
zoomprospector.com

Abundant choices

Michael Miller came to the islands several years ago with friends, a family of four. They all shared a dream — a quiet bungalow by the ocean. They were sure they'd found it in a rented cottage in a quaint Polynesian community on the north shore of O`ahu, but within a few months the glow of paradise began to fade.

The father, a building contractor, could not find a job. Michael, a waiter, and the mother, a physical therapist, secured work, but it was in busy Honolulu — more than an hour's drive each way in rush-hour traffic.

Meanwhile, the two daughters, 10 and 14, had trouble adjusting to new schools, where they were among only a handful of Caucasians. They began to skip classes. Within a year, the family returned to California. Only Michael remains on the islands.

Today, the chances are that a building contractor would be able to find work here, but this family's experience holds some valuable lessons for newcomers: First, the family might have fared better if they had carefully chosen their location. Settling in an area closer to Honolulu, such as Kailua or Kane`ohe, would have put the adults closer to work and the children in school districts with more Caucasian children or a cultural mix with which they might have felt more comfortable.

People in the rest of the world tend to think of Hawai`i as one place, but that is like saying all of the United States is Texas or all of Europe is France. The six populated Hawaiian islands share certain advantages, and problems, discussed in other chapters of this book. Except for those similarities, the islands and towns vary greatly in climate, ambiance and lifestyle.

Choose your climate

Each Hawaiian island is, in effect, a small land mass with many geological variances: a sunny southern side where temperatures typically reach 90 degrees or more in the summer, but rarely drop below 70 degrees in the winter. Each island also has a rainy windward side. Some island neighborhoods are perched on mountains and temperatures can be much cooler, dropping into the 50s on winter evenings. If you don't like the climate in one locale, you can move to another in which you may be more comfortable.

Choose your ambiance

Hawai`i is a neoteric state, with similar people often settling in the same area, thereby creating a distinctive ambiance. Many towns fall into easy categories which reflect the population. When visiting various towns, ask anyone: "Who lives here?" You're sure to receive a simple, accurate answer. Typically, Hawai`i's towns fall into these designations: tourist; surfer/hippie; local; new/developing, or business.

Choose your decade

You have yet another lifestyle choice — one unique to the islands. You may, in effect, choose the era in which to live. The islands vary in the degree to which they have developed. Would you prefer to live on an island reminiscent of the 1980s or 90s (O`ahu); 1970s (Maui); 1950s or 60s (Kaua`i and the Big Island) or 1940s (Moloka`i and Lana`i)? This is not a criticism. Most of us would prefer to live and raise families in a slower, more innocent time. Isn't that part of the island dream for which we search?

    The following is an overview of each island and includes a list of resources for obtaining additional information. The number of McDonald's restaurants and Starbucks Coffee shops serves as a pop culture measurement of development. Population counts are given for four dates, 1980, 1990, 1997 and 2008, to show the growth on each island.

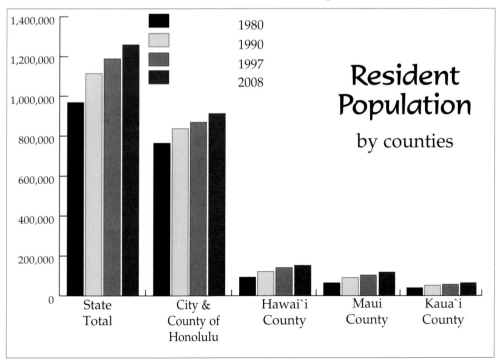

Resident Population by counties

Legend: 1980, 1990, 1997, 2008

Categories: State Total, City & County of Honolulu, Hawai`i County, Maui County, Kaua`i County

The Big Island

Climates vary on The Big Island of Hawai`i. A wild horse grazes in the Waipi`o Valley; a snowmobiler takes advantage of the cold, white stuff atop Mauna Kea.

G Brad Lewis

Photo courtesy of Big Island Visitor's Bureau

Hawai`i the big island

Want to settle in the Hawaiian islands as inexpensively as possible? Consider the island named Hawai`i, called simply the Big Island.

The Big Island lolls at the southern tip of the island chain like a handsome, angry giant — growling, churning, and flexing his muscles. It's almost twice the size of the rest of the islands combined and still growing. Kilauea, an active volcano in Hawai`i Volcanoes National Park has been continuously spewing lava since 1983. The lava flows toward the ocean, mostly through natural underground tubes, spurts into the sea in a hissing cloud of steam, cools and hardens, increasing the Big Island's size and creating its famous black sand beaches. Since 1983 the volcano has coughed up more than 500 acres of new land, mostly hardened lava at the southern and eastern edges of the island — crunchy, "rocky" land, difficult on which to build or farm.

Concerned with the high cost of living, neighbor islanders sometimes consider moving to the Big Island, where land and houses in low-priced eastern areas can cost a

Size: 4,028 square miles

Population in 1980: 92,053; **in 1997:** 144,445; **in 2004:** 158,423; **in 2009:** 192,691

Predominant occupations: resorts, tourist-related business; astronomy; geophysical endeavors; healthcare; cattle ranching; coffee production and exporting; small flower and produce cultivation and exporting; real estate; arts and crafts.

Unemployment in 1998: 10.2%; **in 2004:** about 4.5%; **in 2010** 9.9%

Number of McDonald's restaurants: 9; **of Starbucks Coffee shops:** 6; **of Costco warehouses:** 1.

The best thing about the island: Economic diversification.

The worst thing about the island: Vog and drug use.

What other islanders say about the Big Island: "Land and housing is cheaper... but the drug problems are bad..."

What the Big Island residents say: "We are environmental pioneers! It's invigorating to live on an island that is still forming."

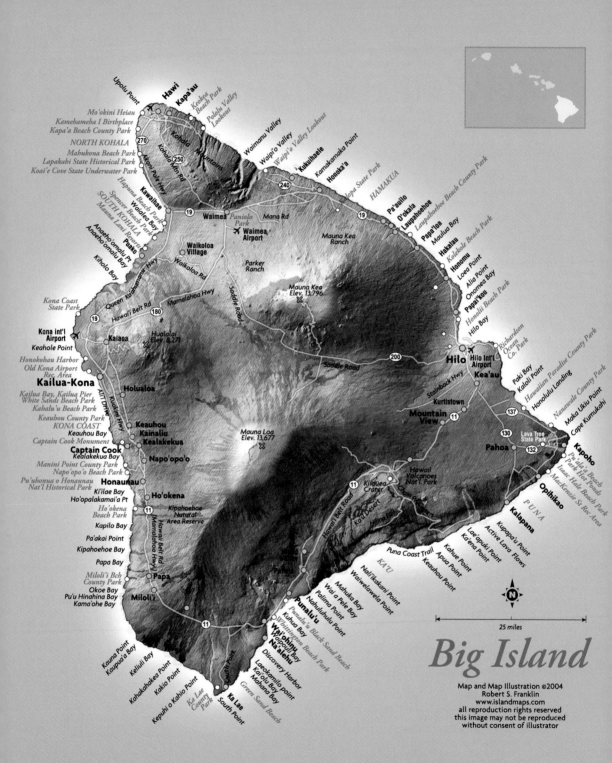

Big Island

Map and Map Illustration ©2004
Robert S. Franklin
www.islandmaps.com
all reproduction rights reserved
this image may not be reproduced
without consent of illustrator

25 miles

fraction of those in high-priced O`ahu, Maui or Kaua`i. There are two reasons land is less expensive here: first, the Big Island is so large more land is available, and second, some of the land is either covered by recent lava flow and or is in the probable path of future flows.

Living with volcanoes

Its geological activity makes the Big Island an interesting, exciting — and somewhat dangerous — place to live. Kilauea's lava production releases gases that mix with moisture in the air to form vog, a smog-like condition that is blamed for decreased crop yields and increased breathing problems for people with conditions like asthma and bronchitis.

The island is also prone to earthquakes. In 1868 a monstrous 7.9 earthquake rocked Ka`u on the eastern side of the island, causing 81 deaths. Earthquakes registering 6 to 7 on the Richter scale shook the island in 1973, 1975, and 1989. In 2003, Big Island Mayor Harry Kim, in a *Honolulu Advertiser* story, warned that another could occur at any time. and urged residents, especially the thousands of new residents who are unfamiliar with quakes, to be prepared. In recent years, building codes have been toughened to make structures somewhat safer.

"People forget that earthquakes of this size are — I hate to say it, but I'll say it — a common, natural occurrence for the island of Hawai`i," Kim told *The Advertiser.*

In addition to the big shakes, small, usually harmless earthquakes also occur often on the Big Island. They sometimes include swarms of "microearthquakes" such as those recorded near campgrounds in the Hawai`i Volcanoes National Park in 1997. In the first four hours of that episode, 60 earthquakes were recorded, along with many additional quakes too small to record. No injuries or damage occurred.

Scary, yes, but all that geological activity is not as unpleasant as it sounds. The Big Island is so vast, and its two major commercial centers so far apart (about 100 miles) that volcanic activity on the Hilo side is hardly noticeable on the Kona side. The Big Island's western coast is enjoying a tourism and real estate boom. Direct flights from Japan to the Kona coast began in the mid-1990s, bringing 60,000 Japanese visitors and an additional $45 million annually.

The Kona side

Along the dry, sunny western Kona Coast the population has doubled since 1980 and new housing developments with prices comparable to those on other Hawaiian islands, overlook the ocean. Life in Kailua-Kona is focused on Kailua Bay, laced with tourist shops and prized for its abundant fishing. Meanwhile, Kona's 2,500 acres of coffee orchards are world famous. Kona coffee, coveted for its intense flavor, contributes about $15 million annually to the Big Island economy.

Kona is the busy, developed, some would say *haole* (Caucasian) side of the island. Queen Ka`ahumanu Road is Main Street, U.S.A. KMart, Costco, WalMart, Ross, Safeway and other stores compete for attention. Farther south, a few small charming towns like Captain Cook greet visitors with quaint coffee shops and boutiques.

North of Kona, past the unique outdoor airport, life gets fancier. Dotted with posh resorts, luxurious estates and high-end developments, the Kohala Coast seems destined to become the Big Island's Diamond Head neighborhood. The resorts are spectacular, but the South Kohala coast is a desolate moonscape of lava — miles of it as far as eye can see. Using white coral stones gathered from beaches, enterprising residents have written messages on the black crust, a unique Big Island graffiti: "Welcome Rick"; "Aloha, Laurie"; and a simple ode to one of Hawai`i's favorite foods: "SPAM."

The Hamakua Coast

On the other hand, the Northern part of the island feels like Paradise Discovered. Just an hour or so from tourist hoopla, the western-style town of Waimea (population 6,000 plus), sleeps peacefully amid misty ranch lands, graceful mountains and sloping green valleys. Farther north, the Hamakua coastline is sprinkled with sleepy villages.

In recent years, thousands of acres of commercial sugarcane land has been converted to other agricultural or residential use. Plenty of rain along the coast makes it a natural for agriculture. Utilities are few, but land is still relatively inexpensive and the Hamakua Coast is an exciting area to watch. You can easily drive to Hilo from here… but there's a more intriguing way to get from Kona to Hilo: Saddle Road.

Strange passage

Residents in a rush use Saddle Road to travel between Hilo and Kona. The three-hour 100-mile ride (locals can, and do, make the trip in one and one-half hours) winds between two dormant volcanoes, Mauna Kea and Mauna Loa. Civilization ends and the Saddle Road adventure begins at Waikoloa Village (population 2,248), a new town of modern houses and condominiums built to house workers for Kohala's hotels.

Recently-repaved Saddle Road is dangerously narrow and curvy in places, with many blind spots and the occasional speeding resident hurling his truck (on sky-high wheels) down the center of the road, toward you. Car rental agencies warn tourists not to travel the road and won't insure cars there. Accidents are common and often fatal.

Ah, but what a beautiful and spooky ride for the strong-hearted.

Along Saddle Road, the verdant pastures of Waimea's beautiful Parker Ranch, the largest privately-owned ranch in the U.S., give way to the barren desert of Pohakuloa Military Training Area, marked on maps as a "High Danger Area." The road winds through years of lava accumulation, finally passing swampy areas where spindly young trees loom like gray ghosts in the mist. No wonder numerous UFO sightings have been reported here. No wonder people whisper of seeing the Night Marchers, ancient Hawaiian ghost troops in full regal attire. Some folks still believe the Hawaiian Goddess Pele dwells in these mountains and the volcanic eruptions are evidence of her wrath.

The Hilo side

Come at last to Hilo, the state's fourth largest city. This charming old town on Hilo Bay is the island's major seaport and its commercial and government center. We're in volcano country. Residents say vog usually heads further south, but today a gray-brown dampness hangs heavy in the air.

With about 140 inches of rain a year, this part of the island has ideal growing conditions, relatively inexpensive land, and is one of the world's foremost exporters of macadamia nuts as well as exotic flowers: orchids, anthurium, ginger and bird-of-paradise. Should you decide to join the new growers in the Puna District, you'll find plenty of support and advice from a mix of big ranchers; longtime small farmers who sell their wares at Hilo's popular Saturday morning open-air farmer's market; local crafters

continues on page 300

7 acres, 3 kids, plenty animals and a trampoline on the Hamakua Coast

Tim Mann has lived on the Big Island for 28 years, even since he sailed 2,400 miles from the Marquesas to Hilo Bay on a boat he made himself. He knew so little about Hawai`i that he pronounced Hilo "high-low," like a thermometer reading.

Today, Mann, a draftsman who designs houses, lives on seven acres of Hamakua coastline at Honoka`a, with his wife Susanne and their children, Victor, 9; Jack, 3; and Lucky, 2.

Their lifestyle is rural and simple. Victor's school is only two miles away. The family goes often to a surfing beach at nearby Waipio Valley. Buying food or clothing means a major drive, but since the opening of Walmart in Hilo (42 miles away) and Costco in Kona (50 miles the other way) shopping is otherwise as it might be in any rural mainland area. The family also patronizes local farmers' markets and grocery stores. But, life on the vast, sparsely populated northern side of this very big island is not for everyone. There's no night life, no restaurants open past 8 p.m.

"You've got to spend time with yourself and if you don't like yourself you are shit up the creek."

"You've got to spend time with yourself and if you don't like yourself you are shit up the creek," Tim says. Still, that can be the best thing about the Big Island. The family has developed a daily custom that takes advantage of their unique environment. They call it "the evening show."

Every year, instead of many small toys, the Manns buy one large Christmas gift for the whole family. Last year, that gift was a trampoline placed on the huge lawn that looks out to the ocean. Their home, like many on the Hamakua Coast, is on former sugar cane land. There are few trees, lights, distractions. Every evening, at about the time mainland families are plopping down in front of their televisons, the Mann family climbs on to its trampoline to await a daily miracle. As the huge Big Island sky begins to paint itself orange and yellow and red, the family lays flat on the trampoline and spends some quiet time staring up at "The Show," appreciating nature... and life... and each other.

Tim Mann, anyone will tell you, is a pretty tough guy. Just look at all those tattoos on his arms and his back. But Tim says he loves the island so much he cries "big, copious, leaking tears" every time he has to leave.

On the Big Island, Tim says, life is about people; not about money. Here, he says, you get a sense of how real someone is.

"It's a lot of small towns. If you cut someone off turning into a street everyone is going to know, three minutes later, that you were less than the optimum human being.

Susanne Friend

Tim, Susanne, Victor, Jack, Lucky and a menagerie of animals.

"Plastic people don't work here. Fake nails, fake tits don't make it," he says. To succeed on the rural parts of the Big Island, you need an honesty, a real connection to the land, a willingness to be authentic, to take time and talk, to value people.

His advice to new residents? "Remember to be a good person. That's what it takes here."

trying to make a living; entrepreneurial businessmen; and another kind of grower who has settled here, where privacy abounds. Historically there has long been a popular crop grown in the Puna district: marijuana. In the 1970s, it was estimated to be the Big Island's third largest source of revenue.

Perhaps Big Islanders are fatalistic, but some believe Hilo, on the quiet eastern shore, is calmly poised for disaster. In 1946 a large tsunami swallowed much of the downtown area. The town rebuilt but was again inundated in 1960 by a tsunami that killed 61 people.

Still, in *The Best of Hawai`i*, writer Jocelyn K. Fujii advises: "Watch this town. It's a sleeper that has much more going for it than meets the eye: new restaurants, from Thai to Italian; a restoration effort that is reviving downtown businesses and attracting new ones; and the abiding charm of one of Hawai`i's last genuine old towns." Business and restoration efforts may or may not succeed, but that last phrase beautifully sums up Hilo: "the abiding charm of one of Hawai`i's last genuine old towns."

The Hilo side of the Big Island has a few small towns too, some simply a few houses clustered along Route 130. Each has unique characteristics. Pahoa (population just over 1,000) looks like a set for a spooky western movie — one part *High Noon,* two parts *Psycho* — and attracts a mix of entrepreneurial locals, aging hippies, recluses, and a few curious tourists who come to see what if feels like to live in the possible path of a lava flow. They visit the once-upon-a-time village of Kalapana, wiped out by lava flow in mid-1990.

'The last great place on earth'

Given the island's geological uniqueness, it figures that the Big Island's *malihini*, newcomers, are unique, especially those who choose the Hamakua, Ku`a and Puna areas. This tough, down-to-earth country, rural and wild, is rife with drug use, islanders will tell you, and the crime drug use brings. It takes a special kind of daring person to carve a life here, to battle nature's threats and man's transgressions. Think of the hazards settlers in the Old West faced and you will get a feel for life here.

Worth it? Certainly. Those who live here successfully love it, but it is not for the faint-hearted.

"This is the last great place on earth," says one small-scale rancher/farmer. "Peace. People leave you alone here."

A gun rack, filled, stands conspicuously in his living room.

The economy: growing

Like the rest of the islands, the Big Island suffers from the demise of the 175-year-old sugar industry, but this island has space and diversification on its side. New businesses and housing developments abound in the Kailua-Kona and Kohala area and some parts of Ka'u. And the island's population has been growing consistently during the past 18 years, from 92,000 in 1980 to about 190,000 today, despite concerns in some areas about sufficient safe water resources and lagging municipal services.

Half of the state's 10,000 farms and ranches are located on the Big Island and its growers account for much of the state's produce. About two-thirds of the beef raised in the state comes from Big Island ranches. It is also the only major coffee producer in the U.S. (some of the other islands are beginning to produce coffee on a limited scale) and the world's largest orchid grower. Most of the world's macadamia nuts are also harvested here.

Looking toward a time when the bulk of the state's fruits and vegetables can be homegrown, Big Island farmers produce everything from coffee and cacao (chocolate) to bananas, papayas, guavas, passion fruit, avocados and cabbages. And they are on the cutting edge of growing new kinds of produce, experimenting with exotic fruits like rambutan (similar to lychee).

G. Brad Lewis

The morning bartering at Suisan Fish market in Hilo is conducted in a melange of languages. Over-fishing by international trawlers has affected the catch, fishermen say, but fishing continues to be an important source of employment — and food — on the islands.

Big Island Visitor's Bureau, Kirk Lee Aeder, Imoco Media

Canoe at Anaeho`omalu Bay, Big Island

Experimental genetic farming also finds a place on the Hilo side of this island.

Usually, nature provides the water necessary to keep the Big Island fertile, but droughts occasionally occur. The island is served by about two dozen municipal water systems, plus a half-dozen private ones. Thousands of residents rely on rainfall for their water, using catchment systems. People in some less accessible areas depend on generators for power.

The Big Island's notorious volcanoes add to its economy, drawing tourists, astronomers and researchers. Several countries from around the world have perched telescopes atop the 13,796-foot summit of sleepy Mauna Kea. In the East Rift Zone of Kilauea Volcano, geothermal energy supplies some of the island's electricity.

On the South Kohala coast, the Natural Energy Laboratory of Hawai`i conducts research using warm and cold ocean water temperatures to generate electrical power. And aquaculture has enjoyed some success in producing fish, lobsters, seaweed and microalgae food supplements. In some of the more remote areas, commercial forestry and eucalyptus tree planting are being attempted.

Alternative medicine, combining tourism with health as a business venture, is seeing some success on the Big Island. The 50-bed North Hawai`i Community Hospital in north-central Waimea offers a combination of Western medicine and alternative therapies.

The Riddle of Kalapana

The state of Hawai'i seeks to attract the film industry — and here is the perfect plot for a factual horror movie. When man and nature conspire to create a psychological/geological disaster like Kalapana, who needs fiction?

I am driving Route 130 in the Puna District on the Big Island. This is the heart of volcano country and Kilauea has been spouting continuously all week, yet there is no sign of mountain or lava — just a hot sun glinting through a veil of grey-brown vog.

The highway sways left, passing a quaint old church, and the ocean glimmers, bright and cool, on the horizon. The road curves gracefully right and comes to a dead stop. A fence bars further travel; a sign warns visitors to stay away. And there is the lava — thick, black twisted coils crawling across the highway, over a beach, and into the sea, cooled and frozen in their tracks.

Once this was the town of Kalapana and the housing development called Royal Gardens. And this is its story:

In the late 1950s, shortly after Hawai'i became a state, a subdividing free-for-all took place in Puna. Authors George Cooper and Gavan Daws in their classic book, *Land and Power in Hawai'i,* describe the land boom. It began when two Colorado businessmen bought 12,000 acres of land between Kurtistown and Mountain View from a local politician and businessman and formed a *hui,* a corporation of investors. The land was divided into 4,000 lots, named Hawaiian Acres. Costing just $500 to $1,000, they were heavily advertised on the mainland for as low as $150 down and $8 a month.

Interest in the exotic new state of Hawai'i was high. The project sold out and more developments followed. According to Land and Power:

"… The developments unique to the Big Island were in the mold of the one in Puna that set off the boom: sizable acreage in remote areas, of little or no real economic use value, subdivided into house lots on which practically no one ever actually built homes…"

For many years, ignored, or even encouraged by government legislators and officials, there was virtually unrestricted bogus development.

Continues…

G. Brad Lewis

Now a desolate lava landscape, this was once the junction of Gardenia and Royal streets in Royal Gardens subdivision.

"By the time the Big Island boom came to a halt in the mid-1970s, something like 80,000 lots of this kind had been created — on an island whose population at the time was somewhat less than 80,000."

Sales brochures painted glorious pictures of paradise:

"Along the southern shores of the Big Island, Hawai`i, largest of the Hawaiian chain lies the historic and legendary land of Kalapana. This is the setting for Royal Gardens. A fertile area directly adjacent to the Hawai`i Volcano National Park with its spectacular attractions, yet only walking distance away from lovely beach and shore areas. Royal Garden lots are all one acre in size, making it possible for the owners to have a small orchard or truck garden or a magnificent garden, as well as a home and a haven for retirement."

Land and Power continues: "…To have a truck garden or magnificent home garden of the kind the brochures talked about, a lot owner would have to catch his own water, possibly haul in his own soil, and anyway use chemical fertilizer."

In truth, Royal Gardens was on volcanic land, a variety of types of recent lava flow. Water was scarce. The brochure was correct in one respect: Royal Gardens was close to Volcano Park — dangerously close. In was near Kilauea's east rift zone. In 1974 a U.S. Geological Survey said Kilauea and its rift zones "must be expected to erupt repeatedly in the future" and "all areas downslope from volcanic vents should be considered vulnerable to eventual burial by lava flows." Royal Gardens was also within a fault zone, making it at risk for earthquakes.

Several state legislators and public employees, including future governor George Ariyoshi, invested in Royal Gardens.

More than 60 people eventually settled in Royal Gardens, optimistic people who worked hard to develop their cheap land and build their homes.

More than 60 people eventually settled in Royal Gardens, optimistic people who worked hard to develop their cheap land and build their homes. For their book, Cooper and Daws surveyed Royal Gardens owners. About 72 percent said at the time of purchase they believed their lots had fertile soil, and 69 percent did not know it was in a zone of serious volcanic hazard.

In 1977 a lava flow nearly wiped out the village of Kalapana, about three miles northeast along the coast from Royal Gardens. Then, in 1985 a total of seven lava flows entered Royal Gardens, destroying altogether 22 homes, about one in three of all residences.

By 1996, the village of Kalapana was entirely destroyed. So was a nearby beach. And much of Royal Gardens. At Royal Gardens, one by one, homeowners watched their work go up in flames as lava slowly flowed this way and that, sparing a few houses while torching others.

"You watch and wait and that's the worst," said G. Brad Lewis, a nationally-known photographer who lives near Kalapana and specializes in photos of volcano eruptions. "Maybe it will destroy your home; maybe it will turn and destroy your neighbor's instead. When your house finally does go up in flames, it's a relief. After waiting weeks, you are just glad the waiting is over."

There are numerous other such developments in the Puna districts.

Continues…

G. Brad Lewis

Some never went beyond the subdividing and selling stage; others became full-fledged neighborhoods, dangerously close to rift zones and fault lines. Today, Volcano Park visitors see signs designating areas in the likely path of flows. Rated 1, 2 or 3, they indicate the chances of various neighborhoods being inundated.

The lava's flow is usually slow. Homes and dreams are destroyed, but few lives are lost. And people who value privacy do build, rebuild, and survive on this vast, exotic land. Many generate their own electricity and catch rainwater for household use.

Leaving the buried town, I head left along an ocean road. There I find a young man constructing his house on a field of black crust north of Kalapana, near what must once have been a beach. As I approach, he puts down his hammer and smiles, glad to see another human in the desolate place.

I want to know why he is building here, how can he live so close to a place of total destruction. Isn't he afraid the lava will come this way again?

The man looks out at the ocean, a few feet from his door, and thinks a moment. Then he says slowly: "It's like a gamble, a big roulette wheel. You always think the lava will flow somewhere else. That you'll be the lucky one who doesn't lose everything."

Advice from Big Islanders:

• **Some of the Big Island's cheap land** lies in the most isolated areas with no utilities and may be three or four miles on a gravel road, difficult to navigate, warns a Hilo real estate agent. "You have to remember you are living in a high rainfall area, very primitive. It's tropical rainforest but not like you think of it. It's isolated and not much vegetation."

• **Never buy property sight unseen,** advises a real estate investor. If you are considering buying property you have seen, talk first to farmers or homeowners in the area, stop at the county agricultural office and the courthouse. Confer with people in the nearest town. Before you buy, find out all you can from independent sources — those who do not stand to make a profit from your purchase.

You'll like the Big Island if:

Kona side: You like tourists, people, fishing — and if big beaches are not necessary to your island dreams. (The west side of the island has a few nice small beaches, including black sand beaches.)

Hilo side: If you like solitude, a rural atmosphere, a tropical feel, and seek relatively inexpensive land for farming. And if you don't mind rain.

RESOURCES

• Workforce Development Division, Kailua-Kona
(808) 327-4770
hawaii.gov/labor/wdd

• Hawai`i Island Economic Development
(808) 966-5416
hiedb.org

• Research and Development
(808) 961-8366
www.co.hawaii.hi.us

• Kona-Kohala Chamber of Commerce
(808) 329-1758
www.kona-kohala.com

• Hawai`i Island Chamber of Commerce
(808) 935-7178
www.hicc.biz
(For $20, either Chamber will send you a directory with specific information.)

• For Information about volcanoes, use these Internet URLs:
hvo.wr.usgs.gov
volcano.oregonstate.edu

Newspapers:

• *Hawai`i Tribune Herald*
355 Kino`ole Street
Hilo, HI 96720
(808) 935-6621
www.hawaiitribune-herald.com

• *West Hawai`i Today*
*75-5560 Kiawe Stree*t
Kona, HI 96740
(808) 329-9311
www.westhawaiitoday.com

Also see Resources at the back of this book

The Garden Island

…deserves its nickname; at left, the overlook at Kalalau Valley; below, taro patches at Hanalei.

G Brad Lewis

G Brad Lewis

Kaua`i the seductive isle

Kaua`i is the seductive "Garden Isle" with which filmmakers have had a passionate affair for decades. The oldest Hawaiian island, it exudes a mystic charm: sharply peaked mountains and sheer cliffs, crashing waterfalls, mist-shrouded valleys and secluded swimming spots. Even a mini-Grand Canyon.

This little island flaunts itself like a maverick, jutting farther out into the Pacific than any of its sisters, vulnerable to hurricanes and other of Mother Nature's whims. In 1982, Hurricane Iwa scoured Kaua`i; in 1992, Hurricane Iniki ravaged the island for five hours, destroying 14,000 houses, gutting more than 4,000 condominium and hotel units. Miraculously, Iniki claimed only four lives. Destruction totaled about $2 billion.

The little island made a brave comeback. Construction and home and condominium sales have been strong, the number of visitor arrivals grows most years, and jobs are more plentiful than they have been since Iniki.

Size: 552.3 square miles

Population in 1980: 39,082; in **1997:** 57,712; in **2004:** 60,747; in **2009:** 63,689

Predominant occupations: Tourism; local business; some agriculture (including sugar plantations and genetic engineering); military; some research, healthcare and social programs

Unemployment in 1997: 11.3%; in **2004:** 4.5%; in **2010:** 9.1%

Number of McDonald's - restaurants: 5; of **Starbucks Coffee shops:** 3; of **Costco warehouses:** 1

The best thing about Kaua`i: Waterfalls and scenery

**The worst thing about Kaua`i:** Traffic through Kapa`a at 5 p.m.

What other islanders say about Kaua`i: "Beautiful, huh? But it rains too much."

**What Kaua`i says about itself:** "We survived (hurricanes) Iwa and Iniki. We can do anything." (A popular T-shirt slogan reads: "Sharks. Centipedes. Hurricanes. Tsunamis. Kaua`i... it's not for wimps.")

KAUA`I

Bob Fijal

Larry and Christine: They persevered

When former Texas construction worker Larry Reisor and restaurateur Christine Ayers opened the Hanapepe Café & Espresso Bar in the ramshackle southwestern Kaua`i plantation town, they were relying on tourists to appreciate their hearty meatless meals. And they knew that every new business needs heavy doses of optimism and perseverance. But they had no idea what fate had in store. On Sept. 11, 1992, just as they were becoming established, Hurricane Iniki hit. Determined not to be done in by the winds that damaged or destroyed nearly every home and business on the island, the partners made repairs and reopened their business within weeks. Despite difficulties in obtaining fresh vegetables (especially important in a vegetarian restaurant), by 1993 and through 1994 they were doing a brisk business, feeding the hundreds of construction workers who had flocked to Kaua`i to help with the rebuilding. But by 1995, their work finished, the construction workers left. Business was slow again, Reisor says, because few hotels had reopened and tourism was down. Reisor and Ayers hung in there, weathering the slow time. Eventually hotels reopened, tourists have slowly returned and business at the café has been steadily increasing, Reisor says.

Kauai's economy

Kaua`i is famous for its excessive rainfall. Mount Wai`ale`ale, with an average annual rainfall of 485 inches, is said to be the wettest spot on earth. All that rainfall keeps the island delightfully lush and green and ideal for farming. Here is tropical Hawai`i as you and the film industry imagine it. The Kaua`i Institute for Communications Media and the Kaua`i Film Commission, a division of the county Office of Economic Development, successfully pursue projects. Movies such as *South Pacific, Blue Hawaii, Outbreak, Raiders of the Lost Ark, King Kong, Honeymoon in Vegas, Waterworld, Jurassic Park* and its sequels, among many others, have been filmed here. During a recent year, film producers spent $4.4 million in Kaua`i and they occasionally hire *kama`aina* as "extras."

Today, Kaua`i strives to take advantage of its beauty to attract filmmakers and tourism, while still attempting to retain its old way of life. Towns were originally developed around sugar mills. Most of the mills are gone and new crops attempt to pick up some of the slack: cane, coffee, corn, sunflower, timber. Genetic engineering of plants such as corn is controversial, but encouraged. Pioneer Hi-Bred International, among other companies, find the Waimea area ideal for research.

Meanwhile, a University of Hawai`i economic survey shows the value of forestry products, much of it produced on former sugar lands, grew from $30 million in 1991 (before Iniki) to over $100 million by 2001. Kaua`i has in recent years begun exporting coffee to the mainland and to other Hawaiian islands and has long exported cookies and taro chips. Like the other islands, Kaua`i hopes to nurture high technology and has had some success there. The island is particularly popular with the military, to the chagrin of some Kauaians. See the accompanying story. (See page 54.)

Kaua`i's wild chickens have become an icon. Some say the hens, roosters and chicks parading along roadways are progeny of poultry released by Hurricane Iniki in 1992.

The good news: public schools on this island are generally considered better than average for Hawai`i. Kaua`i also boasts a thriving local, island-wide bus service, started after Iniki damaged so many cars and roads.

You'll like life on Kaua`i if:
Your family is the center of your life and you don't yearn for a night life. If you enjoy scenery, hiking, snorkeling or surfing. If rainfall doesn't depress you.

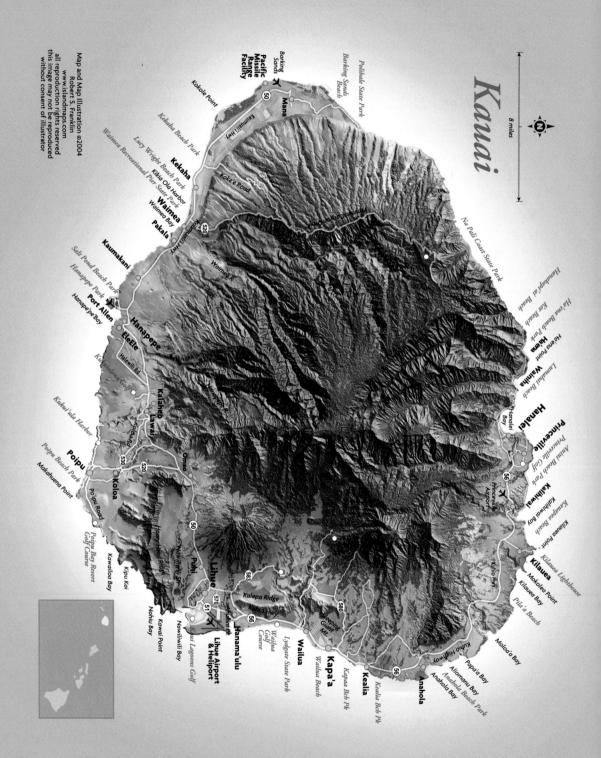

Kauai

8 miles

N

Barking Sands

Pacific Missile Range Facility

Barking Sands Beach

Polihale State Park

Kokole Point

Mana

50

Kaumualii Hwy

Kekaha Beach Park

Kekaha

Kokee Road

Koke'e Road

Lucy Wright Beach Park

Kikia Olo Harbor

Waimea Recreational Pier State Park

Waimea
Waimea Bay

Pakala

550

Kaumualii Hwy

520

Waimea R.

Na Pali Coast State Park

Hanakapiai Beach

Ke'e Beach

Ha'ena Beach Park

Ha'ena
Ha'ena Point

Lumahai Beach
Wainiha

Kaumakani

Salt Pond Beach Park

Hanapepe Park

Port Allen
Hanapepe Bay

Hanapepe

EleEle

Halewili Rd

Kaumakani Golf

Hanalei
Bay

Hanalei
Princeville

Princeville Golf

Anini Beach Park

Princeville Airport

56

Kalihiwai

Kauapea Beach

Kalihiwai Bay

Kaua'i'ula Harbor

Kalaheo
Lawai

Koloa Rd

Omao

530

520

Poipu
Poipu Beach Park

Mokahuena Point

Koloa

Po'ipu Road

Poipu Bay Resort Golf Course

Kawailoa Bay

Kipu Kai

50

Nawiliwili St.

Tree Tunnel Rd

Puhi

583

Lihue

570

51

Nawiliwili Bay

Hanama'ulu

Kawai Point

Nohili Bay

Kalaepohaku Ridge

Kalepa Ridge

Kuhio Hwy

Wailua Golf Course

Lydgate State Park

Kauai Lagoons Golf

Lihue Airport & Heliport

Wailua
Wailua Beach

Sleeping Giant Mt.

580

Kapaa Bch Pk

Kapa'a

Kealia Bch Pk

Kealia

56

Kilauea Point
Kilauea Lighthouse

Kilauea

Mokolea Point
Kilauea Bay

Pila'a Beach

Moloa'o Bay

Papa'a Bay

Aliomanu Beach
Anahola Bay

Anahola Beach Park

Anahola

Kuhio Highway

Kuhio Hwy

Toni Polancy

The northwestern part of Kaua`i has a down-home, country feeling. Teens share cotton candy at a Waimea celebration.

An island tour

Strung along the ocean like shells on a lei are at least 20 towns, some so small you may miss them. **Lihu`e** (population 11,200), near **Nawiliwili Harbor** on the eastern coast, is the county capital and site of most business activity. It has the ambiance of a 1940s small town and closes early. To the southwest, **Koloa**, a quaint, historic town of plantation houses, is the site of one of Hawai`i's first sugar mills. Days and evenings, Koloa throbs with tourists. Small housing developments, old and new, are scattered throughout this part of the island, some half-hidden in cane and bush.

Up on Highway 50, **Kalaheo** is a "local" town, nearly devoid of tourists. Further west are `**Ele`ele, Hanapepe,** the *paniolo* (cowboy) town of **Waimea**, and **Kekaha**, where newcomers and locals provide plenty of *aloha* to visitors on their way to misty **Koke`e State Park** and **Waimea Canyon**, a colorful 10-mile-long gorge called "the Grand Canyon of the Pacific." On the western shore of the island sprawls **Barking Sands,** a civilian-run U.S. naval facility, and the **Pacific Missile Range Facility**, an important, if not large (260 military and civilian personnel) employer on this small island.

To the north of Lihu`e is **Wailua**, a tourist area along Wailua River, Hawai`i's only real river and site of the famous Coconut Palms Hotel, where the Elvis Presley movie *Blue Hawaii* was filmed. **Kapa`a**, a modern center of commerce, hosts a 4 p.m. traffic jam every workday. A long stretch of Kuhio Highway through pasture and valley takes you to the Anahola Mountains (where *King Kong* was filmed) and tiny **Anahola,** little more than a stopping place on the highway. Further along is **Kilauea,** with its lighthouse, quaint stone churches and manager's houses, survivors from plantation days. Here, newcomers and locals share a quiet, dreamy life.

The northern tip of Kaua`i provides a visual treat: the posh **Princeville Resort** with its elegant Princeville Hotel overlooking breathtaking **Hanalei Bay.** The resort is a major newcomer/ part-time residents' housing area, with a variety of condos and houses on wide green lawns overlooking ocean cliffs. Princeville also boasts a luxurious modern spa offering inexpensive membership and a world-class golf course.

Highway 56 winds spectacularly down to **Hanalei Valley,** ringed by waterfalls after heavy rains which feed the taro beds patching the valley floor. Bustling **Hanalei** town with ramshackle historic buildings is quaint and pleasantly touristy. The road climbs sea cliffs, passes a tempting variety of private, pristine homes in sheltered coves and bays tucked between mountain ridges, and finally comes to an abrupt halt just past **Ha`ena,** at the Na Pali cliffs and one of Kaua`i's many quiet beaches.

This end of the island is pricey and exemplifies one of Hawai`i's major concerns: that so many wealthy people moving here, "regular" folks, middle-incomers, will not be able to afford housing or life here. But, as a rule, the average Kaua`i *kama`aina,* born or transplanted, doesn't ask for much from life beyond that which nature offers: a perfect wave and a golden sunset to share with family and friends at the end of the day.

A shelter for pets and people

Kaua'i learned a lot from Hurricane Iniki. After the hurricane, building codes throughout the islands were tightened. There was an unexpected lesson, too.

"We learned from Iniki that people will not go to a shelter without their pets," says Dr. Rebecca Rhoades, executive director of the Kaua'i Humane Society. That's why Kaua'i's new Humane Society is the first shelter in the nation to allow both pets and their owners.

From Kaumuali'i Highway north of Lihu'e, the society's new $3 million building looks like a fort: sterile, cement-walled, set on seven acres and surrounded on two sides with parking lots. The American Red Cross and state Civil Defense-approved facility contains 30,000 square feet of concrete and a 5,000 square foot basement. The shelter has its own well, assuring a water supply after a disaster, as well as a generator, drainage system, hurricane shutters on windows and hurricane doors bolted in three places.

When a disaster looms, pet owners can come to the shelter, ideally bringing their pets in kennels or crates, Rhoades says. During the hurricane, pet owners will stay in the basement and pets will be in their crates stacked in hallways and rooms. After the disaster, the society will continue to house the pets if necessary, Rhoades says, giving owners time to find more permanent shelter or to repair damaged homes without having the added stress of worrying about their pets. The facility has become a model for the nation. Out of devastation, comes a better way.

(*This story first appeared in* The Hawai'i Pet Book.)

The Valley Isle

...is famous for its beautiful beaches, like Wailea's Elua Beach. Longtime residents are likely to live in towns, like Wailuku, tucked into mountains.

Steve Strand

Steve Brinkman

Maui the lucky island?

Maui is called "the Valley Isle," but it might better be called the "lucky island." Maui blends, so far successfully, some of the best of busy Honolulu and the more placid life of the other islands.

Chosen "Best Island in the World" by Condé Nast Traveller magazine for several years and consistently racking up credits from travel magazines, the island draws more than two million tourists annually.

Maui is also blessed with what seems to be a more stable economy than some of her sister islands. And her population is growing faster, nearly doubling since 1980.

Whereas tourist numbers fluctuated or declined in the rest of the world after September 11, 2001, on Maui they rose. About 40 percent of Maui's jobs are in the service industry.

Continued

Size: 728 square miles

Population in 1980: 70,991; **in 1997:** 122,772; **in 2003:** 135,734; **in 2008:** 143,691; **in 2008:** 181,598 (Those figures include Moloka`i and Lana`i, part of Maui County. Lana`i has 3164 people and Moloka`i has approximately 7500.)

Predominant occupations: Tourism, real estate, small and large agriculture, small businesss and business development, technology, arts.

Unemployment in 1998: approximately 7%; **in 2004:** approximately 3.5%; **in 2010:** 8.8%

Number of McDonald's restaurants: 11; **Starbucks Coffee shops:** 8; **Costco warehouses:** 1

The best thing about Maui: a blend of small rural island community and worldwide sophistication.

The worst thing about Maui: Watching the island lose its beaches and pristine areas.

What other islands say about Maui: "Too expensive. Too developed. It's the next Waikiki."

What Maui says about itself: "We've learned from O`ahu. We'll control our growth."

The second-largest Hawaiian island (after the Big Island) also has a somewhat diversified economic base. The sugar and pineapple industries, which have left or reduced production on other Hawaiian islands, continue on Maui in a limited capacity, to the chagrin of environmentalists who decry sugarcane smoke and pineapple field runoff. At the same time, ranchers and small-time farmers ply their trades on the gentle slopes of dormant Haleakala volcano. Small, specialized farms sell herbs, flowers and high-end produce to hotels and restaurants, and a *hui* (partnership or organization) of ranchers supplies fresh beef.

In the boom town of Kihei, the Maui High Performance Computing Center houses the world's most powerful parallel-processing computers, and the Maui Research and Technology Park is incubator to innovative businesses during their early development. At night, the U.S. Air Force beams laser imaging systems from the skies over Maui as part of its ongoing development of remote-controlled aircraft for the U.S. war arsenal. And looking down from its perch atop the summit of Haleakala is Science City, a research facility that draws some of the world's top astronomers to the world's most advanced telescopes.

Jobs. Development. Growth. *Lucky* island. But perhaps more than any other island, Maui faces Hawai`i's notorious Catch 22: managing enormous growth while maintaining the natural beauty that draws people and spawns that growth. Already resort developments blot out some of the island's spectacular ocean views, and ever more "cookie-cutter" houses creep up the jagged West Maui mountains. Traffic is a major concern. And a water shortage stutters, but rarely stops, development as the county fails to control water use and the state takes over management of the island's main water source, the `Iao Aquifer.

Tourists arriving at Kahului airport will eventually be enchanted by eerily beautiful `Iao Valley, by Haleakala's immense crater, by the mesmerizing underwater world of Honolua Marine Preserve, by Ka`anapali's posh hotels and by Wailea Resort's breathtaking beaches. But first those tourists must traverse a condensed, intense version of mainland U.S.A.: used car lots, shopping strips, fast food chains and big-box stores.

As for living on Maui? If you are coming from a large city, you'll find the atmosphere still quiet and polite, for the most part. About 75 percent of the island remains wilderness, with breathtaking vistas and plenty of hiking trails. And Maui has a rich cultural life that enhances its

MAUI

Steve Brinkman

From the air, The Maui Research Park, including the Maui High Performance Computing Center, seems isolated amid kiawe trees and desert; it's actually near the center of busy Kihei.

sophisticated image. The Maui Arts and Cultural Center, between urban Kahului and Wailuku, is a striking mini-cathedral to both the visual and entertainment arts. It draws international performers who relish their time in Maui's sun-drenched elegance. The rambling Mediterranean-style mansion of a former missionary, Hui No`eau Visual Arts Center in rural "upcountry" Maui, is a friendly grassroots art center. The Lahaina Art Society, located in a former jail under the state's largest banyan tree, contains a lovely gallery for local artists' work. And several artists' co-operative galleries dot the island, giving Maui an international reputation as an art center.

An island tour

West Maui is a tourist area unabashedly devoted to fun, sensuous and languid. Golden sunsets reflect on store windows along Front Street in the quaint old whaling port of **Lahaina**, once the center of island government. The entire town of about 11,000 residents is on the national historic record.

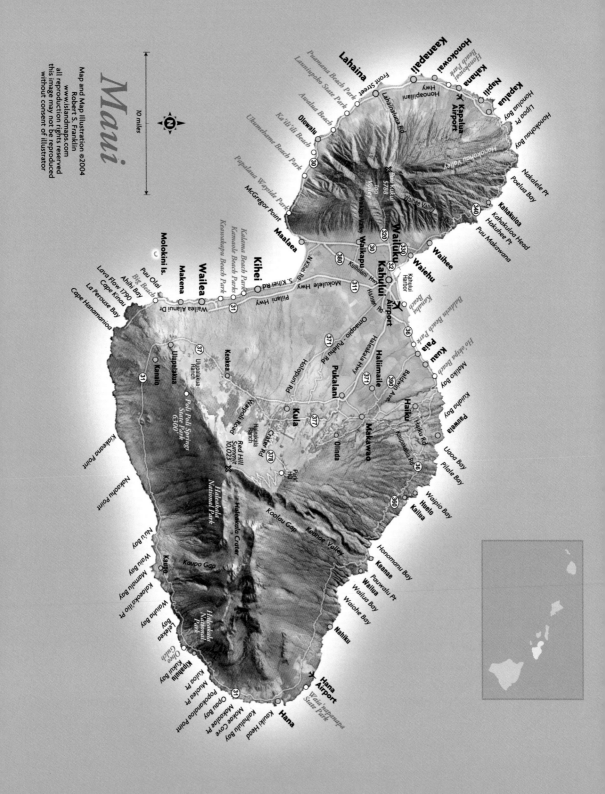

Maui

N

10 miles

Lahaina
Puamana Beach Park
Launiupoko State Park
Awalua Beach
Olowalu
Ka ili ili Beach
Ukumehame Beach Park
Papalaua Wayside Park
McGregor Point
Maalaea

Kaanapali
Honokowai
Kahana
Napili
Kapalua
Kapalua Airport
Honoapiilani Hwy
Lahainaluna Rd
Front Street
Honokohau Bay
Lipoa Pt.
Honolua Bay
Nakalele Pt.
Poelua Bay
Kahakuloa
Kahakuloa Head
Hokuhee Pt.
Puu Makawana
340

Kihei
Wailea
Makena
Molokini Is.
Puu Olai
Big Beach
Ahihi Bay
Lava Flow 1790
Cape Kinau
La Perouse Bay
Cape Hanamanioa
Kalama Beach Park
Kamaole Beach Parks
Keawakapu Beach Park
Wailea Alanui Dr.
S. Kihei Rd.
Mokulele Hwy
N. Kihei Rd.
Piilani Hwy
31
380
311

Wailuku
Kahului
Waikapu
Iao Valley
5788
Waihee Valley
320
30
32
330
Waihee
Waiehu
Kahului Harbor
Kanaha Beach
Baldwin Beach Park
Paia
Kuau
Kuhio Hwy
Hansen Rd.
Haleakala Hwy
36

Kanaio
Ulupalakua
Ulupalakua Ranch
Keokea
Kula
Olinda
Makawao
Pukalani
Haliimaile
Haiku
Kaupo Gap
Koolau Gap
Keanae Valley
Haleakala Crater
Red Hill Summit 10,023
Poli Poli Springs State Park 6,300
Haleakala National Park
Park HQ
Naholoku Point
Nuu Bay
Waiu Bay
Mamalu Bay
Kaleeokiilio Pt.
Waiohu Bay
Lelekea Bay
Oheo Gulch
Kipahulu Pt.
Kukui Bay
Kuloa Pt.
Mokae Pt.
Makaeao Point
Opuu Bay
Kahoolui Head
Kauiki Head
Hana
Hana Airport
Waianapanapa State Park
Nahiku
Waiohe Bay
Waiiua Bay
Wailua
Keanae
Honomanu Bay
Pauwalu Pt.
Kailua
Huelo
Waipio Bay
Pilale Bay
Uaoa Bay
Paiwela
Kuiaha Bay
Maliko Bay
Hoolawa Bay
Ho'okipa Beach
Baldwin Ave.
Kula Hwy
Crater Rd.
Waipoli Road Road
Haleakala Ranch
Omaopio-Puleho Rd.
Kuihelani Hwy
Olinda Rd.
Kaupakalua Rd.
Hana Hwy
Haiku Rd.
378
377
371
390
360
36
37
31

West Maui sometimes seems to be an island unto itself; people who live on the west side travel the 27 miles to Kahului, the island's commercial center, reluctantly. Single-family homes are scarce here and tend to be more costly than in some other areas of the island.

A strip of condominium hotels extends up the western shoreline from the lush green golf courses of **Ka`anapali Resort** to the town of **Napili**, with homes tucked cozily along the shoreline. Carefully planned and lushly landscaped **Kapalua Resort** sits majestically atop West Maui. The total west side population (including visitors) is about 45,000.

In South Maui, **Kihei** (population 25,000), sandwiched between busy Pi`ilani Highway and South Kihei Road, has the nasty reputation of being a hectic community of tourist condos. But those who live in its residential neighborhoods find it family-oriented, friendly and convenient, if increasingly busy and noisy. The Kama`ole beaches, three lovely open vistas along busy South Kihei Road, offer views of breathtaking sunsets. Standing in awe of them and listening to the sound of a conch shell, cocktails and beers in hand, is a nightly tradition for tourists and *kama`aina.*

Kihei post office, the busiest rural post office in the state, is a neighborhood meeting place. Patrons in business dress and bathing suits stand in long lines, trade gossip and listen to friendly clerks explain postal regulations to tourists who speak no English.

There's a saying in this part of Maui: You can measure a person's income by how far south he lives. There is a graduating scale of *malahini* (new-comer) lifestyles, from Kihei Villages, a high-density condominium complex in north Kihei through a variety of residential areas and condominiums of increasingly higher cost, to **Wailea** resort, exclusive and lushly landscaped. **Wailea** is composed of upscale townhouses and small mansions set amid golf courses and tennis complexes, most with ocean views. Heading south to **Makena** and newly developed areas, prices continue to climb. How far they will go is every real estate investor's speculation.

On Maui's northern shore, **Spreckelsville**, named for a sugar baron, includes pricey newer homes near a golf club and a sheltered beach. Up the road, **Pa`ia** is an old sugar town transitioning from hippie enclave to tourist mecca. With crayon-colored plantation houses and a variety of interesting shops, it retains vestiges of each era.

Farther north, **Haiku,** is rural, wet, jungle green and lovely. With mostly two-acre lots, it appeals to people who want privacy and space.

Farther, 45 corkscrew miles away, is rustic **Hana**, small, tropical, and isolated. A few celebrities who cherish their privacy live peaceably here among the many longtimers and passing tourists.

"Real Mauians," *kama`aina* will tell you, eventually move "upcountry," halfway up Haleakala mountain, to areas like **Pukalani, Makawao** and **Kula** with a wide variety of home prices and almost no condos. This is *paniolo* (cowboy) country. Horses graze on broad pastures, an occasional cow crosses Haleakala Highway, buses carry kids to better-than-average schools and smoke curls from chimneys on cool winter nights when temperatures can dip into the 40s. Ball games, polo matches and rodeos are the talk of the town. Jobs include big-scale ranching, small agricultural enterprises and home businesses. And it all plays out against a panorama of the isthmus and ocean below. Artists and writers are also drawn to cool, serene, beautiful Upcountry Maui.

The central valley includes two small, busy towns, **Wailuku** and **Kahului,** that spill into each other. Wailuku, the county capital, is a picturesque historic community tucked against the West Maui Mountains. Its downtown was nearly abandoned in the 1980s and 90s, as car dealer-ships moved to more commercialized Kahului and local stores closed in deference to incoming national chains. But housing and commercial developments are replacing pineapple fields outside of town, creating a new Wailuku. And Old Wailuku may eventually find a niche as an attractive locale for boutiques, galleries and antique stores.

Kahului, the center of commerce, is a busy port with a mostly "local" population — families of longtime *haole*, Filipinos, Chinese, Japanese and other ethnic groups who originally came to work the sugar fields. In the mid 1960s, plantation workers began an exodus from camp housing to a development just outside the Pu`unene plantation. Nicknamed "Dream City," the development comprises much of the residential area of Kahului. Originally costing about $20,000, these cement block homes surrounded by gardens and fruit trees now sell for hundreds of thousands of dollars. Nearby is the Saturday morning swap-meet at University of Hawaii Maui campus where *kama`aina* pick inexpensive flowers and produce, and tourists select souvenirs at half of boutique prices.

An influx of mainland stores has swamped Kahului in the past few years. Costco, Walmart, Home Depot, and others bring prices down and assure a supply of goods, but erase island atmosphere. Symbolically, an over-sized Krispy Kreme donut shop hails tourists arriving at Maui airport.

Longtime Mauians complain about the island's traffic and rapid development, even as they shop in Kahului's mainland-type stores. A local *tutu* (grandma), pushing two toddlers in a cart at Kmart, remembers calmer times 40 years ago, before investors from around the world began to build hotels and condominiums.

"You could go Kihei, go to beaches and not hear nothing, no one there. Private," she says. "Not like now. Noise. Cars. People." She pushes the cart up the Little Caesar's pizza aisle and places her order.

You'll like Maui if:

You're the kind of person who keeps a bathing suit, snorkel gear or surfboard in your car. (Maui has 120 miles of coastline, more of it easily accessible and swimmable than any other island.) If you like a touch of sophistication along with peace and natural beauty.

- Small Business Development Center 590 Lipoa Parkway, Kihei, HI 96753 **(808) 875-2402** www.hawaii-sbdc.org

- County of Maui **(800) 272-0026** www.co.maui.hi.us (Includes job postings)

Newspapers

- *The Maui News* **(808) 244-6363** www.mauinews.com

- *The Lahaina News* **(808) 667-7866** fax (808) 667-2726 www.lahainanews.com

Also see the Resource section at the back of this book.

Toni Polancy

Surfing dominates life for some Mauians. A Haiku resident made a fence of old surf boards.

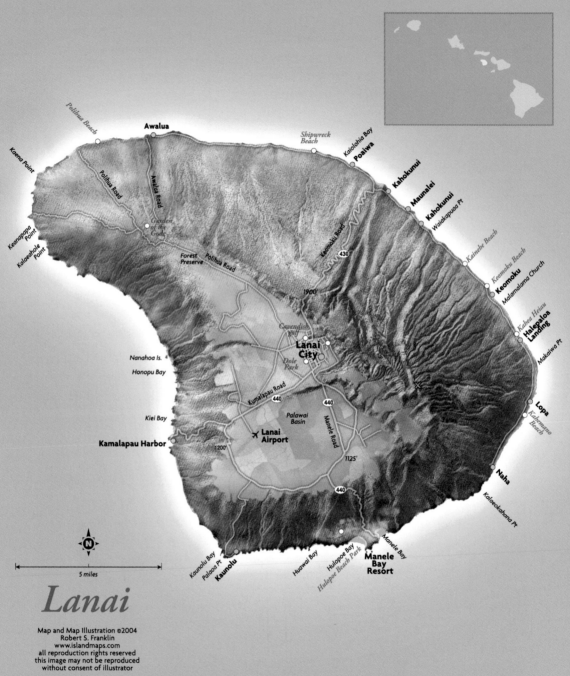

Polihua Beach

Awalua

Shipwreck Beach

Kaiolohia Bay

Poaiwa

Kaena Point

Polihua Road

Awalua Road

Kahokunui

Maunalei

Kahokunui

Waiakapuaa Pt

Garden of the Gods

Keanapapa Point

Forest Preserve

Polihua Road

Kainehe Beach

Keomuku Road

430

Kalaehohe Point

1900

Keomuku Beach

Keomuku

Malamalama Church

Kahea Heiau

Halepaloa Landing

Cavendish golf

Lanai City

Makaiwa Pt

Nanahoa Is.

Dole Park

Honopu Bay

Kumaipapa Road

440

Palawai Basin

440

Manele Road

Lopa

Kalemano Beach

Kiei Bay

Lanai Airport

1200'

Kamalapau Harbor

1125'

Naha

Kaleeokahana Pt

440

N

5 miles

Kaunolu Bay

Paloaa Pt

Kaunolu

Huawai Bay

Hulopoe Bay

Hulopoe Beach Park

Manele Bay

Manele Bay Resort

Lanai

Lana`i

the private island

It's afternoon. Except for a few birds chattering, all is quiet in Lana`i City, a grassy oasis atop this small, round, desert-like island. You could hear a needle drop from one of the many Cook pines in the two-block-long town square circled by small shops and brightly painted plantation houses. School lets out at one end of the square and children scamper through the park, sunlight dancing on their faces, their tinkling laughter hanging in the air. Lana`i City seems a town suspended in time, an Andy Hardy movie.

But is this a place where you'd want to live? In one of the Hawaiian islands' most remote villages, on a "company-owned" island? Surprisingly, the answer may be "yes."

For nearly seventy years, Lana`i was the world's largest pineapple plantation — 18,000 acres owned and operated by Dole Food Co. In 1985 Castle and Cooke, Inc., chaired by entrepreneur David Murdock, bought Dole's share of the land with an eye to exclusive tourism and christened Lana`i "The Private Island."

Today, the tiny island has almost achieved Murdock's goal. Built in the early 1990s, its two resorts, The Manele Bay Hotel and The Lodge at Ko`ele, are so grand *kama`aina* (longtime residents) from throughout the islands go there for second honeymoons — most can't afford Lana`i for first honeymoons.

Size: 140 square miles

Population in 1980: 2,426; **in 1997:** about 2,800; **in 2000:** 3,164; **in 2010:** about 3,000

Predominant occupations: Approximately 70% resort hotel and restaurant; the rest, civil service, teaching; nursing; some small business; airport.

Unemployment in 1998: 6%; **in 2004:** .07%; **in 2010:** 10.1%

Shopping: Three grocery stores, three restaurants, a hardware store, one movie theater (recently reopened).

Number of McDonald's restaurants: 0; **of Starbucks Coffee shops:** 0; **of Costco warehouses:** 0

The best thing about Lana`i: Community spirit.

The worst thing about Lana`i: Small and confining.

What other islanders say about Lana`i: "It's for rich people."

What Lana`i says about itself: "Peaceful. A great place to raise kids."

The Lana`i golf courses are world-renowned, and in addition to resorts, The Lana`i Company is developing chic condominiums and town-houses for those who want (and can afford) the kind of seclusion the island offers. Buyers usually have primary residences elsewhere, says Kay Okamoto, longtime Lana`i Realtor.

When Microsoft magnate Bill Gates wed on the island in the early 1990s, a reporter covering the event was "escorted" from the "private island," causing a national uproar. In truth, Okamoto says, "People are free to come and go. We have the same state and county services other islands have. Roads, beaches, harbors open to the public. It's just most of the land (98 percent) is owned by Castle and Cooke." And more than half of Lana`i's workers are employed by The Lana`i Company.

Life on a tiny island

A woman, raised in the rural northeastern U.S., spent six years on the tiny island, working as a "server" (waitress) for The Lana`i Company. She says she loved life there, where everyone knows each other and families gather for Friday evening *pau hana* (done working) barbecues at the beach. She also volunteered a few hours each month at an art co-op, selling her ceramic ornaments to tourists and earning several hundred dollars a month in addition to her generous wages.

"Still, it's a company town," she points out, "so if an employer becomes unhappy with you, you're screwed. And if you quit or lose your job you have two weeks to vacate your home. That gives the bosses a lot of power." Most often, she amends, bosses are fair and island life is ideal.

There are a few inconveniences. Lana`i has no air tower; when skies are very overcast, planes can't fly for a few hours and travelers can be delayed. Also, expectant mothers must travel off-island to give birth. Lana`i Community Hospital director John Schaumburg explains the hospital does not have the advanced technology to handle emergencies. And because airlines don't like to carry mothers-to-be during the last month of pregnancy, women usually leave a month before their due date, staying with friends or relatives on more populated islands.

It would be difficult to start your own business on an island owned by one company, which also owns all the commercial property. There's a waiting list of potential commercial renters.

Overall, the perks to living on this 10-mile-wide island far outweigh the inconveniences. Most resort employees belong to unions, and their wages are on a par with other Hawai`i workers, yet rent in company-owned housing is discounted to about half the cost of rentals on other islands.

Entertainment includes hunting Mouflon sheep, deer and game birds in the desert-like scrub that surrounds Lana`i City, and snorkeling off a couple of pristine beaches. A four-wheel drive vehicle is the best way to get around the island's many unpaved roads and paths.

Cultural activities consist of a guest artists series at The Lodge at Ko`ele. Internationally known musicians, writers, lecturers (like humor writer Dave Barry) and chefs visit. All events in the guest lecture series are free to residents as well as visitors.

RESOURCES

Lana`i is part of Maui County.

See also Maui.

- The Lana`i Co.
  Main number
  (808) 565-3000

  Employment
  (808) 565-3876

- Lana`i Community Hospital
  (808) 565-6411
  www.lch.hhsc.org

- Lana`i Schools
  (808) 565-7224
  hawaii.hi.schoolwebpages.com/
  education/school/school.php

Jobs available

Sound like an ideal life? The good news: you may be able to find a job here. "Jobs are pretty basic and are often available," says one resident. "You either work for the state, as a teacher, or a nurse at the hospital. Other than that, you work for the hotels — that's The Lana`i Company."

The world is still discovering this unique little island, and it is a fascinating place to watch.

You'll enjoy life on Lana`i if:

You are a recluse, perhaps an artist or writer or if you are healthy, wealthy enough not to have to earn a living, and can just fly in and out for a spell. Or, if you are looking for an interesting job assignment in a friendly place.

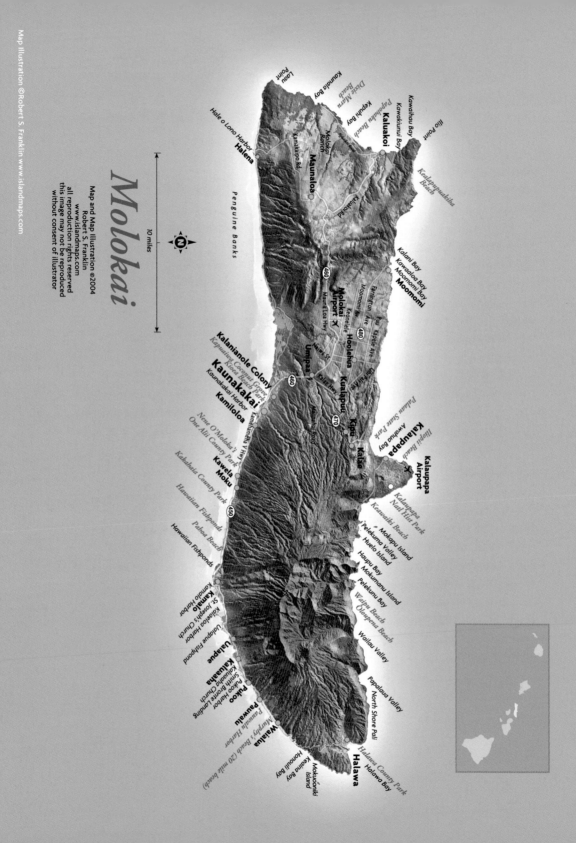

Molokai

Map and Map Illustration ©2004
Robert S. Franklin
www.islandmaps.com
all reproduction rights reserved
this image may not be reproduced
without consent of illustrator

10 miles

N

Penguine Banks

L100 Point
Kaunala Bay
Desk Maru Beach
Kepuhi Bay
Papohaku Beach
Kawaihou Bay
Ilio Point
Kawakiunui Bay
Kaluakoi
Kaupoa Beach
Hale o Lono Harbor
Molokai Ranch
Halena
Kamakaipo Rd
Maunaloa
Kaluakoi Rd
Keonelono Beach

Kolani Bay
Kawaaloa Bay
Moomomi Bay
Moomomi
Farrington Ave
Moomomi Rd
460
Puu Kapele Rd
460
Maunaloa Hwy
Kaunakakai Harbor
Molokai Airport ✈
Kaunakakai St
Hoolehua
Kualapuu
Kalae Hwy
Puu Pelauu

Kalanianole Colony
Kapuaiwa Coconut Grove
Kiowai Beach Park
Kaunakakai
Umipaa
Kamiloloa
460
470
Maunaloa Road
Kipu
Palaau State Park
Kalaupapa
Iliopii Beach
Awahua Bay
Kalaupapa Airport ✈
Kalaupapa Natl Hist Park
Kalae
Kamehameha V Hwy

Nene O'Molokai?
One Alii County Park
Kakahaia County Park
Hawaiian Fishponds
Kawela
Moku
Pahoa Beach
460
Hawaiian Fishponds
Kamalo Harbor
Keawaiki Beach
'Pelekunu Valley
Mokapu Island
Huelo Island
Haupu Bay
Mokumanu Island
Pelekunu Bay
Waipu Beach
Oloupena Beach
Kaloako Harbor
St. Joseph's Church
Kamalo
Ualapue Fishpond
Ualapue
Kaluaaha Church
Kaluaaha
Smith Bronte Landing
Pukoo
Pukoo Harbor
Pauwalu
Papouku Beach (20 mile beach)
Murphy's Beach
Wailau
Wailau Valley
Papalaua Valley
North Shore Pali
Keana Bay
Honouli Bay
Halawa County Park
Halawa
Halawa Bay
Mokuooniki Island

Moloka`i the Hawaiian island

Moloka`i has many nicknames: "The Lonely Island," "The Most Hawaiian Island," "The Friendly Isle" and "Hawai`i as it Used to Be." It is all of these.

Half of Moloka`i's residents are of Hawaiian extraction. And here is Hawaiian life as you probably picture it: secluded, bucolic. On Moloka`i, many Hawaiians and *hapa* (half) Hawaiians live off the land as their ancestors did — harvesting the ocean, gathering fruits and plants, hunting deer, pigs and goats.

It's a simple life, yes — but not necessarily ideal. A struggling economy and high jobless rate means some residents must live off the land and sea; 18.9 percent receive some form of public assistance. A few jobs are available on Moloka`i, but, in the words of one long-time resident, "They don't pay enough to make it worthwhile for people to get off welfare." The Moloka`i Ferry carries workers (and tourists) twice daily to Lahaina, Maui, at discounted rates, but few workers take the long, costly trip.

The 52,000-acre Moloka'i Ranch comprises roughly one-third of the island. After losing money for several decades, the Molokai Ranch closed in 2008, laying off 120 workers. Molokai Ranch had run the only resort hotels

Size: 260 square miles

Population in 1980: 6,049; **in 1997:** about 7,000; **in 2000:** 7,404

Occupations: Teaching; healthcare; social work; farming; fishing; tourism

Unemployment in 1998: Approximately 14% **in 2004:** 9.5%; **in 2010:** 15%

Number of McDonald's restaurants: 0; of **Starbucks Coffee shops:** 0; of **Costco warehouses:** 0.

The best thing about Moloka`i: Axis deer dancing across a dewy meadow.

The worst thing about Moloka`i: The threat of change.

What other islanders say about Moloka`i: "Beautiful. Quiet. But so poor, no?"

**What Moloka`i says about itself:** "Leave us be. We are old Hawai`i and we like it that way."

'Nature Scott': At home on the friendly island

Scott Hemenway, 35, came to Moloka`i in 1993, one of 50 new teachers. From upstate New York, he had never been to Hawai`i. Scott looked down from the island-hopper at the majestic Maunaloa Mountains, at neatly planted fields of pineapple, groves of coffee trees, at the ocean surrounding it all like a sparkling blue blanket... and thought he was about to land in heaven.

With about 7,000 population, Moloka`i is bucolic and quiet. There are no movie theaters. No bowling alleys. No fast-food chains. Kaunakakai, the island's

only real town, barely four blocks long, looks like a setting for a cowboy movie — false-fronted buildings and cars that pull up perpendicular, like tethered horses. Most of the kids hang out at the community pool and gym, a block away. They go home to small plantation houses set in clusters overlooking stunning views.

Weekends, there's an ocean to swim in, mountains to climb, fish to catch and deer to hunt. Moloka`i's deer are so tame they stop and stare at you, interrupting their graceful ballets in fields misty with early morning light. Late nights, line up in the alley behind Kanemitzu Bakery. Knock on the door and a friendly baker will serve up, by the slice, baked bread, warm from the oven, with cream cheese, honey, peanut butter, jelly.

Still, the alluring charm and peace tend to wear thin after a spell. Within two years after he arrived, Scott was the only one of those 50 teachers still on Moloka`i. The rest left, most back to a less costly life on the mainland, or to O`ahu or Maui, where life is more exciting.

Not Scott. Scott teaches eighth-and ninth-grade science at Moloka`i High. In his spare time he umpires little league and interscholastic baseball. On weekends, he conducts tours at the Nature Conservancy, where volunteers call him "Nature Scott."

Scott's mom once visited Moloka`i. She noted how happy Scott seemed and the night before she left she looked at him wistfully. "You're never coming home, are you?"

"No." Scott shook his head. "I'm staying. As long as they will have me."

G. Brad Lewis

A swimmer walks Moloka`i's deserted Papohaku Beach, largest in the state.

on the island and maintained the island's only golf courses. In effect, the closure also shuttered Maunaloa town, closing its gas station, movie theater, cattle ranching and related maintenance work.

A Moloka`i tour

Moloka`i is shaped somewhat like a shark. The back fin is Kalaupapa Peninsula, a Hansen's Disease colony. Modern drugs have controlled leprosy and patients are no longer incarcerated. Fewer than 20 patients choose to remain at Kalaupapa, which is now a national park and a memorial to the disease that was once the scourge of the islands.

The center of Moloka`i contains two towns and the only airport. Neat little Kualapu`u (population 1,661) is the center of the budding agricultural community experimenting with coffee and exotic fruits. Kaunakakai (population 2,658) is the island's commercial center, boasting a dock, small hospital, library, three markets, one bakery, two gas stations, two banks, and a sizeable liquor store that stays open late, as well as several small churches queued along Kamehameha Highway. In between lies the Molokai Plumeria farm, Hawaii's largest supplier of plumeria blossoms for *lei*. During peak season, the 10-acre orchard produces 100,000 new blossoms a day.

Tiny Moloka`i has something many larger cities do not: two newspapers. Both are weeklies, very down-home, personal and strongly opinionated.

This island also has several sandy beaches, the state's highest waterfall, mountains, a few small condo developments and a resort, Kaluako`i, long closed. Nearby is Papohaku Ranchlands, a planned community with roads and underground utilities in place, but few houses as yet.

Papohaku's white sand beach — three miles long and 100 yards wide — is deserted, devoid of footprints. A few small estates lounge on a rise above the far end of the beach. At one home, a gracious resident says, "Yes, it's peaceful here, but this very quiet life is not for everyone." She and her husband have trouble keeping household help. Several mainland couples have come to work and stay in a cottage on the premises, but they soon get bored and leave. She has now hired a local couple, who are accustomed to this quiet life. She praises the standards and efforts at Maunaloa Elementary, the public school her sons attend.

A small island where everyone knows each other, Moloka`i is easy to love. For some, it is a perfect place to live.

RESOURCES

- Moloka`i is part of Maui County. See Maui

- Federal Job Information Center, O`ahu: **(808) 541-2791** www.usajobs.gov

- Hawai`i State Workforce Development Division, Kaunakakai: **(808) 553-3281** hawaii.gov/labor/wdd

Newspapers

- *Moloka`i Advertiser-News:* **(808) 558-8253** www.molokaiadvertiser-news.com

- *The Moloka`i Dispatch:* **(808) 552-2781** www.themolokaidispatch.com

You'll like life on Moloka`i if:

You like to hunt, hike or hide out. If you love nature, silence. And if you have a way to support yourself. If you long to go back to rural small town life as it was in the 1930s. (Remember, that was the decade of a major depression.)

Moloka`i

The "Friendly Isle," more than any other Hawaiian island, eyes tourism warily. Concerned volunteers carefully conduct treks across Kamakou Preserve, the highest point on Moloka`i at 4,970 feet.

Toni Polancy

Lana`i

The bright lights of Maui beckon just a few miles away, but most residents of "Privacy Island" prefer a simple life, including fishing at Kaumalapau Harbor.

Steve Brinkman

The Gathering Place

…has collected three-quarters of Hawai`i's population. Honolulu, the state capital, often gets a bad rap for crowding and traffic. Yet it is one of the most livable and lovely cities in the world.

G. Brad Lewis

G. Brad Lewis

Matt Thayer

On the windward side, a world away from the rush, the Ko`olau Mountains shelter a rural lifestyle. At right, silver-painted mime Johnny Ginbeny, an English transplant, awes onlookers in Waikiki every night.

O`ahu the gathering place

Want to enjoy all the things you are moving to the islands for — perfect weather, sunshine, beauty — and still have a rich cosmopolitan life? In addition to swimming, surfing and soaking up sun, would you like to enjoy big-name concerts, well-stocked libraries, and Broadway-caliber plays? And maybe you'd like a serious career too, in banking, commerce, law, politics, business.

Consider O`ahu.

About 70 percent of the state's nearly 1.3 million population is crammed on this third-largest Hawaiian island. Nearly 400,000 people live in Honolulu, the capital and largest city in the island chain, and the nation's 11th-largest metropolis. Neighbor islanders deride busy, teeming O`ahu, vowing to learn from the island's over-development: too many skyscrapers, too much traffic, too much bustle.

True, in Honolulu, you will look out from your high-rise at houses spilling down mountains like sauce on giant ice cream sundaes. You may stare out the window of your condominium into the window of another apartment. You will gaze down from your *lanai* at lines of cars and hear, not the sound of conch shells serenading the sunset, but police and ambulance sirens. Never mind.

Size: 600 square miles

Population in 1980: 762,565; **in 1997:** 886,711; **in 2003:** 902,704; **in 2009:** 934,262

Predominant occupations: retail business (both local and tourist related); government, importing, exporting, healthcare, some agriculture

Unemployment in 1998: 5.3%; **in 2004:** 3.3%; **in 2010:** 6%

Number of McDonald's restaurants: 51; **of Starbucks Coffee shops:** 40; **of Costco warehouses:** 4.

The best thing about O`ahu: Plenty to do

The worst thing about O`ahu: Traffic

What other islanders say about O`ahu: "Too noisy! Too crowded! Can't wait to get home."

What O`ahu says about itself: "We are the Hawaiian islands. We house three-quarters of the population."

All those high-rises allow you to live within walking distance of work, world-class shopping, some very fine dining, beaches and parks. A recent comparative study of the "quality of life" in 300 American metropolitan areas ranked Honolulu in the top third.

As large cities go, Honolulu is lovely, clean and relatively safe. A 2004 survey by Farmers Insurance Group ranked the state's capital as one of the safest cities in the nation. Honolulu was No. 14 among 213 U.S. metropolitan areas judged on crime, the risk of natural disasters and jobless statistics.

Here, you are residing in the very heart of the islands. Stand still and you can feel it pulsating beneath your feet. During the day, downtown Honolulu is the center of power for the island chain. In tall business buildings and small historic palaces, decisions are made that will intimately affect the lives of all residents of every island.

After dark, the city lights up like a massive fireworks display stopped in mid-explosion, providing breathtaking scenes from balconies. A carnival atmosphere shimmers Kalakaua Avenue in Waikiki. Mimes and musicians, hucksters and prostitutes, artists and drug dealers, ply their trades next to posh boutiques, open into the wee hours. O`ahu's 85,000 tourists (on any one day) can get anything they want nearly all night long.

Big city economy

O`ahu has the highest employment rate of the islands (except the private island of Lanai`i) and a wider variety of both blue-and white-collar positions. It is the shipping hub and the government center of the islands and the landing point for most tourists. Here are the islands' major television studios, banking centers, hospitals, advertising agencies, commercial and shopping centers. This is headquarters for the nation's Pacific military fleet, which generates $2.6 billion annually and provides jobs, directly and indirectly for an estimated 27,000 civilians.

A tour of O`ahu

In addition to high-rises, Honolulu's neighborhoods contain an eclectic mix of old plantation-style houses and modern homes. Stand near the Ala Wai canal in Waikiki. Look up at the mountains. These are mostly desirable, but costly older neighborhoods with sparkling views, just far enough away from town to offer respite from the busy highways, yet close enough to avoid long, stressful commutes. If you can afford it, consider **Manoa Valley,** location of the University of Hawai`i; **Makiki, Nu`uanu, Kamehameha Heights** or **Pacific Heights.** Your neighbors will be an interesting mix of longtime residents and newcomers. Home prices start at about $700,000; rentals abound.

Beginning at Waikiki and heading south, Kalakaua Avenue becomes Diamond Head Road and proceeds through the glitzy neighborhoods of **Diamond Head, Black Point** and **Kahala.** Homes are expensive here, from about $1,000,000, but rents can be comparatively reasonable, so don't discount these affluent neighborhoods.

Houses pour down an O`ahu hillside

Matthew Thayer

Diamond Head Road bypasses H-1, meets Kalaniana`ole Highway and zooms through the neighborhood of `**Aina Haina,** with its eclectic mix of architectural styles. A few very busy miles beyond is one of the most popular areas for newcomers, the planned community of **Hawai`i Kai.** The bustling, planned community was created in part via the vision of developer/dreamer Henry Kaiser. A man who once worked for Kaiser says that in the 1960s the multi-millionaire looked down at the valley of pig farms, declared the land would one day be covered by homes, and commanded his employees to make it happen at any cost. It has — and the price is rising. Hawai`i Kai includes marina townhouses for water enthusiasts, as well as hillside homes and condos for view-lovers — all set

Characteristics of O`ahu Neighborhoods

Neighborhood	Resident population	Median age	House-holds	Average house-hold size	Average Family size
O`ahu total	876,165	35.7	286,450	2.95	3.46
1. Hawai`i Kai	27,657	42.1	9,666	2.86	3.21
2. Kuliouou-Kalani Iki	18,271	45.1	6,204	2.93	3.29
3. Waialae-Kahala	7,118	46.1	2,728	2.61	3.08
4. Kaimuki	18,063	45.4	6,362	2.78	3.34
5. Diamond Head/Kapahulu/ St. Louis Heights	19,137	42.7	7,698	2.44	3.18
6. Palolo	13,091	41.7	4,373	2.97	3.53
7. Manoa	21,184	39.3	7,051	2.59	3.13
8. McCully/Moiliili	26,122	38.9	12,670	2.04	2.92
9. Waikiki	19,720	42.2	11,397	1.72	2.59
10. Makiki/Lwr Punchbowl/Tantalus	30,145	41.0	14,998	1.97	2.84
11. Ala Moana/Kakaako	14,186	42.9	7,797	1.78	2.65
12. Nuuanu/Punchbowl	16,494	43.5	6,180	2.63	3.32
13. Downtown	14,575	40.9	6,818	1.87	2.78
14. Liliha/Kapalama	19,905	44.4	6,495	2.93	3.58
15. Kalihi-Palama	37,987	36.3	10,258	3.57	4.34
16. Kalihi Valley	17,937	36.5	3,941	4.42	4.93
17. Moanalua	11,748	36.0	3,219	3.08	3.36
18. Aliamanu/Salt Lake/ Foster Village	36,572	33.4	11,732	3.09	3.67
19. Airport	18,163	25.7	5,001	3.32	3.37
20. Aiea	31,221	37.6	10,580	2.89	3.52
21. Pearl City	47,794	37.7	14,369	3.13	3.53
22. Waipahu	62,402	34.1	16,937	3.60	4.10
23. Ewa	53,099	30.8	14,324	3.68	4.08
24. Waianae Coast	42,333	28.5	10,554	3.97	4.47
25. Mililani/Waipio/Melemanu	34,592	35.4	11,038	3.13	3.49
26. Wahiawa	39,553	26.2	10,603	3.30	3.68
27 North Shore	18,380	31.3	5,893	3.05	3.60
28 Koolauloa	14,546	27.6	3,682	3.75	4.40
29 Kahaluu	14,732	36.4	4,476	3.29	3.66
30 Kaneohe	36,736	38.1	11,348	3.18	3.60
31 Kailua	43,780	39.6	14,628	2.96	3.44
32 Waimanalo	10,919	32.9	2,657	4.03	4.46
33 Mokapu	11,827	22.0	2,332	3.21	3.25
34 Makakilo/Kapolei/Honokai Hale	15,545	32.7	4,589	3.38	3.77
35 Mililani Mauka-Launani Valley	10,622	32.8	3,852	2.76	3.23

Source: City and County of Honolulu Planning Department, tabulations from the 2000 U.S. Census as quoted in the Hawaii Data book. For updated statistics see http://www2.hawaii.gov/dbedt

around **Koko Marina**, a tasteful shopping center. Today, amidst an island building boom, residents are decrying the continued development in this area, and adequate infrastructure is a concern.

As a rule, the farther from Honolulu you travel, the less expensive housing becomes. Hawai`i Kai is Hawai`i's version of moderately expensive, in the $500,000 to $900,000 range, at this time.

Kalaniana`ole Highway clutches the *pali* (ocean cliffs), winding through beautiful, tranquil scenery to wide ocean vistas. Tucked around a corner and down a hill is **Hanauma Bay**, a popular marine preserve, and **Halona Bay,** where Burt Lancaster and Deborah Kerr rolled on the beach in the movie *From Here to Eternity.*

Terrible traffic?

Busy and bad as it seems, Honolulu is actually one of the few places in the country where traffic congestion is getting better, not worse, according to a national study. The 2003 Urban Mobility Report, an annual survey of transportation trends, showed Honolulu had the best improvement of 75 major metropolitan areas in recent years. Honolulu drivers spend an average of 50 hours a year stuck in traffic jams, about the national average. Los Angeles has the worst record: an average of 90 hours.

Starting again at **Waikkiki** and heading northwest on Highway 1, homes are less expensive, but the area is crowded. **Pearl City, `Aiea, Salt Lake** and **Waipahu** include military and government-subsidized housing, as well as the older homes of longtime residents, and more shopping strips. Condominiums here can be purchased for from about $200,000. If you have children, pay particular attention to the public schools in this area; some are overcrowded and have more than their share of problems. (See chapter 9: Children.)

Farther north off Highway 1 are several new planned communities like **Mililani Town** and **Kapolei,** (O`ahu's "Second City") with condos and single-family homes, mostly situated on small lots with shopping centers nearby. **Waikele,** an outlet center, has become the commercial hub of this area and more commercial developments are planned. This could be Anytown, U.S.A, plunked down in paradise between major highways. But, close up, these high-density developments are mostly clean and neat and provide an opportunity for middle-income families of all ethnic

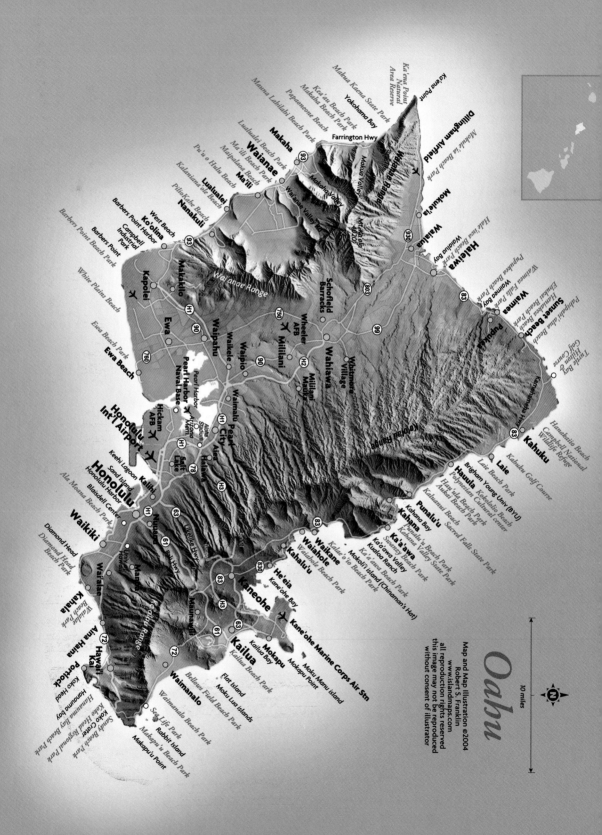

Oahu

Map and Map Illustration ©2004
Robert S. Franklin
www.islandmaps.com
all reproduction rights reserved
this image may not be reproduced
without consent of illustrator

10 miles

N

groups to own a brand-new house or attached "townhome" at prices that begin at about $400,000 at this time. Life here appeals to many modern families: there are bike paths, community parks, a golf course with clubhouse and other amenities. Relatively reasonable rentals also abound. Schools here are generally considered sufficient, if over-crowded.

Heading to the **"Windward side"** of the island, traverse the Pali or Likelike Highways and you are in for a treat. You'll pass through the deeply ridged and majestic Ko`olau Mountains to the town of **Kane`ohe,** overlooking Kane`ohe Bay. Just ahead, **Kailua** nestles near Kailua Beach, considered one of O`ahu's most beautiful. These two suburbs are *haole* (Caucasian) enclaves, featuring newer developments as well as a few older homes (older, in Hawai`i, meaning just 20 years or more) that tend to be medium-priced for the islands, in the $500,000 to $700,000 range (and up, of course). Although these towns have grown rapidly and haphazardly, with an overabundance of shopping strips and car dealerships, they retain much of their natural beauty and are a relatively easy commute to Honolulu. The public schools here are generally considered above average, an important consideration.

O`ahu's hidden treasures lie just beyond Kane`ohe: the Windward and North shores. Kamehameha Highway winds away from the busy modern world to a quieter time. The rural Windward shore is sheltered by the Ko`olau Mountains, a fortress against modern madness. Here, cows graze in meadows against a curtain of verdant cliffs and children hawk bananas, pineapples, *lei* and farm produce from roadside stands. Old plantation houses huddle in tropical cul-de-sacs or perch on narrow beaches. In tiny beach towns like **Kahalu`u, Waiahole, Ka`a`awa, Hau`ula** and **La`ie,** *haoles* and locals live together, most of the time, in relative peace. Some newcomers can be uncomfortable, or at least lonesome, in the heavily local atmosphere, but others thrive.

Fifteen miles up the road, at the North Shore, **Hale`iwa** (population 2,442 and growing) is a quaint tourist town. Here, serious surfers tackle the waves of the famous Sunset Beach and Pipeline as the well-to-do look down from the mini estates of **Pupukea.**

While the **North Shore** and the windward side of O`ahu remain somewhat pristine, many residents complain that these areas are too far from Honolulu (at least an hour's drive) for daily commuting. Excess speed along the narrow, tortuous Kamehameha Highway makes for many traffic accidents. More than 330 were reported in one 18-month period; crosses and flower-laden shrines mark the spots where people have lost their lives in auto crashes. Another kind of traffic, drugs, had made inroads in this area in the past few years, as it has on much of the islands.

An island away, past the Ko`olau and the Waianae mountain ranges, the dry leeward side of the island is less lush. Here, a heavily "local" population deserves the right to call this area its own — if not by possessing the land, at least by living there peacefully. **Makaha, Wai`anae** and other small towns are tucked between the ocean and arid chunks of the Wai`anae Mountains. Most housing is older, smaller, and less expensive, from $300,000, but the commute to town is long, arduous and dangerous.

RESOURCES

- City job information line
  (808) 523-4301
  www.honolulu.gov/HR/labor.htm

- Business Action Center
  808-586 2545
  hawaii.gov/dcca/bac/

- *Rentals Illustrated*
  magazine
  808-949-3686
  rentalsillustrated.com

- Chamber of Commerce of Hawai`i
  (808) 545-4300
  1132 Bishop St., Ste. 200
  Honolulu, HI 96813
  cochawaii.com

- Kailua Chamber of Commerce
  (808) 261-2727
  P.O. Box 1469
  Kailua, HI 96734
  www.kailuachamber.com

- For many other Hawai`i and O`ahu sources of information, see the Resources section at the end of this book.

You'll enjoy life on O`ahu if: you like beaches, warm weather, shopping, tourists, high-rises, traffic and don't mind a lot of other people. If you'd like life in a tropical New York City — or Los Angeles as it was in the smog-free 1950s.

A valuable addition to your library is a copy of the *Atlas of Hawai`i*, third edition, loaded with facts about culture and environment. Produced by the department of Geography at the University of Hawai`i at Hilo, the book is published by the University of Hawai`i Press and is available at bookstores.

Kapu: Two forbidden islands

The small islands of Kaho`olawe and Ni`ihau loom softly just offshore the main island chain — shadowy seductresses. But forget living on either of these islands. They are kapu: forbidden.

Kaho`olawe: the unfortunate isle

Poor Kaho`olawe. This small, shy island, hunching red and barren just offshore of southern Maui, has a sad past. Archaeological evidence suggests the island — windy and dry and just 45 square miles in size — once supported a small community, decimated in the 1700s by disease or island wars. In the mid-1800s the island became a penal colony, and next served as a place for Maui ranchers to graze cattle and sheep. The cattle devoured the vegetation, allowing high winds to blow off much of the topsoil.

Adding injury to insult, the United States military used the island as a practice bombing site during World War II and for many years after. In 1990, bowing to protesters, the U.S. government returned "Target Island" to Hawaiians and committed $400 million to clearing away unexploded bombs and debris. Contractors removed 92,000 pieces of unexploded ordnance and 8.5 million pounds of metal scrap, but, money spent, the government gave up the effort, leaving about ten percent of the little island a minetrap of unexploded ordnance.

Kaho`olawe was the first unexploded-ordnance removal project ever undertaken by the Navy. Navy officials say they did the best they could given the money and time limitations set by Congress.

Today, Kaho`olawe is destined to become a spiritual and cultural preserve, returned to the Hawaiian people in 2004 by formal agreement with the government. The Kaho`olawe Island Reserve Commission, which has $30 million from the government in a trust fund for island management, would like to see trails, campsites and education centers for visitors. Ideally, a pier would be constructed to allow vessels to bring people to and from the island. Realistically, it is unclear how many people will actually ever be allowed to visit. Visitation may be limited to people who want to advance the mission of the reserve, including those who practice Native Hawaiian traditions, volunteer for environmental work or engage in preservation or archaeological activities, according to a story in *The Honolulu Advertiser*.

Those who have visited so far say the island has something special going for it: dramatic views. On a clear day, you can see four of its more fortunate sisters: Maui, Moloka`i, Lana`i and O`ahu.

Ni`ihau: the forbidden island

Ni`ihau, the "The Forbidden Island" has been more fortunate, but could face a future as dreary as Kaho`olawe's past. A cattle and sheep ranch, owned by the Robinson family since 1864, Ni`ihau is private property. Visiting its 230 residents, mostly Ni`ihau natives, is by invitation only. Islanders lead a primitive life with no stores and few modern conveniences, dining on the fish they catch and the vegetables they grow.

The little island has an interesting, unique history. Eliza Sinclair, widow of a Scottish sea captain and 63 at the time, brought her family to Kaua`i from New Zealand in the 1860s and purchased Ni`ihau from King Kamehameha IV for $10,000. Later, she bought the ahupua`a of Makaweli on Kaua`i. (Hawaiian kings divided the islands into *ahupua`a*, a pie-shaped tract of land that runs from the ocean to the top of a mountain.)

Sinclair's heirs, the Robinson family, have so far scorned development of Ni`ihau and strive to protect its residents and its rural way of life. For over a century, they kept the island off-limits to visitors. For a time in the late 1990s, despite the protests of islanders and some Kaua`i residents, the U.S. Navy (while at the same time cleaning up Kaho`olawe's bombing mess) considered Ni`ihau as a site for missile launchings. As part of a $50 million upgrade to the Pacific Missile Range Facility on Kaua`i's west side, the Navy would build several test launch sites and a 6,000 foot-runway on Ni`ihau. Nothing, to this time, has come of the plan.

na mea `e a`e
e no`ono`o ai

other considerations

Your decision determines

your entire future...

and the lives and happiness

of family and friends, too

Larry and Maria:
He wanted to come; she didn't

When her husband Larry said he wanted to move to Hawai`i, Maria Lospinuso was definite: she did not want to come. The third-generation American/Italians had fallen in love as teenagers and married young. Bonded by their love and their religion, and encircled by large, close-knit families, they had remained married for over 20 years and had happily raised a daughter, Stephanie, 19.

Then in 1999, Larry and Maria vacationed in Hawai`i.

"It was like Larry fell under some kind of spell," Maria remembers. "When we got back home, he kept talking about moving to Hawai`i. I thought he was crazy, but he just kept insisting.

"I seriously considered divorcing him," she adds. "But I had to put my marriage first. We are Catholic and once you are married, that's it."

Maria reluctantly went along with plans to move. The process included another trip to Hawai`i to try out life here, investigate jobs and housing, set up bank accounts. Planning for the move took months, and Maria used that time to say long, fond goodbyes to family, co-workers and lifelong friends. She was depressed. Sad.

"I knew what the move entailed. We would be so far away. Financially, we could not go back and forth to visit very often."

"On the other hand, I was on a high," Larry says. "All I could think of was getting here, starting over, in beautiful Hawai`i. My only real concern was leaving my daughter. She seemed too young to be on her own."

The Lospinusos encouraged Stephanie to come with them to Maui. Larry described the island's beauty and assured her that she would easily find a job here. But Stephanie had grown up in New Jersey, already had a job and a serious relationship. Her family would have to go to the islands without her.

Meanwhile, Maria's father was appalled that she would move so far from her family. He refused to speak to her. Before leaving for Hawai`i, Maria visited him in a nursing home one last time. He was sleeping and she waited patiently, watching him. When he awoke, she said she loved him and asked his forgiveness. He hugged her goodbye.

And so Larry and Maria climbed into their car, drove off and left a lifetime of jobs, family and friends behind. Traveling cross-country to take their car to Los Angeles for shipment to Hawai`i was a vacation of sorts. By the time their plane landed in Hawai`i, Maria was at peace, optimistic about the move.

But now, it was Larry's turn to "freak out." He became anxious about the move. Nervous. Crying.

"He had been on this high. Excited about coming," Maria remembers. "Suddenly, the reality of the move just hit him, full force."

"I panicked. I mean I really panicked for a day or so," Larry says. "Everyone, friends, family were so far away, especially my daughter. What if she needed me again? And you couldn't just pick up the phone and call if you got lonesome for them — there was that six-hour time difference."

"I panicked. I mean I really panicked. Everyone, friends, family were so far away,... And you couldn't just pick up the phone and call it you got lonesome for them — there was that six-hour time difference."

"You need to know about this," Maria says. "You need to know there is the real pain of loss. You need to face that and deal with it. You have to weigh

what you are giving up against what you are achieving...and decide whether it is worthwhile."

Family needs drew the Lospinusos back to the mainland after a year on the islands, but they eventually returned to Maui to live.

"You have to weigh what you are giving up against what you are achieving...and decide whether it is worthwhile."

Making your decision: Answer these questions

So, you've read all the chapters in this book — and reread the ones on costs and working. You've used a computer and the URLs in the Resources sections to learn about life here. You have a realistic idea of what it is like to live in Hawai`i. And you probably have at least a good idea about what you will do to earn a living here. A counselor, who has twice moved back and forth from the mainland, suggests you now hone in on the personal and emotional side of your decision. It's time to ask yourself and your loved ones some hard questions.

- **Why are you moving?** Are you escaping California's traffic? Washington state's rain? Pennsylvania's snow? Family problems? Or do you just want a fresh start? Are you attracted by the ocean? Hawai`i's natural beauty? In a clean notebook, separate from your daily input, write down your reasons for wanting to come. Review them in a week, in a month, in a few months, as you make one of the most important decisions of your life.

- **Who wants to move?** In any relationship, it's usually one person who most wants to make a change. Others — children, a spouse or lover — go along, eagerly, willingly or reluctantly.

- **What about those left behind?** Remember the people you are leaving behind. You are euphoric, excited about your move. But your parents, your children, your siblings and friends do not have that happy anticipation to bolster their spirits now. Most likely, all they can see is that you are leaving. Set definite dates when mom or dad or children from a former marriage, for example, can look forward to coming to visit. Make it a holiday — Christmas or a birthday — a time when they are apt to miss you most.

- **What are your expectations?** You've decided why you are coming… now decide what you hope to achieve in paradise. Set goals and a plan to achieve them. The goals don't have to be monetary. You may be seeking a more peaceful lifestyle, more time to spend with your family. List the goals in that notebook and refer to them in the hectic days and months to come. Setting your sights on those goals will help you keep your perspective. Refer to the list again in five years. Have you achieved what you set out to do?

Tell us

For future editions of this book, we'd like to know about your experiences moving to, or from, Hawai`i. Is island life what you expected it to be? E-mail polancya@hawaii.rr.com

Set a time to ask, listen... ho`onoponopono style

A loved one, spouse or child doesn't share your enthusiasm for living on a tropical island. Maybe you should talk about it, and more importantly, listen and ponder their concerns, a counselor suggests. Try this talk-think session, a variation on the Hawaiian custom of *ho`onoponopono*, in which families and friends who love each other talk out problems. Here are some guidelines:

- **Gather together** all the people involved in your move. Schedule an hour or more, depending on the number of people. During this time there should be no interruptions.

- **Choose a facilitator.** Ask an uninvolved person to act as timekeeper and moderator, also recording the session or summarizing in notes.

- **Let each person speak.** Each person will have a maximum of five minutes to talk without being interrupted. The person who most wants to move should begin speaking and he or she should express exactly why the move means so much. Then listen carefully as others, including children, discuss any feelings or fears they have about the move.

- **Talk a little.** Now spend about half an hour discussing among you what you have heard, answering everyone's concerns, but make no decisions during that meeting. Spend the next few days thinking about what you've heard.

- **Compromise, solve.** Schedule another meeting, a few days later, after everyone has had time to consider each others' responses. Now you know how everyone feels and why they feel the way they do. Respond to each other. Can you compromise? Can you do anything to make those around you more comfortable with the move?

- **Carefully consider** your decision again. If your spouse or teenage children really don't want to come, you should probably delay or reconsider the move. Starting a new life here will be difficult enough without negative feelings. If you do decide to come, at least you know where everyone stands, how everyone feels. Even those who come reluctantly will appreciate that you cared enough to listen.

The One-Week Experiment

Many people who move here make the same mistake: they are so smitten and sure they will never want to leave the islands that they burn all their bridges behind them, perhaps giving up a lucrative job and saying a final farewell to friends and neighbors.

Months later, after sampling island life, many newcomers — as many as 40 percent, some statistics show — leave the islands, sadder and, surely, poorer.

So, you'd be wise to come to the islands for a time and try out life here. If you can't arrange an extended "living period," come to Hawai`i for at least one full week. Use this time, not to enjoy your island as a tourist, but to live as a resident. In a visit as short as one week, you can learn a great deal about life here.

Yes, it will be costly… but not nearly as costly as a mistake might be. The information you gain will be well worth it.

- **Three months before your trip**, order a week's subscription to the newspaper from the island you are considering, or scroll it daily on your computer. Newspapers are listed in the Resources section at the back of this book and are also accessible on the Internet.

- **Rent a place to live.** From the newspaper or Internet ads, find houses, cottages, condominiums or studios for rent and call those that seem to offer what you desire as a long-term rental. Chances are, the owner or rental manager will be trying to rent it for six months or a year. Discuss what you are doing — trying out Hawaiian life — and offer an extra 50 percent above the rental price for just one or two weeks occupancy. If the first few owners reject your offer, keep trying. You'll instigate some lively discussion about life in Hawai`i... and chances are you'll find a willing landlord within four or five calls.

- **Live your life** just as you would if you had moved here. Maintain a daily schedule. Drive or take TheBus to wherever you expect to work every day and do it at about the time you would leave for your job. You will actually be going to work in the sense that you will use this time to visit the places where you'd like to be employed and the people with whom you'd like to work. Spend a minimum of five hours each day looking for a job in your field and finding out all you can about employment here. Visit the state employment office, private employment firms and businesses, offices or resorts at which you can realistically expect to work. This is extremely valuable time. Talk to human relations directors. Talk to the people in jobs similar to yours. Are they adequately paid? What are the chances of finding a job in your field? You will learn a great deal and you may even find a job, as one person who tried this approach did. "The best time to find a job is when you don't really need it. When you aren't desperate," he commented.

- **If you expect to be self-employed**, use these six hours a day to pursue information. Talk to economic development directors, business and tourism officials, rental agents, suppliers, and people in businesses related to the one you are considering.

- **Your spouse and family** should be spending at least part of their days in ways they would if they lived here. Will you need childcare? Visit childcare centers. Visit schools, talk to students and teachers. Encourage your teenage children to interact with peers at youth centers.

- **Food shop** to fill the larder for your stay. Plan to prepare food and dine as you do in your current life. No restaurants, unless you dine out often now. You're not on vacation: your goal is to sample real life here.

- **Spend your leisure time** as you would enjoy it if you lived here. If you are into sports like softball, find a diamond. Tennis? Most islands have plenty of public courts. Golf? The links are great places to pick up job leads and information. Interested in community service? Check out newspaper events calendars and get in touch with people with interests similar to yours.

- **Finally**, each evening, spend 10 or 15 minutes writing down your impressions of the day. Take time to assess the information you've gained and your feelings about what you've learned. Talk over the day's experiences with your spouse or family.

- **On the seventh day, rest.** Review your impressions. You've sampled a little of real life in paradise. Do you still want to move here? If you do, you will have developed some good contacts, advice and valuable firsthand knowledge.

The Wichers: leaving paradise

Not everyone is rushing to the islands; some people are quietly paddling away. The Wichers are selling their Maui home, taking profits garnered in Hawai`i's booming real estate market, and moving far away, to Norway.

The couple has lived on Maui since they met on a Hawai`i beach in 1998. Elin was a medical technologist on vacation with girlfriends; Vern was a windsurfer and sign shop owner. There are several reasons for the move back to her homeland, but the primary one, says Elin, is the frustrating Catch 22 she has encountered in getting a Hawai`i state license to practice medical technology. Despite passing federal licensing requirements, Elin cannot obtain a

Perhaps the move is most difficult for Dewey, the Wichers' one-year-old Jack Russell terrier. Like Hawai`i, Norway has no rabies, and its regulations include six months of quarantine or extensive vet visits to meet qualifications.

license to work as a medical technologist here until she has practiced in the state for one year. And she cannot get hired to practice until she has a license.

"It is really stupid, because we really need this kind of work in Maui," she says.

Over the past few years, the Wichers experienced the ups and downs of island business. He ran his sign shop; she operated a small visitor accommodations service. Both businesses were adversely affected by the terrorist acts of 9/11.

"If you don't bring your own money, there's nothing you will earn here. It is very hard," Elin says.

"Word of mouth, networking, is really important here," Vern comments. "The first two years in business we were really scraping."

But he is feeling a bit of "rock fever: too. "I like Maui a lot, but I reached a point where I felt isolated. I want to see the rest of the world."

Erica's story continues: Will she stay?

Toni Polancy

Erica's perseverance impresses members of Ewalani Hula Maids halau.

How long does it take to feel welcome, comfortable in a new place? To feel as though you belong?

"Stay two years and you will stay forever," offers one longtime transplant.

"No," says another. "To truly break away from the place you grew up takes years and years. Seven years at least."

Some people, in fact, can never really feel comfortable anyplace but where they were raised. And sometimes we have to go away to discover which kind of person we are.

Erica Maluski, the art therapist from New York, whose story appears in earlier chapters of this book, had been in Hawai`i only 18 weeks when we first interviewed her. She was miles away from her family for the first time.

Like many young people, she had wanted an adventure in an exotic place and Hawai`i fit the bill. Re-interviewed later, nine months after she moved to Hawai`i, Erica still loved her job as art therapist at a leeward area psychiatric

Continues...

facility, but was experiencing some difficulty adjusting to life outside the hospital. She was lonely and having trouble meeting people.

"Anyplace else I've ever gone," she said, "school, college, I made friends easily. Here, it's hard to connect. I don't mean romantically. I mean just friends. The romance part, well, that will come if it comes. I just want some friends to hang out with."

Part of Erica's problem may be that she works and resides in an area of O`ahu where there are few *haoles* her age. And the apartment complex in which she lives consists of mostly families, many involved in the military.

"Neighbors are nice. They say hello when we meet," she says, "and people at work invite me to their houses. 'Come for dinner every Thursday,' they say. But we are at a different point in our lives. I want friends like me."

Erica could easily drive to Honolulu's many singles bars, but that doesn't interest her. Keeping busy helps with the homesickness. She surfs at nearby Barbers Beach, runs nearly every day, participated in the 8.5 mile Aloha Run and was practicing for the Hawai`i marathon.

She also joined a *halau*, and did what many of the mostly-Hawaiian dancers have not done: learned a long chant to be sung in perfect Hawaiian for the *kumu hula*, the teacher. It took five attempts for Erica to do it correctly and her efforts are appreciated. Her older dance mates smile gently at her efforts to master the graceful sways and movements.

And all the activity has paid off in a way Erica never anticipated: she has lost 30 pounds since she's been here.

Still, even after nine months, even with a job she loves and plenty of hobbies to keep her busy, Erica was depressed, homesick again, after several mainland friends who visited her on O`ahu left. Toughest, she says, are the evenings. "You can't just pick up the phone and call a friend back East. It's six hours later there, the middle of the night."

Will Erica "make it" in Hawai`i? Will she fulfill her commitment to stay two or three years? Or will she pack up and leave the islands as many newcomers do?

Erica shakes her head and looks pensive. "I don't know," she says. "I'll probably stay the two or three years. Probably. And even if I do leave, this will always be a special place."

Make friends with your new neighborhood

So, how do you learn to fit into a neighborhood where everyone is transient, or speaks a foreign language, where, maybe, you are the only newcomer?

- **Go for a walk.** Instead of leaping in and out of your car for every errand, try walking to the store. If the store is too far, just go for a daily walk. You'll get to know your neighborhood and, maybe, your neighbors.

- **Smile.** Be the first to speak. A smile is a universal sign of friendship. A simple, very general statement can start a conversation. "Your tree has big mangos." "Your garden is beautiful." "Weather is so warm. Yes?" There's about an 80 percent chance you'll be met with a smile in return, and your neighbor appreciates the gesture, even if he does not speak English. If you are met with a lack of enthusiasm, no big deal. Back off politely. Nothing ventured; nothing gained.

- **Offer to help.** Let your neighbors know that you are there for them if they need your help. Walk over, put out your hand for a shake, and introduce yourself. "I'm Steve Smith. I live across the street. Since we live so nearby, I thought I'd let you know. If you ever need us, we are willing to help." Exchange phone numbers. This is especially important if you have elderly neighbors who may need you in an emergency. And vice-versa.

- **Noisy?** Planning a party or having guests who may make a bit of noise? Knock on your neighbors' doors and apologize in advance. Assure them that you are aware they may be inconvenienced and will break up the party early. Most times, this works well, defusing potential problems.

The Eoffs: A sad coming, a gentle staying

"The Islands will either welcome you and embrace you, or they will spit you out, and send you back to where you came from."

We hear that statement often in regard to *malihini*. As tough as the islands can be on newcomers, they can be equally gentle and welcoming. Just ask the Eoff family. Their journey here was a painful one, in circumstances that still bring tears, but the Eoffs say they were destined to live here, where they have experienced great love and caring.

Daughter Terrel Williams, Terry and Janey Eoff.

The Eoff's son David was an adventurer who, by the time he was 27, had visited much of the world. He came to Hawai`i in 2001, fell in love with the land and with a lady, got a construction job, and vowed to stay. He encouraged Terry and Janey Eoff to move from Colorado, writing: "Mom and Dad, you would love it here."

In April 2002, everything changed when an aggressive driver forced David's Jeep off Mokulele Highway in Maui. The Jeep overturned and David's head struck the roll bar. David played down the injuries, but he could not remember things he had said in previous conversations, could not drive, and was experiencing seizures. The Eoffs soon suspected he was seriously hurt. Janey and David's brother Taylor,10, came to Maui to help care for David and Janey then learned how seriously ill her son was. Doctors said blood clots had affected some parts of his brain. Very worried, Terry Eoff gave up his job and came to help care for his son. David's sister, Terrel Williams, also came. Six weeks later, David died during a seizure.

As word of David's death traveled the coconut wireless that day, friends and co-workers began appearing at the home where the Eoffs' were staying. By evening, 100 people had come to show love and support to a family most of them had never met. With them, they brought a house full of food.

"Someone even brought a case of Kleenex," Terry remembers, "and we passed it around and used it all up."

Overwhelmed by the kindness of strangers, the Eoffs decided to stay on the island. Terry was soon hired to engineer Lahaina's famous Sugar Cane Train. Janey signed on to sew for Sig Zane, clothing designers. Both are employed at jobs they enjoy.

Terry says the secret to living happily here is not to try to "Californicate Hawaii," but to "gel with the local people. They will take care of you."

You know you are *kama`aina...*

• when Hawaiian and Japanese words begin to dot your conversation. "Did you enjoy your *musubi?* Has anyone taken the dog *shi shi?* Are you *pau?*"

• when you automatically remove your shoes before you enter a home — even while you're visiting relatives in Boulder and it's 10 below.

• when you put Spam and shoyu on your grocery list under "staples."

• when you slide into pidgin during everyday conversations.

• the day you give all your winter clothes to the Salvation Army.

• when you never take your bathing suit off entirely.

• when you automatically walk out of the ocean facing it.

• when a two-inch long cockroach flies at you and you don't duck.

• when you know the difference between shave ice and *guri guri.*

• when you know what an *okole* is.

• when you find yourself smiling unexpectedly, for no good reason except that it's great to be alive.

Toni Polancy

Tourists and residents line up for fresh bread each evening behind Kanemitzu Bakery, Molokai. Page 330.

Our wish for you:

May you always be a tourist at heart.

Jim Powell

A Ni`ihau resident walks a deserted beach on the privately-owned island. Page 344

Toni Polancy

Awed tourists gaze at the Pali lookout, windward O`ahu. Page 339

resources

Resources

Living
- *Landlord Tenant Code*
  For a booklet on state rental laws,
  send a check for $2 to:
  Cashiers Office
  P.O. Box 541
  Honolulu, HI 96809
  call **(808) 586-2630** or via the internet at
  hawaii.gov/dcca/ocp/landlord_tenant

- *Homes & Land* real estate magazines
  Free full-color magazines with photos
  and prices of homes, condos and land
  for sale throughout the islands and
  the nation, call toll-free **(800) 277-7800**
  or via the Internet at
  www.HomesAndLand.com

- *Rentals Illustrated*
  Free twice-monthly pictorial of
  apartments and homes
  (808) 949-3686
  1240 Ala Moana Blvd.
  Honolulu, HI 96814
  www.rentalsillustrated.com

- National realtor network via the
  internet: **www.realtor.com**

Business
- For a free workbook *Starting a
  Business in Hawaii* call:
  The Business Action Center
  (808) 586-2545
  Provides entrepreneurs with information, business forms, licenses
  and permits:
  **www.Hawaii.gov/dbedt/bac/
  business.html**

- Professional and Vocational Licensing
  Division, Department of Commerce
  and Consumer Affairs **(808) 586-3000**
  pvl.eHawaii.gov/pvl

- High Technology Development
  Corporation **(808) 539-3839**
  www.htdc.org

- Small Business Information Service
  (808) 541-2990 or via the internet:
  http://www.sba.gov

- Retail Merchants of Hawai`i
  (808) 592-4200 or via the internet:
  www.rmhawaii.org

- Small Business Hawai`i
  (808)396-1724 or via the internet:
  www.smallbusinesshawaii.com

Living
- Newcomers Club **(808) 944-3310**

Crime
- The Honolulu Police Department's
  annual report. Helpful for choosing
  neighborhoods. Available at Hawai`i's
  main library or at the main police
  station, 801 Beretania Street, Honolulu

General
- *The Hawai`i State Data Book*
  published through the Hawaii State
  Department of Business, Economic
  Development & Tourism is available:
  hawaii.gov/dbedt
  Get the information on a CD. Write:
  Department of Business, Economic
  Development & Tourism
  P.O. Box 2359
  Honolulu, HI 96804
  or via the internet:
  **hawaii.gov/dbedt/info/economic/
  databook**

- For further information about data
  and sources, call the Research and
  Economic Analysis Division's
  Business Resource Center Library
  (808) 586-2424
  hawaiieconomicdata.com

Newspapers and periodicals
- *Honolulu Advertiser*
  call **(808) 538-6397** or write
  Honolulu Advertiser
  Attention: Circulation
  Post Office Box 3350
  Honolulu, HI 96801 or via the internet:
  www.honoluluadvertiser.com

- *The Honolulu Weekly*
  Contains a comprehensive arts and entertainment guide, **(808) 528-1475**
  2100 College Walk, Suite 214
  Honolulu, HI 96817
  www.honoluluweekly.com

- *Honolulu* magazine, a monthly chronicle of lifestyle **(808) 524-7400**
  fax (808) 531-2306
  36 Merchant Street
  Honolulu, HI 96813
  www.honolulumagazine.com

- *Island Family.* A free monthly newspaper includes a calendar of family events **(808) 689-0000**
  P.O. Box 2429
  Ewa Beach, HI 96706-0429
  www.islandfamilymagazine.com

- *Hawaii Filipino Chronicle*
  A free twice-monthly newspaper
  (808) 678-8930
  1449 North King Street
  Honolulu, HI 96817
  www.rrhi.com/hfci

Politics and taxation

- Send for Government in Hawai`i a booklet by the Tax Foundation of Hawai`i. Call **(808) 536-4587** or fax (808) 536-4588
  126 Queen Street, Suite 304
  Honolulu, HI 96813
  or via the internet:
  www.tfhawaii.org

O`ahu

Business and jobs

- The Chamber of Commerce of Hawai`i **(808) 545-4300**
  1132 Bishop Street, Suite 200
  Honolulu, HI 96813
  cochawaii.com

- Kailua Chamber of Commerce **(808) 261-2727**
  P.O. Box 1469

Kailua, HI 96734
www.kailuachamber.com

- City job information line:
  (808) 523-4301 or via the internet:
  www.honolulu.gov/HR/labor.htm

- Business action line: **(808) 586 2545**
  See also the working section of this book

Big Island

Business

- Hawaii Island Economic Development **(808) 966-5416**
  or via the internet:
  www.hiedb.org

- Research and Development **(808) 961-8366** or via the internet:
  www.co.hawaii.hi.us

- Kona Kohala Chamber of Commerce **(808) 329-1758**
  www.kona-kohala.com

- Hawai`i Island Chamber of Commerce **(808) 935-7178**
  or via the internet:
  www.hicc.biz
  For $20, either Chamber will send you a directory with specific information

Information about volcanoes:

- Use these Internet URLs
  hvo.wr.usgs.gov
  volcano.oregonstate.edu

Newspapers:

- *Hawaii Tribune Herald*
  355 Kinoole Street
  Hilo, HI 96720
  (808) 935-6621
  www.hawaiitribune-herald.com

- *West Hawaii Today*
  75-5560 Kaiwe Street
  Kona, HI 96740
  (808) 329-9311
  www.westhawaiitoday.com

Maui

Business

- Small Business Development Center
  590 Lipoa Parkway
  Kihei, HI 96753
  (808) 875-2402 or via the internet:
  www.hawaii-sbdc.org
  E-mail **dfisher@maui.com**

- The Business Information Center
  590 Lipoa Parkway
  Kïhei, HI 96753
  (808) 875-2400 or via the internet:
  http://www.hbrl-sbdc.org
  E-mail **corn@maui.com** or
  sonia @maui.com

- County of Maui **(800) 272-0026**

Newspapers

- *The Maui News* **(808) 244-6363**
  www.mauinew.com

- *The Lahaina News* **(808) 667-7866**
  Fax: **(808) 667-2726**
  www.lahainanew.com

- *The Maui Weekly*
  (808) 875-1700
  Fax: **(808) 875-1800**
  wwwmauiweekly.com

Moloka`i

Moloka`i is part of Maui County.
Also see Maui.

Business, working

- Federal Job Information Center,
  O`ahu: **(808) 541-2791**
  www.usajobs.gov

- Hawai`i State Workforce
  Development Division,
  Kaunakakai: **(808) 553-3281**
  hawaii.gov/labor/wdd

Newspapers

- *Moloka`i Advertiser-News*
  (808) 558-8253
  www.molokaiadvertiser-news.com

- *The Moloka`i Dispatch*
  (808) 552-2781
  www.themolokaidispatch.com

Lana`i

Lana`i is part of Maui County.
Also see Maui.

- The Lana`i Co.
  Main number **(808) 565-3000**
  Employment **(808) 565-3876**

- Lana`i Community Hospital
  (808) 565-6411
  www.lch.hhsc.org

- Lana`i Schools **(808) 565-7224**
  **hawaii.hi.schoolwebpages.com/
  education/school/school.php**

Kaua`i

Working

- County of Kaua`i Office of Economic
  Development,
  (808) 241-6390
  www.kauai.gov/OED

- University of Hawai`i
  Small Business Development Center
  at Kaua`i Community College
  (808) 246-1748
  www.hawaii-sbdc.org/index.htm

- State Department of Labor and
  Industrial Relations,
  Lihue: **(808) 214-3421**
  Fax: **(808) 241-3518**
  www.workwisekauai.com

- State Department of Education
  (808) 274-3507
  www.doe.k12.hi.us

- County of Kaua`i Personnel Services
  Office **(808) 421-6595**
  www.kauai.gov/personnel

- Kaua`i Business Guide and
  Membership Referral Directory,
  Kaua`i Chamber of Commerce
  P.O. Box 1969
  Lihue, Kaua`i, HI 96766
  (808) 245-7363

Newspapers

- *The Garden Island*
  P.O. Box 231, Lihue, HI 96766
  (808) 245-3681
  thegardenisland.com

Additional Reading

Religion
- *Hawai`i's Religions* by John F. Mulholland © 1970 by Charles E. Tuttle Company, Rutland, Vt., and Tokyo, Japan.
- *Hawai`i's Missionary Saga* © 1992 by Piercy LaRue. Mutual Publishing.

Living
- *Pests of Paradise* By Susan Scott and Craig Thomas, M.D. 2000 University of Hawai`i Press, Honolulu.
- *What's Bugging Me?* By Gordon M. Nishida and Joann M. Tenorio 1995 University of Hawai`i Press, Honolulu.
- *What Bit Me?* By Gordon M. Nishida and Joann M. Tenorio 1993 University of Hawai`i Press, Honolulu.

Business
- *Mason on Management* – 65 columns on business management from *Pacific Business News* magazine's former editor and publisher George Mason. Down to earth and helpful advice. Crossroads Press, Inc. P.O. Box 833, Honolulu, HI 96808 or phone (808) 596-2021.
- *Business Basics in Hawai`i* by Dennis Kondo 1992 University of Hawai`i Press. General business knowledge.

Politics, history and costs
- *Land and Power In Hawaii* by George Cooper and Gavan Daws. Paperback edition published by University of Hawai`i Press 1990; Originally published in 1985 by Benchmark Books, Inc. The deals and doings that forever changed Hawai`i during the Democratic years of government.
- *Hawaii State and Local Politics,* James C. F. Wang, University of Hawai`i at Hilo, 1982

- *Hawaii: The Sugar-Coated Fortress* by Francine du Plessix Gray. 1972. Haddon Crofsmen, Scranton, Pa. This beautifully written essay sensitively probes the military and business influence in the Hawaiian islands.
- *Hawaii, Compass American Guides*, by Moana Tregaskis. 2001. Fodor's Travel Publications, Inc. This ultimate tourist guide book includes concise history of each island, details about many towns and cities and contains spectacular photos.
- *Notable Women of Hawai`i* edited by Barbara Bennett Peterson, @1984 University of Hawaii Press
- *The Best of Hawaii*, by Jocelyn K. Fujii, 1994, Three Rivers Press
- *The Peopling of Hawaii*, Eleanor C. Nordyke, the University Press of Hawaii, 1977
- *The Price of Paradise, Volume I*, Randall W. Roth, editor. 1992. Mutual Publishing, Honolulu. A must-read collection of editorials, articles, written by a variety of specialists in their fields. Great cartoons. Overview of some of the more controversial aspects of island life from politics to taxes to government efficiency.
- *The Price of Paradise, Volume 2* 1993. See above. This volume less diverse than first volume. But still important reading. Heavy government.
- *The Land of Aloha* by Carl Giampolo, editor. 1983. Paradise Books. Good maps and overview of each island. Excellent articles on Hawaiian history and the advent of each ethnic group to the islands.

Pamphlets, other publications

Available at most libraries or by calling directly, or on Amazon.com

- **A Practical Guide to Divorce in Hawaii.** by Peter J. Herman, University of Hawaii Press, 1991

- *Crime in Hawai`i.* State of Hawai`i, Department of the Attorney General annual report.

- *Government in Hawai`i.* A handbook of financial statistics by the Tax Foundaton of Hawai`i. Write Tax Foundaton of Hawai`i, 126 Queen Street, Suite 304, Honolulu, HI, 96813 or call (808) 536-4587.

- *Handbook for Employers on Unemployment Insurance.* Hawai`i Department of Labor and Industrial Relations, employer services **(808) 586-8926.**

- *Hui `Imi Task force for Hawaiian services.* Report of the state of Hawai`i Office of Hawaiian Affairs, 1991

- *Hunter's Guide to Hawai`i.* a labor market information publication of the Hawai`i Department of Labor and Industrial Relations.

- *How To Find A Job.* The Research and Statistics Office, Department of Labor and Industrial Relations.

- *Population growth, policies and strategies; a public opinion.* Commission on Population and the Hawaiian Future, 1977.

- *Sex Discrimination and the Law in Hawai.* A guide to your legal rights by Judith R. Gething (The University of Hawaii Press 1979)

- *People at Work, the City's Heartbeat, City Civil Service opportunities*, City and County of Honolulu, **(808) 523-4301.** (Internet: **www.cohonolulu.hi.us/depts/per)**

Useful Internet sites

Use the Internet and the worldwide web to learn about life on Hawai`i's islands. Here are a few helpful Internet locations:

www.mauigateway.com/msgs.html
"Ask a Local" questions about Hawaii life

www.mapquest.com
See maps, including street maps, for anywhere in the nation. The Esbensens used this to locate possible rentals on the islands.

www.HomesAndLand.com or www.realtor.com
See homes and their prices around the nation, including Hawaii.

www.hawaii.com/move
For information on relocating.

www.honoluluadvertiser.com/ www.starbulletin.com
Read portions of Honolulu's newspapers.

www.usnpl.com/hinews.html
Link to other Hawai`i newspapers and TV stations.

www.hawaiiantravelclub.com
For fares and accommodation bargains.

www.visitmaui.com
For Maui County information.

www.maui.com
For information on Maui about Business Resources, relocation and Hi-Tech info.

wwwhawaii.gov/dbedt/index.html
Access the Hawaii Data Book.

www.maui.com/~hpd or www.honolulupd.org
See the Honolulu Police Department's Annual Crime report.

www.gohawaii.com
Short term rentals on the islands:

⚞ Chambers of Commerce ⚟

Hawai`i has at least 19 Chambers of Commerce, including several with ethnic links. For a list of websites, see **www.globalindex.com/chamber/hi.shtml**

A complete list of chambers:

Chamber of Commerce of Hawai`i
(808) 545-4300

Junior Chamber of Commerce (aka Honolulu Junior Jaycees)
(808) 941-5266

Hawai`i Island Chamber of Commerce
(808) 935-7178 fax (808) 961-4435

Kona Kohala Chamber of Commerce O`ahu
(808) 329-1758 fax (808) 329-8564

Kaua`i Chamber of Commerce
(808) 245-7363 fax (808) 245-8815

Maui Chamber of Commerce
(808) 871-7711 fax (808) 877-6646

Moloka`i Chamber of Commerce
(808) 553-3773 or (808) 567-4248

African American Chamber of Commerce, O`ahu
(808) 623-2911

Australian American Chamber of Commerce, Honolulu
(808) 526-2242

Chinese Chamber of Commerce, Honolulu
(808) 533-3181

Filipino Chamber of Commerce, Kalihi, O`ahu
(808) 843-0322 or (808) 847-6089

Hawai`i Hispanic Chamber of Commerce, Honolulu
(808) 545-4344 fax (808) 682-5101

Hawai`i Korean Chamber of Commerce, Honolulu **(808) 526-0999**

Honolulu Japanese Chamber of Commerce **(808) 949-5531**

Kailua (O`ahu) Chamber of Commerce
(808) 261-2727

Native Hawaiian Chamber of Commerce, Honolulu **(808) 531-3744**

Portuguese Chamber of Commerce, Honolulu **(808) 523-5030**

Vietnamese-American Chamber of Commerce, Honolulu
(808) 531-7174 fax: (808) 228-2969

Japanese Chamber of Commerce of Hawai`i, Hilo, Big Island **(808) 934-0177**

Irish Chamber of Commerce, Honolulu
(808) 533-0033

Tourist Bureaus

Hawai`i Visitors Bureau-Big Island
(808) 961-5795

Kaua`i Vistors Bureau **(808) 262-1400**

Maui Visitors Bureau **(808) 244-3580**

Moloka'i Visitors Bureau **(808) 553-3876**

O`ahu Visitors Bureau **(808) 524-0722**
www.hawaii.gov/tourism

Speaking the Language

There are actually two original "languages" spoken in Hawai`i. The first is Hawaiian. Brought by early Polynesians who settled the islands, it was much changed by outside influences. The second language is pidgin, a blend of words and colorful phrases that originated in plantation days as a way for the mix of nationalities to communicate with each other. Pidgin, which can be as difficult to understand as a foreign language, is still so commonly spoken today it is the bane of the public school system. Here are some common Hawaiian words:

aikane (aye-KAH-neh) - friend

akamai (ah-KAH-my) - wise or smart

ali`i (Ah-LEE-ee) - chief, nobility

hana hou (HAH-nah-HO) - do it again, encore!

hale (HA-leh) - house

hanai (ha-NY) - adopted

haole (ha-O-leh) - Caucasian

hapa (HAH-pa) - half or part as in hapa-haole, half or part Caucasian

heiau (HEH-ee-ah) - ancient Hawaiian burial ground or place of worship

holoholo (HO-lo-HO-lo) - to travel around visiting, as in "go holoholo"

hui (HOO-ee) - club or association, especially to do business

hula (HOO-lah) - Hawaiian dance

imu (EE-moo) - pit for roasting

kahuna (kah-HOO-nah) - priest or teacher

kai (KI) - sea

kama`aina (KA-mah-EYE-nah) see page 13

kanaka (ka-NAH-kah) - a native Hawaiian

kane (KAH-neh) - boy or man

kapu (KAH-poo) - keep out, taboo

kaukau (KOW-kow) - food

keiki (KAY-kee) - child

kiawe (kee-AH-vay) - mesquite tree, prolific "weed" tree

kupuna (koo-POO-na) - ancestor

lanai (lah-NI) - porch or balcony

lei (LAY) - necklace of flowers, feathers or shells

lu`au (LOO-ah) - traditional feast

mahalo - (ma HA lo) thank you

mahu - (MA-hoo) homosexual or gay

makai - (MA-kai) toward the sea

make (MA-kay) - dead

malihini (mah-lee-HEE-nee) , see page 13

mauka (Mau-ka) - toward mountain

mauna (Mau-nah) - mountain

Mele Kalikimaka (ME-leh kah-lee-kee-MAH-ka) - Merry Christmas

menehune (meh-nee-HOO-neh) - legendary dwarfs, nocturnal workers

nui (NOO-ee) - big

`ohana (oh-HAH-nah) - family or adopted family

`okole (oh-KO-lay) - rear, buttocks

`ono (OH-no) - delicious

pali (PAH-lee) - ocean cliff

paniolo (pah-nee-OH-lo) - cowboy

pau (POW) - finished, done as in *pau hana*, done working

poi (POY) - soft food from pounded taro root

puka (POO-kah) - hole, opening, cubicle

pupu (POO-poo) - hors d'oeuvres or appetizers

shishi (shee-shee) - to urinate, childs phrase

tutu (TOO-too) - grandmother, term of endearment for old person

wahine (wa-HEE-neh) - girl or woman

wikiwiki (WEE-kee-WEE-kee) - quick, fast

Index

Notes

Notes

Mahalo

Mahalo

Thank you…

Friends and strangers who, over years of gathering material for this book and its revision, answered endless questions, sharing emotions, lifestyle details and financial information.

Government, business and university researchers, most of whom went an extra step to provide information Very few said, "I don't know." Most said, "I'll find out."

G. Nishida at the University of Hawai`i, and Grant K. Uchida at the state Department of Agriculture; Allen Hoe, attorney and activist; Sam Slom, state senator and small business reformer, and Marcia Sakai, attorney at the Hawai`i state tax department.

To University of Hawai`i at Hilo and Maui Community College for translations.

Author Gavan Daws for permission to quote abundantly from *Land and Power in Hawai'i*. Every time I read *Land and Power* I remembered what journalism should be and I push myself to do better.

The original editors: Christine Flanagan in New Jersey and Honolulu, who knows so much about Hawai`i; Bob DiNicola in Indianapolis, encouraging when I needed it most; and Francine Godzwa in Erie, Pa., a tough taskmistress.

Jonathan Scheuer, Honolulu, who so diligently edited and commented on the first edition after it was printed. His corrections are reflected in this second edition.

Second edition editors: Meg Skellenger, so talented and thorough; and Harry Eager whose comments keep us clear and accurate.

Talented writers Matthew Thayer, Blair Thornike, Meg Skellenger and Mary Chase.

Ann Greenwood for the original design and production and Kellee LaVars for production on the revised edition. Both required organization and patience.

Jody van Aalst and Melody Draney for checking details and resources on the second edition; Laurence Christopher and Rene Panzer for proofreading.

Literary agent Roger Jellinek for steering me in the right directions.

Photographers Matthew Thayer, Maui, a fine photo journalist; and Brad Lewis on the Big Island who so abundantly shared his excellent work.

Family and friends who tolerated my reclusiveness and offered their resources.

About the author

As reporter, editor and columnist at newspapers in Pennsylvania and Florida, Toni Polancy covered news stories that ranged from murder to meatballs and politics to polygamy. She won many awards and held several titles, from cub reporter to managing editor of the *Erie* (Pennsylvania) *Daily Times*.

As she ascended the wobbly corporate ladder, Polancy was climbing farther and farther from her first love, writing. By 1991, her 10-hour workdays had become a series of business meetings and she did what many other middle-agers consider doing: look for stimulating change. Hawai`i beckoned, but the islands had a nasty reputation for luring newcomers only to cast them adrift on a treacherous sea of high prices, low wages and scarce jobs — so Polancy brought her own business. She collected all her savings, cashed in her IRAs, and purchased a franchise for *Homes & Land* real estate magazines, which she established on Maui and Kaua`i.

Along the way, Hawai`i was full of surprises — both jolts and joys. There was a lot to learn about life, friendships, business and survival on tiny islands in the middle of an ocean. Tourist brochures and travel books did not tell the story. And very little truthful, practical information on day-to-day life was available in a concise form. Polancy began saving notes and articles in a large cardboard box. Accompanied by two years of research and over 200 interviews, they became the basis for

So You Want to Live in Hawai`i
A Guide to Settling and Succeeding in the Islands

First published in 1999, the book has sold 85,000 copies and influenced the decision of at least 100,000 people.

This revised edition was updated in 2010.

You are invited to communicate with the author at polancy@hawaii.rr.com

Visit liveandloveinhawaii.com

To order copies of

The Hawai`i Pet Book

Keeping your dog and cat healthy, happy and housed in the islands

or

So You Want to Live in Hawai`i

A Guide to Settling and Succeeding in the Islands

Send $19.95 by check or money order, plus

$4 postage and handling for each book to:

Barefoot Publishing, Inc.

815 Kupulau Drive

Kihei, HI 96753

Your books will be sent via priority mail at no additional cost.

Visit liveandloveinhawaii.com

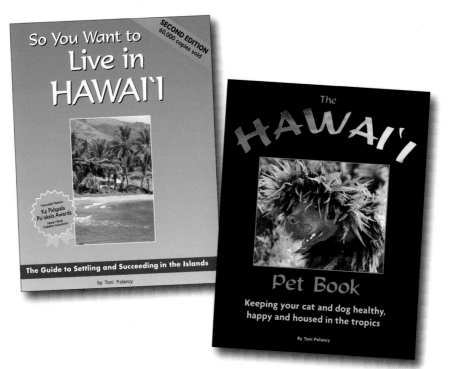

Barefoot Publishing: *Practical Books About Paradise*